MAINSTREA

C000067823

'66

THE REAL STORY OF ENGLAND'S
1966 WORLD CUP TRIUMPH

ROGER HUTCHINSON

MAINSTREAM
PUBLISHING

EDINBURGH AND LONDON

To

The West London Unattractives, 1973–75 and 1994;
Stanley Bowles;
and Sleat Football Club, 1978–1992
for the best times

First published in Great Britain in 1995 by
MAINSTREAM PUBLISHING COMPANY
(EDINBURGH) LTD
7 Albany Street
Edinburgh EH1 3UG

ISBN 1 84018 603 8

This edition, 2002

A catalogue record for this book is available
from the British Library

Typeset in Times Roman
Printed and bound in Great Britain by
Cox & Wyman Ltd

CONTENTS

PREFACE TO THE 2002 EDITION

When this book was first published (originally entitled '. . . *It Is Now!*') on the 30th anniversary of the 1966 World Cup finals in 1996, among the universally kindly reviews was to be found one friendly suggestion that I had perhaps taken too dark a view of the long-term negative influence of Alf Ramsey's team. After all, it was pointed out, 1966 was followed by 1970, whose World Cup featured Brazil, possibly the most exciting international side of the century, amongst the winners. That is true – and the Brazilians were in their turn followed by the incomparable Dutch. And as the century drew to its close there was nothing much wrong with the French side which won in 1998, nor indeed with the tournament in which they triumphed. By the time of the 2000 European Nations Championship in Holland and Belgium, it seemed that international soccer, especially in Europe, was improving in quality almost by the week.

Nobody welcomed this more than myself. But we would be deluding ourselves if we failed to recognise that there was one unhappy spectre at the feast – England, who unlike Holland, and unlike France prior to 1998, had actually won the World Cup once and had joined the small, elite band of international prefects, but never looked like doing so again. What was arguably the nation's most talented group of footballers since 1966 did well, under a sympathetic and intelligent manager, to reach the semi-finals of Italia '90. But typically and predictably, this half-triumph was instantly pursued by the horrors of the Taylor years and failure even to qualify for the 1994 tournament.

While I was writing this book Terry Venables became the manager of

5

England. This was the same Terry Venables who had made the penultimate 40, but not the final 22, of Ramsey's 1966 squad, and who had conquered his dismay at hitting the final hurdle by rigorously attending as an eager spectator (with his friend George Graham) as many matches as it was possible to reach. The same Venables who had progressed, at Queen's Park Rangers, Barcelona and Tottenham, to become one of the most inventive English club managers of his generation. And the same Terry Venables who, in the first major international tournament to be staged in England since 1966, defeated the Dutch 4 –1 at Wembley before being beaten in a penalty shoot-out by a united Germany in the semi-finals of the 1996 European Championships. (Tellingly, the Dutch were more surprised than humiliated by their mauling at the hands of a side they had previously considered to be incorrigibly stupid. They would be intelligent and effective again in the morning, the orange-clad players consoled themselves. Whether the English could sustain this unprecedented spasm of brilliance for another 24 hours was another matter altogether.)

It is tempting, but ultimately impossible to talk here of so many steps forward being followed by so many steps back. The steps forward have been too tentative and inconclusive and the steps backward too baffling and traumatic to permit any accurate or logical graph of England's halting progress since 1966. But what has clearly been underway is a battle to haul the English national side – and, in fact, English soccer as a whole – away from the precepts and received wisdoms of the late 1960s and '70s. The fact that this battle occasionally seemed to be raging within the single personality of individual managers such as Bobby Robson and Graham Taylor only confused the issue. The astonishing success of English club sides consisting largely of English players in Europe in the late 1970s and '80s complicated matters further. If Clough's and Paisley's lads could do it for Forest and Liverpool, then why not for England?

Those were diversions, which the long shadow of the post-Heysel club ban from Europe and the humiliations of 1993 did much to expose. By the 1990s it was widely accepted that the English national team had for 20 years been fighting the First World War with the tactics of the Crimea. When the England of Venables so thoroughly trounced the

Holland of Guus Hiddinck in 1996 it seemed at last to be employing modern ordnance. Where Ramsey had introduced a system and picked the best players to work it, Venables seemed finally to be selecting the best players and doing what, with some inevitable compromise, all successful modern international coaches had agreed upon – he was using his own imagination to craft a winning line-up from their talents.

His line-up did not win, of course. Another penalty shoot-out in another semi-final against Germany saw to that. But the fact that Venables was then replaced by another imaginative former player and club manager, Glenn Hoddle, seemed designed to continue the good work. A fresh course had apparently been set which could not have been predicted as recently as 1994.

What happened next becomes less easy to comprehend as the years go by. Having fought his way over the back of Italy to the 1998 World Cup finals and then been eliminated in semi-heroic fashion by Argentina at those finals (on penalties again, after having played most of the match and extra time with ten men), Hoddle confessed in a newspaper to his belief in a form of reincarnation which many found unorthodox and offensive. No disability or failure is accidental, thought Glenn. We pay, or are rewarded for, our behaviour in one life by our experiences of another life. So it was that Glenn Hoddle was reincarnated firstly as Howard Wilkinson and then as Kevin Keegan. And so it was that the national football team of the country which had controversially beaten West Germany in the final of the 1966 World Cup was defeated at Wembley by an insubstantial German side in the early qualifying stages of the 2002 World Cup, with its manager sitting in the dug-out telling himself and anybody else who cared to listen that he didn't have a clue what was going on out there, beyond the broad white touchline.

If this thirty-year war has been a battle for the direction, or the soul, or the style of English football, then it has been a contest with a foregone conclusion. Innovations in sporting technique and tactic are as impossible to disinvent as the atom bomb: you adapt to them or die. By the year 2000 the English Football Association had been helped gently on the road to adaptation by a European Court ruling that almost instantly flooded its own premier division with continental footballers.

The Bosman Case changed England more than anyone else in Europe, for the simple reason that nowhere else in Europe was so much in need of change, so thirsty for change, so *dying* for change, as England.

Within a couple of years of the Bosman ruling, the FA Cup was won by a London club with a foreign manager and a team of foreign players. When Kevin Keegan walked out of a hissing Wembley, and out of Sir Alf Ramsey's former job, the English FA was uniquely able for the first time in its history to look overseas for a replacement.

It was also desperate. On one level the war had been won. The ground was laid for a change as dramatic and far-reaching as Alf Ramsey's insistence in 1962 that he – and not the old buffers of the International Committee – should pick the England team. By accepting that it had to look abroad for a manager, the country which invented the game of soccer and which had been world champions just 34 years earlier was implicitly accepting that it had allowed itself to drift so far behind the rest of the world that not even its domestic league, the richest and the busiest on earth, could provide a trustworthy national team coach.

Sven-Goran Eriksson was widely expected to fail in his appointed task of getting England to the World Cup finals in Japan and Korea. He certainly was not expected to beat Germany 5–1 in Munich. But he was expected by all intelligent judges to respect the talent which was available to him and to work with that talent, to harness and deploy it rather than squeeze it protesting into some straitjacket of a system which had been overtaken by decades of innovation, improved technique and – not least – changes in the rules.

Eriksson's England may not equal Alf Ramsey's England; it may not win the World Cup. But its legacy, we can finally allow ourselves to believe, may be a team which will never again look inwards and backwards for the answers to questions posed by a sport which has long ceased to be centred in the British Isles, but which is now the plaything of the world's intelligence.

Roger Hutchinson
Isle of Raasay, 2002

PREFACE

Like most people who will have just turned 47 years old when England host the European Nations Championships in 1996, I had just become 17 when Bobby Moore held up the World Cup on 30 July 1966. And, like most, I remember the occasion well. Obliged against my will to watch the game at a family gathering rather than at the home of a friend, I suffered the most common experience of all teenaged football fans that afternoon: being surrounded by aunts and cousins who were there for the shared national experience rather than the match.

For two hours, football was like a royal wedding. No sooner had Gottfried Dienst blown his whistle at three o'clock than the conversation and tea and cakes began. They faltered slightly in their flow when Bobby Charlton was announced by Kenneth Wolstenholme as being on the ball (my aunts and cousins came from a Tyneside mining family: they not only knew about the Charltons and Milburns of Ashington, they even tried hard to enjoy *House Of The Rising Sun* because The Animals were local boys), but hardly at all when a goal was scored.

I remember the last 13 minutes of normal time only as dizzy moments of extreme terror: Peters having put England 2–1 in front, nobody else in my vicinity seemed quite aware of the imminence of the unthinkable. I sat like an alien in a trance on the edge of a chair while creatures from another world talked over my head of illnesses and the price of mince, and when Weber equalised I fell to the floor moaning. Concerned, they looked at me, and then at the television set, and as Wolstenholme did what he was paid to do and explained to aunts all over Britain the significance of West Germany's goal, they tutted in commiseration.

9

And after that I remember hardly anything. I did not hear Wolstenholme's famous lines as Hurst scored his third and England's fourth goal. I had passed through all of that. I was on the disembodied eighth level of consciousness which is known well to football fans (it is just two levels below an ecstatic death); my ears and voice had ceased to function in any normal way. Only my eyes worked, and they told me that both of the extra-time goals had been given, and I was released. You will gather that my critical faculties were suspended. I would not have cared at that moment if England had won the World Cup with eleven androids carrying machine-guns. Alf Ramsey knew all about people like me.

Eight years later I was in the happy condition of being able to watch football matches in the company of my choice. And like most young men who had been 17 in July 1966, my chosen company of friends and myself wanted Alf Ramsey sacked; had wanted Alf Ramsey sacked for a number of years. English football was moribund and the blame was laid squarely at the door of the man who had dropped Jimmy Greaves. When the news came through from Lancaster Gate on 1 May 1974 that Ramsey was out and Joe Mercer – who was by then the avuncular general manager of Coventry City, but who had earlier worked on an exciting Manchester City side with one of Ramsey's greatest critics, Malcolm Allison – was to replace him temporarily, my heart took a holiday.

It was a short holiday. There followed Don Revie, and the failure to qualify for the 1978 World Cup finals, and the cheerless neglect of a whole new generation of talented English footballers, and it became apparent that however responsible Alf Ramsey may have been for introducing some sort of extreme dry rot to the game, his removal had not been its cure. It was chronic.

What happened? Where did it all go wrong? How did the footballers from one of the strongest leagues in the world, whose club sides dominated European competition, drift so quickly from being World Champions to being tearfully grateful for a place in the semi-finals of the worst World Cup in living memory? What did you do to our game, Alf? Could you go back and start again?

Ramsey himself had been in the meantime more discreet than his former employers had the right to expect. He was treated badly, no doubt about it. They spat him out and left him with his knighthood and his golf and a season ticket to Portman Road, and he kept his counsel. His unshakable sense of his own dignity never served him better than in forced retirement.

But he had taken hold of the English national side at a time when it was desperate for success, and in achieving that success he drove our game of football up a cul-de-sac. His influence, through his World Cup-winning team of 1966, has been immeasurable. And it has always been difficult to see how, once the damned trophy had been won and then honourably lost four years later, it was a beneficial influence. In all of that, I agree with Denis Law, and Pele, and Di Stefano, and a million others.

The outstanding unanswered questions for my generation and others were: what exactly did he do, and why, and how? The answers could only be groped towards by writing this book. It did not turn out exactly as I had expected. Naturally, I anticipated all of the painful conclusions about the deliberate suffocation of the wild unfettered flair of football in its pomp. But I had not intended to find myself writing about an honest man who made a promise, and to keep that promise was ultimately obliged to build a football team absolutely in his own image: resolute, taciturn, often haughty, occasionally profane, and capable when the occasion demanded of something which we should hesitate to call brilliance, but which certainly walked briefly with greatness. A football team which, when push came to shove, turned out, like Alf Ramsey himself, to be unbeatable. I was made glad at the time by that emotional stroll with grandeur in the last two matches of the 1966 World Cup and – despite everything – I am still grateful today.

Roger Hutchinson
Skye, 1995

1 THE PROMISE

'Although England's victory in the World Cup final was
obviously a great achievement which at the time gave the
game a badly needed boost, I think that in the long run it
was a bad thing for British football. It was the beginning
of the end of football as we knew it.'

— DENIS LAW

He arrived slowly at the famous assurance. Upon the announcement
of his appointment in October 1962 he told John Arlott: 'England can
do well in the 1966 World Cup, even win it. Certainly some overseas
sides control the ball better: I would say the players in the hotter
countries move better, move quicker, perhaps think quicker than
ours. But I am not sure they would be so effective in English conditions.'

And shortly before his first game in complete control, against
France at the Parc des Princes in February 1963, he had contented
himself with telling the world that 'I am sure we shall do very well in
1966. We shall be playing in our own conditions, before our own
people.'

Three months later, following a dour draw at Wembley against a
Brazilian side missing Pele, Zito and Garrincha, he committed
himself to one further step. 'With four, five or six of today's players,'
he said, 'I hope it will be possible to find a team good enough to win
the World Cup.' He had not yet won a single match.

But in the July of that year, after an extremely successful tour of
Europe which had brought him not only his first win, but also three
good wins in succession, back at home in Ipswich he relaxed suffi-

ciently in the company of a local journalist to come right out with it, boldly and brooking no misinterpretation. England, said Alf Ramsey, will win the World Cup in 1966.

There was no going back. Alf Ramsey could never retract. It may have been, as he said, 'the sentence which created more pressure for me than any other in my career', but he would not withdraw it. How could he? At the next available opportunity – an official press conference at a London hotel on 21 August 1963 – the national media clamoured for confirmation. This compact, urbane, impenetrable man whose slow, clipped tones had betrayed for years the starching effect of elocution lessons on his native Essex twang, looked levelly at the hungry journalists and repeated the haunting words.

'I say it again,' he pronounced, 'I think England will win the World Cup in 1966. We have the ability, strength, character and, perhaps above all, players with the right temperament. Such thoughts must be put to the public, and particularly to the players, so that confidence can be built up.'

The press was scornful and the public puzzled. Jimmy Leadbetter, the Scot who had been the unlikely lynchpin in his all-conquering Ipswich Town side, heard the news with amazement. 'He made only one slip-up,' Leadbetter would muse later of his boss's England career. 'He said that England would win the World Cup. It wasn't in character – he's so cagey, watching out all the time.' Leadbetter laughed and shook his head at the thought. 'He must have been daft that night. He must have been drunk!'

It was a rod for his back, of course, and it was a mistake. 'I don't think I really meant it when I said it,' Ramsey admitted later. 'The pressures at that time were enormous. It was probably a question of saying the first thing that came into my mind, something I don't normally do.' It was an error, but it was no flushed and tipsy footballer's boast at midnight in a foreign town. 'It was an expression of fierce desire and a subsequent conviction that it could be done,' said Arthur Rowe, his former manager at Spurs, when the promised deed had been accomplished. 'It was no cheap, throwaway phrase: it was studied.'

Only in its persistent repetition was the celebrated promise studied. Having over-committed himself, he simply made the best of it. Alfred Ernest Ramsey cared nothing for the press and little for the public. He was addressing a rare breed: he was talking to men such as a young but established international half-back called Bobby Moore, who would declare that: 'We began to believe in him when he showed that he believed in us. That seed was sown when he first said "England will win the World Cup". He came to regret it because it put himself and his players under great pressures. In fact, it built up within us the very confidence we needed.'

He was speaking from afar, from the conference room of a distant London hotel, to such characters as a certain uncapped defender who was about to be promoted from the Second Division with Leeds United. Professional footballers thrive on success and detest the faintest whiff of failure. Along with Bobby Moore and a crucial couple of dozen of their kind, Jack Charlton read the words of Ramsey, stopped to think, and nodded to himself. It did not occur to him to mock, or to disbelieve. 'He could be right,' thought Charlton with growing respect. 'He could be right.'

* * *

And then when all the happy accidents were history, and he had no need to say 'I told you so' because everybody else was saying it for him, football's Age of Innocence was over. 'After 1966,' George Best, the most brilliant footballer ever to be produced by the United Kingdom, would say, 'the game stopped being a pleasure, the fun went out of it.'

World Cup matches, said Hilton Gosling, the Brazilian team doctor since 1958, had become 'gladiatorial contests fit only for a Roman circus . . . There is a new style of play coming into favour in Europe. It is a tougher style. We must learn to play it.'

Led by the champions, who scored 11 and conceded just three goals in their six tournament games (four and two of them respectively in the 120 corrosive minutes of the final), the 1966 World Cup finals bottomed out at an all-time low of 2.7 goals per game. One thousand, five hundred and thirty-six goals were scored in the 462 English First Division games in season 1962–63; 1,571 in '63–64; 1,543 in '64–65. In 1966–67 the total instantly slumped to a post-war low of 1,387. By 1970–71 it was 1,089. Fear had arrived in association football, and it was there to stay: fear of losing; fear of conceding; fear of relegation; fear of elimination; and fear of dropping the away draw bonus.

'Money was the cause of the trouble,' said the great Dutch referee Leo Horn after a violent Inter-Cities Fairs Cup clash between Leeds United and Valencia in 1966. 'You could almost smell it on the pitch.' Money or not, fear or not, the Age of Innocence had gone and the Modern Era flexed its ruthless muscles. In the June of 1969 the Brazilian team manager, Joao Saldanha, shared a flight between Montevideo and Rio de Janeiro with the touring England team. Saldanha had been doing his international homework in preparation for the 1970 World Cup finals.

What he had seen, he told the England squad, had horrified him like nothing that he had seen before in association football. He had been to Belgrade and seen the Yugoslavs – who were already eliminated – set out to avenge themselves against Belgium – who had already qualified – for an earlier defeat in Brussels. 'The tackling began at navel-height and got higher, until the Yugoslavs were 2–0 up.' He had seen six players booked in Hamburg when West Germany met Scotland, he said, and only Tommy Gemmell sent off when any strict interpretation of the rules would have seen all six dismissed. 'If someone does something brutal,' the Brazilian manager told his wrapt English audience, 'nothing to do with football, then we are not playing football.'

Casting his mind back, no doubt, to Goodison Park, Liverpool, on 19 July 1966, and the spectre of Pele limping helplessly for the last hour of Brazil's last match in the World Cup which England won, this extraordinary man warned: 'It is a battle and so we fight. Not just one of my players or two, but all eleven. No, maybe 12, because I will be there with them.

'I do not ask men to take treatment like that without hitting back. We do not care if the match ends after only five minutes. Why try to play to a conclusion when it is no longer a football match anyway, when the laws have been thrown into the rubbish bin, and instead we have the law of the jungle?'

The Modern Era, Saldanha was signalling in those, the saddest of

16

words, had begun. It would produce great players, of course, and great matches, and great teams. Just as there were large islands of sinfulness in the game before 1966, so it is impossible to draw a neat line between soccer's early and later history. Saldanha's own Brazil would, in 1970, reclaim their game for a fleeting hour or two; Holland in 1974 would seem to point the sport back towards the light. But these, we can see now, were twitchings of the corpse; after 1966 something quite definable was lost to soccer. No more would World Cup games between well-matched opponents routinely finish with scorelines of 7–3, 4–4, 5–2 and 6–3. No 17-year-old, however gifted, would ever again be allowed to score hat-tricks in the semi-finals of the World Cup and then get a further two in the final itself – in fact, the next great 17-year-old to follow Pele, Diego Maradona, would be kept out of his first World Cup altogether for the sake of his health. Never again would the regulations be so relaxed as to allow the best footballers in the world to jump like happy-go-lucky Corinthians from one international side to another as the passing mood took them, as Alfredo Di Stefano jumped between Spain, Argentina and Colombia, as the Hungarian Ferenc Puskas felt free to become Spanish, and as several Argentinians of Italian descent transferred from one country to the other in between World Cups. The days were numbered when English First Division goalkeepers would spend their summers bowling in county cricket. Few players would be selected solely because of their flair, if they were simultaneously incapable of fitting into a game-plan, and a whole generation of the best English players would be lost to international football because of their individuality. Centre-forwards would no longer shake hands with opposing goalkeepers. Wingers would no longer plough their lonely furrow up and down each touchline; inside-forwards had to learn to tackle back; full-backs to get forward; centre-halves to sweep behind men who used to be half-backs; centre-forwards to lay off and go, or simply to stay up there alone and chase, and chase, and chase while their ten team-mates addressed the urgent task of retaining a one-goal lead.

After 1966, that was how you reached World Cup finals. For good or for bad, innocence had no part of it. Planning, preparation and sound defence was all. The emphasis shifted openly from starting play to stopping it. Managers – once mere selectors of talent – became Napoleonic generals. 'Football is a noble game,' Alfredo Di Stefano would say. 'It is spoilt because players have to bow to the knee of coaches instead of expressing themselves.'

And out of all of this came the professional foul, and the cultivated draw, and the penalty shoot-out, and what had for a century been largely a contest of impromptu skills, telepathic understanding and individual brilliance, became once and for all a clash of tactical nuances. And the sport shuddered into decline, with its ruling bodies wildly shuffling the laws in an attempt to remedy the irremediable; as if the old offside or pass-back legislation had been responsible for the loss of innocence and the rise of cynicism; as if three-point wins could revive the sport, or away goals counting double, or time-outs, or larger goals.

England's finest sporting hour – a triumph of discipline, fitness, pride, power and planning – was achieved at the cusp of soccer's long arc; at the very watershed of the game that she had given the world. After it had passed, nothing in soccer would ever be the same again. 'The world always copies the winners,' says Geoff Hurst. 'Half the defeated nations flew away at the end of July with films of England's six matches in their baggage. You can be sure that in training camps anywhere from the Sierras to Siberia players were being looked at in a new light: "Can Jose So-and-So do the job Stiles did . . .?"'

Less sympathetically, Michael Parkinson added: 'Ramsey's robots won the World Cup and British soccer managers, not renowned for their individuality, slavishly followed his pattern of creating teams in which stamina counted for more than skill and mediocrity, given a willing heart and strong legs, was rewarded while more artistic but less muscular attributes were rejected.'

How did Alf manage it, this drastic re-routing of the world's most popular sport? 'I'm not a dreamer,' he said back in February 1963. Nor was he. He was only a boy from Dagenham, trying to keep a promise.

2 DAGENHAM, SOUTHAMPTON, TOTTENHAM AND IPSWICH

'Without wishing to belittle the achievements of any
club I believe certain methods of attaining success have
influenced British football too much and in the wrong
direction. I am thinking of the power game. Results are
achieved by placing too much emphasis on speed, power
and physical fitness. Such teams now have many
imitators. We are breeding a number of teams whose
outlook seems to be that pace, punch and fitness are all
that is required to win all the honours in the game. They
forget that without pure skills these virtues count for
precisely nothing.'

– MATT BUSBY, *1960*

Alfred Ernest Ramsey was born on 22 January 1920 in a small
wooden cottage at Five Elms Farm, Dagenham, Essex.

For 20 years of adulthood he lied about his age. In the book
Talking Football which he published in 1952 he re-asserted what he
had always told his footballing employers: that he had been born in
1922. He repeated the deceit later in *Who's Who*, and it appeared and
reappeared like a bad penny in numerous newspaper articles. Only
after his knighthood did he set the record straight. Sir Alfred Ramsey
could not bring himself to fib to *Debrett's*. People who fib to
Debrett's, he may have told himself, did not deserve to be there in the

first place. Who knew what happened to chaps who were less than honest with *Debrett's*? If discovered they may actually – disgrace upon disgrace – find themselves being removed. Barons might lie to *Debrett's*, earls and the sons of earls might cheerfully deceive their own, but working-class men never could. The chronicle of the peerage was given his correct date of birth.

It was a white lie and it was perfectly understandable. It was not vanity. The Second World War robbed Alf Ramsey, like so many of his generation, of six prime footballing years. When he emerged from the conflict and gained at last a professional career he was 26 years old. By the time he won a regular first-team wage, he was 27. A minor perfidy in 1946 made him 24, and gave him the possibility of two more salaried years. Alf Ramsey was not to know, in the late 1940s, that 20 years later he would become the most severely scrutinised football manager in the world.

The straw and hay dealer, Herbert Henry Ramsey, and his wife Florence, gave birth to a daughter and four sons: Albert, Len, Cyril and Alfred. At the ages of seven and nine respectively Alf and Len played inside-left and inside-right for the Becontree Heath School team which won the Dagenham Schools junior championship. In 1933 – when Alfred was, of course, 13 – he was sent off for querying a referee's decision while playing for the same school. The Dagenham Schools FA ordered him to apologise in writing to themselves and to the referee. He did so, promptly, and was selected to play for Dagenham Schools against West Ham Schools.

School offered little to Alf Ramsey, other than soccer ('I seem to have spent more time pumping up footballs and carrying goalposts on to the common'), and at 14 he left and tried for a job at the Ford Motor Plant. He was rejected and went to work at the Co-op as an errand boy. The job was a six-day week, which claimed his Saturday afternoons, which, in turn, meant no more legal football, because Sunday football was, at that time, outlawed by the Football Association.

So Alf broke the Sabbath. He joined a Sunday outfit called Five Elms United which played in the back garden of The Merry Fiddlers public house. Officially, Alfred Ramsey should have been obliged to seek reinstatement with the FA following this transgression. The reinstatement application would have been accompanied by a payment of 7s 6d. Alf never applied, never paid, was never reinstated. The 1966 World Cup was won by an ineligible manager.

He played centre-half for Five Elms and was spotted by a Portsmouth scout named Ned Liddell. Liddell persuaded him to sign amateur forms for the First Division club, which he did, then he waited for the call which never came. Portsmouth did not so much as invite him to train.

And then came the war, and Alf Ramsey left Dagenham – and his family, and their embarrassing accents, and their humble home, and the creeping suburban sprawl, and its empty future – forever. 'Are your parents still alive, Mr Ramsey?' a radio interviewer would ask the new England manager in the early 1960s.

'Oh, yes.'

'Where do they live?'

And Alf Ramsey, whose contorted attempts to betray or to dismiss certain grey areas of his past, whose efforts to reconstruct himself in a strangely perceived image of gentility seem now eerily to foreshadow those of another upwardly mobile tradesman's child, Margaret Thatcher, replied as if he'd hardly heard of the place: 'In Dagenham, I believe.'

In Dagenham, I believe!

He joined the Duke of Cornwall's Light Infantry in June 1940, was posted to an anti-aircraft unit, and as Company Quarter-Master Sergeant he enjoyed an uneventful war, with the exception of one seminal event. Stationed in Hampshire, his battalion side was invited to play against Southampton Football Club. The battalion lost 10–0, but Southampton, impressed with Ramsey and desperate for wartime players, took him – still on amateur forms – from Portsmouth. He played inside-left and took away 30 shillings 'expenses' per match.

Alf Ramsey was demobbed in 1946, and Southampton offered the player whom they believed to be 24 years old £4.00 a week in the summer, £6.00 during the season, and £7.00 if he made the Second Division team. Alf refused, and threatened to go back to the Co-op. The Southampton manager, Bill Dodgin, increased his offer to £6.00, £7.00 and £8.00, and Alf signed.

He played his first league matches in the post-war season of

1946–47 in the position which he was to hold for the remainder of his playing career: right-back. He was slow, unfit and naive. Newcastle United's left-winger Tommy Pearson ('ball control I have never seen since') spun the 26-year-old professional novice like a top. (Ramsey would be plagued by Newcastle left-wingers. Pearson's replacement, Bobby Mitchell, caused him so much pain that in a later season the full-back was seen before a match inspecting the duelling area – his right flank and Mitchell's left – on a rain-sodden pitch, searching for the deepest puddles. After kick-off he spent much of the game trying to jockey Mitchell into this quagmire – 'Even the world's greatest player cannot play in mud.') And Sam Barkas of Manchester City made him look and feel like a fool ('seeing him play changed my whole life'). But thoughts of retire-ment never entered his mind. There would be no going back to the grocery round, to the Co-op, to Dagenham, no leaving 'a comfortable living for those who want to get paid for doing something they enjoy above all else'.

So Alf Ramsey took the only other option, the option which he was to pursue throughout his footballing career, and the option which required qualities which he would at all times in the future most appreciate in others: he worked. He was not and could never be one of the naturals, one of the blessed, one of the indolent greats; so he worked, and thought hard, and worked some more, and talked to the experienced Southampton left-back and captain Bill Rochford (who told him to put in all the extra training he could handle), and dredged the well of knowledge of the club's trainer, a former full-back named Sid Cann, and discussed tactics with Bill Dodgin; and he tried to force some strength and accuracy into his weak left foot, and because they were the one way that he might contribute to his side's Goals For column without the benefit of Heaven-sent genius, he practised penalty kicks until his goalkeeping colleagues grew weary, and then he practised penalty kicks by himself, and he slogged away at his sprint bursts and turns and recovery . . . and when the 1947–48 season came around the superhuman efforts had paid off. Alfred Ramsey looked like a professional full-back. He took his revenge slowly and deliberately; containing Pearson (whose Newcastle United were about to be promoted) in a 3–1 Southampton win at St

22

James's Park. And when the 42nd game of the season was finished, Southampton FC had lifted themselves from mid-table anonymity to third place in the Second Division, missing promotion by four points.

And Alf was asked to join the England squad.

It was an extraordinary compliment to a 28-year-old Second Division full-back of 18 months' experience, even if the selectors did think he was only 26. This was England in its pomp, an England which had never been beaten on home soil by a team from without the United Kingdom, an England which had since the end of the war played 16 internationals and won 12 of them, the England of Lawton, Mortenson, Finney, Matthews, Mannion, Swift and Wright. Alf Ramsey was not called upon to play with these gods on his first European tour. He sat and watched in Turin as they put four past Italy without reply. And he considered, simply and significantly, that the victory had been so easy because England 'outlasted' the Italians. They were fitter.

In September 1948 Alf Ramsey won his first representative honour. He was picked for the English League against the Irish League, and he shared a room with another debutant, the Newcastle United centre-forward Jackie Milburn. Milburn – two of whose young relatives, Jack and Bobby Charlton, were already showing promise in the park games of the family's home town of Ashington, Northumberland – got a hat-trick in the Football League's 5–1 win. But later, when he came to talk of that weekend, it was his puzzling, intense room-mate who came immediately to mind. Alf Ramsey insisted on staying up half the night talking tactics. 'Alf was never a great one for small talk when he was with England parties,' said Milburn. 'Football was his one subject of conversation. He was always a pepper-and-salt man, working out moves and analysing formations with the cruet on the table.'

In the game itself, Ramsey found himself to be pleasantly surprised by the English League's right-winger, the forward directly in front of him. That right-winger's name was Stanley Matthews, and he had more than a decade of international experience. He none-the-less played the game, Ramsey was keen to tell others without a hint of self-consciousness, in a properly disciplined fashion. When Ramsey told him to hold the ball, Matthews held it. 'To my surprise, he played football as I believed it should be played between winger and full-back.' There was no self-doubt, no levity, no time or room for indecorous disorder in the thick-set, beetle-browed frowning full-back who played behind Stanley Matthews and told him what to do. His new England colleagues were amused by his seriousness, but impressed despite themselves. 'I found it a little disconcerting at first,' the captain and right-half Billy Wright would say later, 'to have a full-back behind me who was always as cool as an ice-soda . . . I soon learned that nothing could disturb this footballer with the perfect balance and poise: no situation, however desperate, which could force him into abandoning his immaculate style.'

The Arsenal and England right-back Laurie Scott was injured in the winter of 1948, and that December Alf Ramsey put on Scott's England shirt for a home game against Switzerland. England won 6–0, and Ramsey would retain that number two shirt for another 31 internationals – a couple of them being quite unforgettable games for all concerned with English football. And Alf Ramsey was very concerned with English football.

On 15 January 1949, after 90 successive club games, Alf injured his knee in a friendly match at Plymouth. The right-back whom he had replaced at Southampton two seasons earlier, Bill Ellerington, stepped back in. Southampton were six points clear at the top of the Second Division, Ellerington was playing well and Bill Dodgin assured Ramsey that he would have to fight to regain his place. In fact, added Dodgin, the way things were he might easily fail to displace Ellerington for a second time.

This was desperate news for a 29-year-old. Alf first proved his fitness in the reserves, then failed to spot his name on the first-team sheet and promptly asked for a transfer. Sheffield Wednesday came in first, but Dodgin wanted their inside-forward Eddie Quigley in exchange. Wednesday refused, the manager of Tottenham Hotspur, Arthur Rowe, stepped quickly forward with cash and a nippy little Welsh winger named Ernie Jones, who was anxious to join a seaside club because the doctors had advised him that his daughter's chest complaint required extra ozone, and on 14 May 1949 Alf Ramsey went to White Hart Lane. The total value of his transfer was estimated at between £20,000 and £21,000, making him the most expensive full-back in the history of British soccer. Southampton unaccountably slipped back down to third place in the division, missing promotion by one point. Bill Dodgin, who was watching football in Brazil when his board agreed to the Ramsey sale, would leave Southampton shortly afterwards protesting that he had never intended to alienate Ramsey, and had never wished to see him go. But Arthur Rowe had found his General, and the irresistible rise of Spurs was underway.

They actually did call him 'The General' at Tottenham back in the late '40s and early '50s. (It was that wonderful age when nippy little forwards carrying the surname White were invariably dubbed 'Chalky' and hard-tackling centre-halves 'Crusher'. *Roy Of The Rovers*, which first appeared about that time, invented very little.) And, apparently, he was that influential. He didn't look the part. He was not a natural athlete, let alone a natural footballer. He would never have got a sniff of the Brazilian or Italian national sides. His heavy lower body was cruelly described as pear-shaped; his jowls were emphasised by a Nixonian two-shaves-a-day stubble; and he looked every hour of his 29 years.

But Arthur Rowe was a manager with a brain, and that suited Alf Ramsey. It seems fantastic now, but Rowe's epochal tactical innovation was chiefly to induce Spurs to play a passing game. His Tottenham team became known as the 'push and run' side, on account of their constant use of ten- and 15-yard short balls played between ever-supporting players – 'Play it the way you're facing,' Rowe would say, 'short and quick.' He would frequently cite the example of a tug-of-war team who, pulling together, could overcome a stronger opposition who were disorganised and less confident of each other.

This suited Alf down to the ground. Calmness was part of his character, positional sense came easily to him, and he had taught himself how to play a ball accurately. 'Alf Ramsey,' the great Tom Finney would say later, 'must rate as one of the greatest right-backs of all time. He lacked speed but had immense skill and judgement. I have never known a player give so much deep thought to the opposition.'

'He thirsted for tactical knowledge,' Rowe would add. 'He wanted to know the whys and wherefores of every movement. He was an out and out perfectionist . . . [*that Spurs side*] wouldn't have been the same without Alf – in fact, it couldn't have been without him. His calm, repetitive passes from the back: that's where it all started.'

Spurs had finished fifth in Division Two in 1948–49, the season that Ramsey was dropped by Southampton. In 1949–50, Alf's first season with Rowe's side, they were promoted as champions, nine points clear of the third placed side. (Southampton slipped down to fourth, and then to 12th, and then to a long and ignominious spell in the mid-table doldrums until they were finally promoted a decade and a half later, in the eventful spring of 1966.)

Alf Ramsey loved that first season in the Second Division with Arthur Rowe and Tottenham. Years later, after Spurs had gone on to win the First Division title, he would say that the promotion-winning side, not the League champions, was the stuff of his fondest dreams, for all the right Ramsey reasons: 'It was a real privilege to play for that team, for a finer bunch of lads never existed . . . nowhere have I found such a team spirit or a will to win.'

The 1949–50 promotion season also contained the match which he would look proudly back upon as his own greatest game as a player. Interestingly, that may have been at least in part because during the away league fixture with Grimsby Town on 19 November 1949, a very rare thing occurred. Alf Ramsey scored a goal from open play. Tactics, when all was said done, were just the foreplay: extremely enjoyable foreplay, particularly for those who were good at little else, but not to be compared with the orgasm gained from a beaten goalkeeper and a bulging net . . .

Spurs were six points clear at the top and unbeaten away from White Hart Lane when they travelled to Blundell Park. Grimsby took the lead within 60 seconds, but then . . . 'This was it,' relished Alf. 'We rolled up our sleeves and went after the equaliser . . .'

It failed to materialise. Instead, Grimsby scored again, and came close to making it 3–0 when Tommy Briggs hit the bar. Spurs right-winger 'Sonny' Walters then pulled a thigh muscle, and in those days long before the introduction of substitutes, Tottenham were chasing a two-goal deficit with ten fit men and a passenger in front of Alfred Ramsey. Lesser teams, lesser generals might have wilted.

Inside-right Les Bennett got them back in the game after a solo run shortly before half-time, and they trooped into the dressing-room 2–1 down. Arthur Rowe's comments there, and Ramsey's delighted recollection of them, are instructive. They would be recalled on a hot afternoon at Wembley 17 years later.

'Well done boys,' said Rowe to his losing side. 'You can do it.' Ramsey and the other players had been half expecting a rollicking. 'The confidence his words inspired,' Ramsey would remember, 'was wonderful . . . Every one of the lads had the utmost confidence in his ability successfully to diagnose a game and to prescribe some sort of success medicine.' And . . . 'When Arthur said something in that quiet manner of his, you knew he wasn't talking for talking's sake. He had said we could win, and after that I don't think anyone in that dressing-room was in doubt about the outcome.'

Rowe certainly motivated Ramsey. Eight minutes into the second half he collected the ball on the halfway line, saw Sonny Walters unmarked on the right flank, remembered the winger's pulled muscle, broke with protocol, ignored him and drifted forward. The Grimsby defence peeled away before the Tottenham full-back, the left-half covering Walters, and the left-back and centre-half unsure of how to cope with this entirely unprecedented sight: Alf Ramsey bearing down on goal. 'Then it was that the realisation that I had a scoring chance dawned on me, but even at that stage it seemed just too far-fetched to be true.'

Bereft of a right-winger, Alf had no choice. He pushed on, found himself inside the box, and – 'my heart around the region of my mouth' – scored.

'The crowd seemed as surprised as I was, but they gave me a big hand – a Cleethorpes crowd, remember – that I heard dimly as the boys suddenly converged upon me. The ribbing I received after that!' Left-winger Les Medley went on to make it 3–2, and Spurs' unbeaten away run remained intact.

They were happy times at Tottenham. Journalist and Spurs fan Ralph Finn remembered the maximum-wage days when reporters such as himself had cars, but professional footballers did not, and he would drive Ramsey and half of his team-mates from White Hart Lane to Manor House station after home games. 'I used to have three-cornered chats with Arthur Rowe and Alf Ramsey. When I travelled to away matches with them in the days when I was reporting matches regularly, Bill Nicholson [*Spurs' right-half and future manager*] would sit in a corner reading – usually studying, he was a very serious student even in those days – while Arthur Rowe, Alf Ramsey and, when he was present [*England manager*] Walter Winterbottom, or at other times one or other of the reporters making the trip, would talk football. Alf was always intelligent. A deep thinker. A man with ideas of his own.'

Small innovations, small advances: Ramsey got Spurs' goalkeeper Ted Ditchburn to throw the ball to his full-backs' feet rather than punt it hopefully downfield; he himself practised playing it to centre-forward Len Duquemin's capable chest for the big Channel Islander to control and turn; he worked at finding Les Medley on the left wing from free-kicks on the right, while the rest of the forward line decoyed the opposition defence in the penalty area. After England had scraped a lucky 2–0 win over Italy at White Hart Lane in the November of 1949, he commented: 'That afternoon I realised more than ever that it is sometimes more important to watch the man than the ball . . . to watch where the man runs when he has parted with the ball.'

Simple things 40 years later, simple things 25 years later, but breathtakingly intellectual, almost revolutionary in the complacent world of post-war English soccer. And the first truly shocking evidence of the need for revolution was about to be delivered.

It came out of the blue, with no effective forewarning. If anything, it was a disaster in disguise. It crept slowly and imperceptibly up on the Football Association. In April 1950 England travelled north to Hampden Park to play Scotland in a Home International Championship match with a difference. The difference was that England and Scotland had simultaneously decided to enter the fourth World Cup, which was due to be held in Brazil that summer. It would be their first crack at the Jules Rimet Trophy. FIFA agreed that the Home Internationals (which from 1882 until 1984 were contested annually between England, Scotland, Wales and, first, Ireland, and after 1924 Northern Ireland) could be used as a World Cup qualifying group.

Six major teams, including Argentina, Belgium, Peru and Austria had withdrawn (and the two new Germanies, East and West, had, in 1950, other things on their minds), and so FIFA added that the top two British sides would qualify. That was not good enough for the Scots. As reigning Home International champions following a 3–1 win at Wembley in 1949, they proudly announced that they would only travel to Brazil if they won the group, not as runners-up.

The build-up to that Hampden game could not have been more tense. England had beaten Northern Ireland 9–2, Scotland had thumped them 8–2; England had beaten Wales 4–1, Scotland by 2–0. The Scottish FA could be expected to overlook the shame of a runners-up place on goal-average, and so all that was required at Hampden to salvage both sides' honour and book two sets of tickets for Rio was a draw.

England won 1–0 with a goal from Chelsea's inside-left Roy Bentley in the 63rd minute. Right-back Alf Ramsey contained for once the Scottish danger-man, left-winger Billy Liddell of 'Liddellpool', the player who, along with Pearson and Mitchell, routinely caused him most grief in the English League. The secretary of the FA, Stanley Rous, begged the Scots to change their minds and travel; the English captain Billy Wright repeated the request to his opposite number George Young, stressing that the England team would benefit by some neighbourly company in South America; but to no avail. Scotland stayed put and England became the first United Kingdom team to enter the World Cup.

Two months later they were wishing they'd stayed at home. England fitted in a couple of May friendlies, beating Portugal and Belgium comfortably in Lisbon and Brussels, and arrived in Rio de Janeiro as joint favourites with the hosts, Brazil. Everybody, including the bookies, still believed in the Founding Fathers. On 25 June an England team which was selected not by the manager Walter Winterbottom, but in the absence of the rest of his international committee solely by the travelling FA chairman, Arthur Drewry, a fish-processing millionaire from Grimsby with a lot of free time on his hands; which was looked after by a hired Brazilian doctor who handed out sedatives like sweeties; which was given £2.00 a day to spend on themselves; and which was coached, effectively, by a man –

Winterbottom – who had no decisive voice in the personnel or formation of the side, played its first group game, against Chile at the Maracana Stadium. England won 2–0 despite Chile's superior performance. It was their seventh successive international victory. It seemed that England may not have the fancy tricks of the South Americans, and may be missing not only a doctor, but also a team selector with any valid experience, but they could still depend on those roast-beef qualities of the English professional league: gritty defending and a couple of bludgeoning centre-forwards to see them through times of difficulty. Most pundits saw no reason to alter the odds.

Four days later Drewry's lads arrived in a cool, brisk mining town high in the mountains named Belo Horizonte to claim two points from the bankers of their group, the United States of America. The pitch at Belo Horizonte was small and bumpy, the grass was uncut, it was hemmed in on three sides by a concrete wall, and it was bordered by a murderous cinder track. There was no suitable dressing-room and the England team changed at their hotel. The Americans, they learned before the game, were in no condition to play an important match, having spent most of the previous night partying. Drewry stuck with the side which had beaten Chile, leaving out Jackie Milburn and – against the expressed wishes of his team coach Walter Winterbottom and the FA's secretary Stanley Rous – Stanley Matthews.

In the 38th minute a Scot called MacIllveney, who had played seven times for Wrexham and who qualified for the USA under FIFA's residency rule, took a throw-in from the right. It reached left-half Bahr, who shot cleanly but innocuously from 25 yards. Goalkeeper Bert Williams had it covered until Joe Gaetjens, a Haitian centre-forward guesting for the USA, dived at it and made the slightest of contacts, and the Americans were 1–0 up.

And that was how it stayed, despite a Ramsey free-kick being headed goalwards by Mullen and cleared off the line, and despite – at the other end – Ramsey himself making a desperate goal-line clearance. Nor was that the end of the matter. Everybody would remember the USA catastrophe ('His face creased,' said a journalist who, decades later, mentioned Belo Horizonte to a member of that

England team, 'he looked like a man who had been jabbed in an unhealed wound.'), but there was more to come. In their last game, a game which England had to win, they went down 1–0 to Spain, who they had last played in 1931 in London and beaten 7–1. Spain consequently qualified comfortably, with maximum points, for the final group, where they were beaten 6–1 by Brazil who, in turn, lost the final 2–1 to Uruguay.

As the Spain match drew to its close, 90,000 Brazilians in the Maracana took out white handkerchiefs and waved them at England. One journalist reported this pathetically to his readers as a 'gallant farewell to gallant losers'. It was not. The Brazilians were waving white handkerchiefs in derision. They were signalling to the hopeless that the time had come for them to surrender.

But then, not many English people drew the proper conclusions from the 1950 World Cup. The press floated headline comparisons with Dunkirk and Gallipoli. There were mutterings about lax refereeing and cynical time-wasting during the last 40 minutes of the game against Spain, and the FA chairman and humiliated team selector Arthur Drewry loudly lamented the USA's 'ineligible' players (eight of the Americans had in fact been born in the States – six of them in St Louis – while the Scot, the Haitian and the Belgian left-back were eligible through residency; and too few back home saw fit to ask Drewry what, in any case, he chose to fear in a failed Third Division half-back, a player from one of the worst equipped footballing countries in the world and a Belgian emigrant who had never played professional soccer).

England did not stay on in South America. Their flight home had originally been booked – revealingly – for the day after the final. They left straight after elimination. What reason was there to stay? To see Uruguay, Brazil, Sweden and Spain play each other? What could be learned?

Alf Ramsey took home two lessons, and two alone. He had much in common with Arthur Drewry and his colleagues, in that he saw no reason, and he would never see any reason, to castigate English football. English football was fine and strong. No matter what they now said in Spain and in St Louis, English football was arguably still the most powerful in the world. But that had been in part its downfall. No

31

opponent, thought Alf, should ever again be underestimated. And the FA's preparations for their trip to South America had been complacent, had left much to be desired. Get those things right, thought Alf, and the rest would surely follow.

Three years followed which would do little to shake Ramsey's faith. That November he temporarily replaced the injured Billy Wright as captain of England (and thereafter served as vice-captain), and as his country settled back into its comfortable, accustomed routine of beating foreigners in friendlies at home, drawing with them away, and losing to Scotland every other year, his club, Tottenham Hotspur, achieved the remarkable feat of winning the League championship on its first season back in the top flight. Alf was never captain of Spurs, but he picked up more than his share of the plaudits. He was 'the soccer intellectual,' enthused the *Daily Mirror* in February 1951 . . .

'To Ramsey, football appears as a succession of chess problems, an exercise of the intellect. For all that, he can produce a lustiness and strength in the tackle when needed . . . He passes a ball with supreme accuracy and precise pace. These are the qualities of Ramsey's game, reflected in himself. He dresses quietly, immaculately. In conversation he is reflective . . . He said one very significant thing to me: "I don't care too much to be told that I have had a wonderful game. I prefer it when someone points out a fault. Then I can do something about it" . . . He spends as much time in ball practice as any inside-forward might. He practises killing the ball from any angle, any height. He concentrates on passing into the 20–30 yard range, and never wants to kick the ball more than 30 yards. All this, he does in addition to laps, sprints and exercises . . . At 28, the boy who was a shop assistant in the Co-op before the war, has come a long way.'

Alf was, at the time of publication, 31 years old.

The ruse was working. He had no thoughts of retirement, and nobody else was suggesting that a 28-year-old international full-back should hang up his boots. Alf Ramsey was conquering time. In November 1951 a strong Austrian team arrived at Wembley, and took a 1–0 lead five minutes into the second half. They held that lead for 20 minutes, and England's home record seemed to be in danger. Then Eddie Baily was brought down in the box. Ramsey placed the ball on the spot, moved back, strode forward, and 'just before my right foot made contact I noticed Zeman move slightly to his right. At once, like a boxer going in for the kill, I sidefooted the ball into the other side of the net.'

The game finished 2–2. Alf liked that one. It was practice paying off.

As 1951 moved into 1952, and Spurs relinquished their League title to Manchester United, some supporters at White Hart Lane did begin to suspect that their right-back was ageing beyond his years. He fiddles about too much, they said. He stands on the ball. He gets into trouble. Ted Ditchburn, the goalkeeper, has to help him out too often. He's slow and he can't tackle. But he survived, with Spurs and with England, until the second famous defeat of the 1950s.

This also came, as great humiliations will, uninvited and unannounced. At the end of 1953 England had been beaten just twice in 24 games since the 1950 World Cup: once – as was only to be expected – by Scotland at Wembley, and once by World Champions Uruguay in Montevideo. In October 1953, the 90th anniversary of the Football Association, they had drawn 4–4 with a FIFA 'Rest Of The World' side at Wembley, thanks to a last minute equalising penalty from A Ramsey. To wrap up the year there was a Home Championship/ World Cup qualifying game against Northern Ireland in Liverpool (3–1 for England), and a friendly against Hungary at Wembley on 25 November.

It should not have been unexpected. Eighty years is a long time to be undefeated on home soil. And the Hungarians of 1953 were one of the great teams of the Age of Innocence. They had not entered the 1950 World Cup, but were 1952 Olympic Champions (these Hungarians were nominally amateur) and in the November of 1953 they were three-and-a-half years into what would turn out to be a six-year run in which they suffered just one defeat – and that in the World Cup final.

They had two forwards, Sandor Kocsis and Ferenc Puskas, who between them would score 158 goals in a combined 152 appearances for Hungary. They had Jozsef Bozsik at centre-half and Nandor Hidegkuti working behind Kocsis and Puskas, and on the left wing they had a fast and immensely talented man named Zoltan Czibor.

Hidegkuti got three against England, Puskas two, and Bozsik the other. Czibor did to Alf Ramsey what his national side did to England in their 6–3 win: he left the full-back looking old and tired, gasping for air and contemplating the end of an era. England replied lamely through Sewell, Mortensen and – in the final minutes, with the score at 2–6 – a last Alf Ramsey penalty for his country.

After 80 years of English international football, nemesis had arrived, and its footsteps echoed throughout the land. At five past three in the playground at the Tom Hood Technical School in Leyton, Essex, a 12-year-old named Robert Moore was told by a school-friend: 'England are one down.'

'You must be joking,' said Robert. 'England one down?' Who are these Hungarians? he wondered.

The news continued to filter through for the remainder of the school day. One each, then 1–3, and on the train back to his home in Barking Robert saw a stop-press latest score in a fellow-passenger's newspaper. England 1, Hungary 4. It must be a misprint, he thought.

It was Alf Ramsey's 32nd and last match for England. Character-istically, he refused to accept the significance – or even the justice – of the result. 'Four of those goals,' he would comment, 'came from outside our penalty area. We should never have lost.'

There is great significance in those two sentences. Alf Ramsey would not until his final days with England, over 20 years later, accept that the national side need ever be beaten by foreign opposi-tion. There was nothing in continental or South American flair, he considered, which could not be overcome by the proper application of sterling English virtues. If, once in a while, those virtues were found to be wanting, it was an aberration, or the opposition had a lucky day. In the gospel according to Alf, England could only defeat itself. He had been brought up in days when that was probably true, and in carrying the confident credo of his childhood and adolescence into international management with a passionate and imperturbable belief, he extended its effective natural life by more than a decade.

Six months later Yugoslavia beat a reconstituted England side 1–0 in Belgrade, and the following week the squad trooped fearfully into Budapest for the return engagement – a warm-up for the immi-nent 1954 Switzerland World Cup, no less! – with the Hungarians.

Puskas and Kocsis got two apiece in the 7–1 win. It remains England's heaviest defeat ever. It was a Sunday afternoon, and commentary was broadcast live on the radio back in Britain. Young Bobby Moore sat glumly by a wireless speaker in Barking. 'Suddenly,' he would recall, 'I sensed that a new age was born. England were no longer the accepted and admired masters of old.' Bobby Moore was wiser, in 1954, than his future boss.

Like Bobby, Alf sat at home and heard the results of England's second World Cup adventure come in. They had qualified with a hundred per cent record on top of the Home International table (and this time second-placed Scotland agreed to travel to Switzerland, where they promptly finished at the bottom of their first-round group), embarked on that disastrous pre-tournament tour of Yugoslavia and Hungary, managed to rally sufficiently to finish on top of their qualifying group, and were then knocked out in the quarter-finals by cup-holders Uruguay. The average age of the England squad was 29, and they had arrived in Lucerne just two-and-a-half days before their opening match. Players too long separated from their loved ones, thought Walter Winterbottom, became dispirited.

And Hungary, the Magical Magyars? They proceeded from their 7–1 pre-championship demolition of England to beat West Germany 8–3 in their opening World Cup tie, before dismissing South Korea 9–0. They then sent Brazil home (4–2), and knocked Uruguay out of the semi-finals by the same score. In the final they would face West Germany, who had somehow recovered from that opening day to sneak through the weaker half of the draw. With eight minutes gone, Hungary were 2–0 up through Puskas and Ramsey's old tormentor, Czibor. West Germany pulled themselves back from the brink and equalised within another eight minutes. Hungary pressed on in the driving rain but somehow failed to score, and five minutes from time West Germany broke away and grabbed the winner. The greatest side that Europe had ever seen, unbelievably went home as runners-up – and to commence another unbeaten run which stretched until 1956.

His international playing career gone, Alf Ramsey's time at Tottenham was running thin. The old tricks could no longer sustain him. His brain still worked but his legs, never the fastest in the world, were going. Left-wingers jockeyed into puddles just got out of them again, and left Alf Ramsey behind. He was dropped – by his mentor Arthur Rowe – from the Spurs first team; he was told by the board that no coaching job could be found for him at Tottenham, although Rowe wanted him as assistant manager (Alf Ramsey, who would become a footballer's manager, was always a manager's footballer); and as a final insult he was denied a seat on the bus for Tottenham's 1955 continental tour, a tour which he had been anticipating with great pleasure as a personal swansong.

His time was up. It had been a good run. During a professional career which had effectively started at the age of 27, Alf Ramsey had won the Second and First Division championships, 32 England caps, and had played in a World Cup. He had no cause to regret the subterfuge which had encouraged an ambitious manager to pay a record fee for a 29-year-old in the belief that he was only 27. Ramsey had gone from those few quid a week at Southampton in the post-war years to £1,000 a year at Tottenham in the thriving '50s – 'not bad pay for doing the job on which I set my heart'.

Having been refused that coaching job at White Hart Lane, Alf Ramsey could go in only one direction. Football had become his life. He bet occasionally on the horses and the dogs, chiefly because other players did so, and for the same reason he played golf without much enthusiasm. But they were the extent of his hinterland. He was obsessed with the game of football, and only one road was open to him in the close season of 1955. He had to become a manager. All of his playing career had groomed him for management. Not only his tactical quizzing of everyone from Jackie Milburn to Walter Winterbottom; not just his careful observance of players and teams; but also the air of dignity, the sense of gravitas which he had cultivated assiduously, and which he felt to be part of a true manager's make-up. He was a model of self-improvement, on and off the training park. 'In the evening,' he said in 1952, 'I usually have a long read, for, like Billy Wright, I have found that serious reading has helped me to develop a command of words so essential when you suddenly find yourself called upon to make a speech. People, remember, are inclined to forget that speechmaking may not be your strong point.

With this in mind, I always try hard to put up some sort of a show when asked "to say a few words".'

In the jargon of a later age, Alfred Ramsey was upwardly mobile. In the manner of his own era, that mobility was not confined to income. Consciously and deliberately, Ramsey deferred to class. His irresistible rise would be marked not only by a steady increase in take-home pay, but also by the improved social mannerisms which he felt should properly accompany new-found wealth. Hence the contorted attempts at a spoken grammar which always eluded him; hence the clipped and constipated accent which he felt to be more suited than the chirpy tones of Five Elms Farm to a man of position. He could have been produced by no other country in the world, at no other point in time.

A venerable but unremarkable club from the Third Division (South), Ipswich Town, were in search of a manager. Ipswich had been founded back in 1878, but had only been elected to the Football League in 1948. They had a cricket pavilion for dressing-rooms, railway sleepers for terracing, and a ground capacity of 24,000 – a third of the big city clubs. Ipswich Town was run by the Cobbold brothers, the Old Etonian sons of a famous brewing family.

Having just been demoted from the dizzy heights of Division Two after one glorious season, their secretary/manager Scott Duncan was anxious to unburden himself of the latter part of his job description. Alf applied, was offered the job, and on 9 August 1955 Tottenham Hotspur released him from his contract. (A month later a factotum with West Ham United called Jack Turner found himself watching Leyton Boys draw 3–3 with East Ham, and left to report of one 15-year-old: 'Whilst he would not set the world alight, this boy certainly impressed me with his tenacity and industry.' Young Bobby Moore was subsequently taken on to the West Ham ground staff at £6 15s per week.)

It took Alf two seasons to get Ipswich back into the Second Division, two seasons during which it is arguable that rubbing shoulders with the Cobbolds gave an added urgency to his ambition to improve his enunciation, and led him into those famous elocution lessons. (This occasion of promotion from the Third Division South in 1957 is remarkable for at least one other thing: it was the last time that a semi-corroborated story would be told of Alf Ramsey cutting loose. He was reported to have been discovered under a table after the Ipswich celebration party, singing *Maybe It's Because I'm A Londoner*.) He then spent three seasons consolidating his side in the middle of the table, and won promotion to the First Division as Second Division champions in 1960–61. This time the Ipswich chairman John Cobbold is said to have gone looking for Ramsey when the manager was not to be seen at the promotion party. Cobbold tracked him down to the deserted stand, where he was watching Ipswich Boys play Norwich Boys. 'Come and get a drink,' urged Cobbold.

Alf looked up at the chairman and replied quietly: 'Not just now, thank you. I'm working.'

In their first season ever in the First Division, 1961–62 (the season after Spurs' second great team of the century had won the double, and the season after a phenomenal 21-year-old, Jimmy Greaves of Chelsea, had topped the goalscoring table with 41), Alf Ramsey's East Anglian minnows won the League championship, thereby repeating Ramsey's feat as a Tottenham player under Arthur Rowe ten years earlier, of taking the Second and First Division titles in consecutive years.

He would never forget those gallant, hardworking, self-improving players from Ipswich, who grumbled at first at the extra hour of daily training but came happily to accept it as the price of their success. Years later, after he had won the most prestigious trophy in world football and worked with the greatest English players of his day, Alf Ramsey found himself on a train between the Midlands, where he had been watching a cup-tie, and London in the company of a group of journalists. Someone asked him to name his ideal forward line. Ramsey paused, and then announced straightfaced: 'Stephenson, Moran, Crawford, Phillips . . .' His old Ipswich Town attack.

Tottenham had been Tottenham, though, one of the big five even then, with cash to spend and the glamour to attract both fans and players. Ipswich Town were church mice. During their season of promotion from the Third Division, Ramsey was told that he could spend £3,000 on new players – one-seventh of what Alf Ramsey alone had cost Tottenham in 1949, and exactly double his own managerial wage at Ipswich.

He spent not a penny of that £3,000. By the end of his seven years at Ipswich, when they had lasted four seasons in the Second Division and one in the First, he had laid out just £30,000 on footballers. Alf Ramsey believed that comparatively ordinary British players – almost any ordinary players, so long as they were British – could, given the correct organisation, motivation and training, win football matches. They did not need to have the grace and vision of Danny Blanchflower and John White, or the predatory genius of Greaves. He himself was walking individual evidence of the success of this theory of application. He would make Ipswich Town the visible collective proof.

'Alf Ramsey had thought about his team,' says Eamon Dunphy, 'and come to the conclusion that his players weren't good enough to compete, in any positive sense, with their betters. His response was a formula which stopped good footballers playing.'

There is a lot of truth in that statement, and it was of course the basis of the anti-Ramsey testimony for two decades and more. It was echoed by Malcolm Allison's judgement that Ramsey was 'a good manager of a bad team, but a bad manager of a good one'. But it was not the whole story. Alf Ramsey certainly made Ipswich successful by building from a powerful defence and a hard-tackling midfield. But he also did so by tinkering brilliantly with their established formation.

Since the last quarter of the 19th century football teams had adopted as a matter of course an outfield playing pattern which was simply described as 2–3–5. This time-honoured shape – which would vestigially, and anachronistically, survive in newspaper match reports until the early 1970s, and in British schoolboy football until even later – consisted of strict positions with clearly defined responsibilities. There were two full-backs, right and left, numbers two and three, whose job was to stop the opposing wingers. There were three half-backs, right, centre and left, numbers four, five and six, whose tasks were to mark the inside-forwards and the centre-forward, and do a spot of creative work in their spare time. And the forward line consisted of right-winger, inside-right, centre-forward, inside-left and left-winger – numbers seven, eight, nine, ten and eleven.

In practice, since 1925 when Arsenal's Herbert Chapman and Charlie Buchan had come up with the idea of dropping centre half-back Alex James back to play as a third defender, they lined up more like 3–2–5, or 3–2–2–3, or even 3–4–3, with the centre-half operating almost entirely defensively between the full-backs, the half-backs and inside forwards playing deep and attacking midfield respectively, and the wingers and the centre-forward committed to outright attack (the result could look at times a little like the ultra-modern 1–4–2–3 sweeper system).

The old formation was, by the 1950s, rooted so deeply in British football that certain clearly defined physical characteristics were demanded of those who pulled on the numbered shirts. Full-backs should be horny handed sons of toil; wingers should usually be nippy, and able to cross a ball accurately. Half-backs were expected to be either fearsome in the tackle, like Tottenham's Dave MacKay, or incisive passers of the ball, such as Fulham's Johnny Haynes; centre-halves were tall and good in the air, occasionally with a permitted dash of elegance. Inside-forwards were above all tricky (Jimmy Greaves), and centre-forwards big, brave and bustling (such as Bobby Smith of Spurs, or Nat Lofthouse). In 1955 an experienced eye could scan the team photograph of a British side and, without seeing it play, place the players in their positions with a 90 per cent chance of accuracy.

By the end of the 1950s it had been agreed in other countries that the system was no longer sacrosanct. The Brazilians were lining up with two in the middle and four up front, and whatever shape the Hungarians were using, with Hidegkuti roaming behind two strikers, it was certainly not 3–2–5.

Some British clubs were receptive, however briefly, to the new notions. It could be a traumatic experience. In the summer of 1960 West Ham United hosted a friendly match against Fluminense of Brazil. That young defender from Essex, Bobby Moore, was, by then, a first-team regular, and he recalled: 'I was at left-half and Noel Cantwell was at left-back. As soon as we had kicked off Noel and I realised that we were up against something rather different to what we were used. The Brazilian right-winger lay very deep and the inside-right played well upfield.

'For ten minutes we stuck to our normal game, the traditional man-to-man marking which meant that I, as left-half, had to lie deeper than Noel to mark the inside man. This was obviously not going to work out.

'"You move out and mark the winger," Noel told me. "I'll take the inside man."'

'This change meant that I was really playing full-back, marking the extreme wing while Noel covered the inside . . .'

West Ham discussed 4–2–4 after the Fluminense game and decided to try it in the League. Bobby Moore would remember the strange, disconcerting feeling of being one of the first British footballers in almost a century of organised soccer to go on to a field wearing a number six (left-half's) shirt, but then actually to play left-back. It felt as if the earth had shifted slightly on its axis. West Ham dropped the system a quarter of the way through the season because, after a mixed series of results, their manager Ted Fenton considered that 4–2–4 was costing them too many goals. How, given that Fenton was managing West Ham United, he knew for certain exactly what was costing him too many goals, has not been explained.

Curiously, a future England team-mate of Moore's, Ramon Wilson, had a similar experience with Huddersfield Town in 1962–63. At a meeting of players and management, everyone 'liked the idea' of 4–2–4. 'Everyone agreed to give it a whirl. For some time we did well playing in this way. The lads seemed to like it, but then it was changed and finally dropped so that from doing above average we started to slide. I could not understand any reason for abandoning the system.'

Huddersfield had experimented with 4–2–4 because England were perceived as having successfully adopted the new shape since 1960. Walter Winterbottom had introduced it almost in desperation. Two bad defeats in the May of that year, 0–3 to Spain in an electric storm in Madrid, and 0–2 to Hungary in Budapest, were followed too quickly for comfort by the return of Spain to Wembley. Winterbottom told his side that they would play 4–2–4; he slotted his two most cultured half-backs, Johnny Haynes and Bobby Robson, in the middle;

and – with an interested Ray Wilson and Bobby Moore both watching with approval – England delivered their best performance in years to win 4–2.

Alf Ramsey did not exactly introduce 4–2–4 to Portman Road in the late 1950s and early '60s, although he came close to it. Anything too revolutionary would not only offend against his own instincts, it would also, he knew, be in danger of not carrying the players with it. 'Any method of play,' he said, 'demands complete understanding of what you, as manager, are trying to introduce and what they, the players, will have to do to make it work.'

He had two big, strong forwards, Ray Crawford and the local boy Ted Phillips, and he had an ageing, wizened, slightly-built, one-footed and extremely slow Scot named Jimmy Leadbetter, who wore the number eleven shirt. Ramsey pulled Leadbetter back into left midfield and used the Scot – whose distribution was excellent and experience invaluable – as a linkman, while he inclined Crawford and Phillips to the left-hand side of the forward line. Second Division, and even First Division, full-backs invariably followed Leadbetter towards the halfway line, leaving their flank open to plunder. In their season of promotion from Division Two, Crawford got 40 of his side's 100 League goals, and Phillips 30. Ipswich scored 93 goals in winning the First Division title. Crawford collected 33 of them and Phillips 28. They got them through a fast build-up which depended on 'a concentrated, well-organised defence', and on Jimmy Leadbetter's speed of thought and positional sense. 'We believe in striking quickly from defence,' said Ramsey. 'A team is most vulnerable when it has just failed in attack. If I had to suggest an ideal number of passes I would say three. It is difficult to generalise on such a fluid game as football, but generally the second pass out of defence I would regard as the most vital.

'Say, for example, we have won the ball by a tackle or interception in our defence. The first pass would be from the defender perhaps to a wing-half, more likely to Leadbetter. It would be the next pass which would put us in an attacking position – provided it were made quickly, accurately and in such a way as to penetrate the defence.'

They were a dull team to watch. In this, Alf Ramsey was indisput-

ably consistent: few if any of his sides would thrill the neutral spectator. But most of the rest of the Football Association was impressed.
Impressed enough to mark Jimmy Leadbetter – 'the basis of all the
Ipswich success,' said Ramsey helpfully – out of every game that he
played for the remainder of his career.

And impressed enough to offer Alf Ramsey the England job.

3 SWEDEN, CHILE AND LANCASTER GATE

'I remembered Walter Winterbottom saying that if you
got eight world class players and stuck them in a team
then they would take care of themselves. But was that the
case? Some world class players need a bit of guidance.'

– BOBBY MOORE

Change had been overdue for years. England's competitive record
since Alf Ramsey's retirement from the international scene after the
Hungary debacle of 1953, and since the disappointing Switzerland
World Cup in the following year, had been miserable. In less than a
decade British soccer players, fans and journalists had progressed
from the absurd assumption that their international squad was easily
the best in the world, to the sneaking, uneasy feeling that it may be
one of the worst. The continentals and South Americans had, by
unfathomable devices, stolen our thunder.

The 1958 World Cup was held in Sweden, and the Home
Internationals were dropped as a qualifying tournament. This initially appeared to favour the British national sides. England, Scotland
and Northern Ireland all won their three-team qualifying groups
(Northern Ireland remarkably seeing off both Italy and Portugal); and
Wales, who finished second in theirs, came first out of the hat in a
sweepstake of runners-up to determine who should play off against
Israel, all of whose Middle-Eastern opponents had withdrawn in
political protest. Wales won, and so for the first and the last time
all four of the home countries travelled to a World Cup finals.
Astonishingly, England were once more joint favourites – with
Brazil and the USSR – to win the Jules Rimet trophy. In their one

previous meeting with Brazil, at Fortress Wembley in 1956, England had won 4–2; and their last warm-up game before Sweden, just three weeks before the real thing, had resulted in a 1–1 draw with the Soviets in Moscow. Surely the bookies knew their job.

Yet again, the English preparations were hilariously bad. While Brazil – who had also yet to win the World Cup – flew in with an extensive back-up team of experts, including a psychologist who got the Brazilian players to draw pictures of a human figure and from the results advised the manager of their fitness to play, and what position would be best for them (the creators of childish stick-figures should be put on one wing and men who drew sophisticated portraits on the other, for balance, considered this expert. Garrincha's and the 17-year-old Pele's stick-figures were, however, apparently so elementary that Dr Joao Carvalhaes recommended that they should not be allowed on the field at all. He was politely ignored.). While most participant countries had the scene scouted and the squad prepared for months before, England once more arrived last, just three days before their first match, to find themselves without a training camp (they put up for the whole tournament at the Park Avenue Hotel in the centre of Gothenburg, while their opponents trained in the country-side of western Sweden), and Walter Winterbottom reputedly spent much of his first week in the country chasing around looking for accommodation.

England had another, graver, cross to bear in 1958. On 6 February a BEA Elizabethan passenger aircraft on its way home from Belgrade crashed in blizzard conditions after refuelling at Munich airport. Twenty-three people died, including eight players from Matt Busby's brilliant young Manchester United side. Four of them were established English internationals. Roger Byrne was the regular left-back. Tommy Taylor had scored 16 goals in 19 games for his country, eight of them in the four qualifying matches. David Pegg had just replaced Tom Finney on the left wing, and the prodigious 21-year-old Duncan Edwards was the central genius – some said the entire future – of both his club and his country. In the shadow of the death of those enormous talents, England travelled to the sixth World Cup that June with just one Manchester United player: a 20-year-old with three caps and three goals to his tally, who had seriously considered giving up football after the Munich disaster. He was one of the nephews of Alf Ramsey's old room-mate Jackie Milburn. His name was Bobby Charlton, and he did not get a game.

England and Scotland failed to get past their first round groups to the quarter-finals. Wales and Northern Ireland managed it, the former beating Hungary of all teams in a play-off thanks to a 25-yard Ivor Allchurch volley which would have ranked as the goal of any tournament other than this one – which was already illuminated by the astonishing feats of France's Just Fontaine and West Germany's Helmut Rahn – before losing creditably to the eventual winners, Brazil, thanks to a single piece of close control and sharp finishing from Pele. Fontaine, on his way to a record 13 goals in the finals, buried Northern Ireland in the quarters. There was some British representation at the final. The Brazilians were presented with the cup by one Arthur Drewry, the Football Association chairman who had eight years earlier picked an England team which lost to the USA, and who had by 1958 been rewarded by a grateful world with the presidency of FIFA.

The Celtic taste of glory only emphasised England's awful bankruptcy. It was impossible to understand. On the face of it, even after Munich the players were there. Billy Wright and Tom Finney were, admittedly, 34 and 36 years old respectively, but Johnny Haynes and Bobby Robson were just 23 and 25, big Bobby Smith was banging them in for Spurs, Don Howe and Maurice Norman were accomplished defenders . . .

They journeyed back wearily, press, travelling public and players alike, to a gloomy country many of whose people had for the first time been able to watch the World Cup on television. (The 1954 series in Switzerland had been broadcast in part on the BBC through Eurovision, but in 1954 television sets were still rare. By 1958 they were much more common, and both BBC and ITV carried live coverage of the games.) Unfortunately, there was still no shortage of excuses. On top of the trauma of Munich, after FIFA scrapped seeding England had undoubtedly been dumped in the toughest group, along with Brazil, the Soviets and Austria. They had drawn with all three, and lost only to the USSR in a play-off.

So they travelled back to a hostile media and a public baying for blood as much with those excuses in mind as reform, and then the worst possible thing happened. Their eliminators in Sweden, the Soviet Union, visited London for a friendly in October, and England won 5–0. What was wrong with that? Was anything wrong with that? The FA's International Selection Committee preened its feathers – not least because it had overruled Walter Winterbottom and recalled to the team the 32-year-old Nat Lofthouse, who had not played in any of the '58 cup games, and Lofthouse had scored – and looked forward to the 1960s.

In 1960 FIFA decided that the the 1966 World Cup finals – the first to take place after the 100th anniversary of the birth of the organised game – would be staged in England. Later that year England played their first qualifying game of the 1962 finals, away to Luxembourg, and won 9–0 with Jimmy Greaves and Bobby Charlton getting a hat-trick apiece.

Portugal – traditionally a soft touch – were also disposed of, and England would be the only team from the United Kingdom to qualify for the seventh World Cup in Chile. They no longer journeyed in hope or in expectation. 'On reflection,' said that Huddersfield Town full-back Ray Wilson, who had first been capped against Scotland two years earlier, 'I know now that we all travelled out there with some strange attitudes and quaint notions. "If only we can do well" – that was the feeling. I do not believe that anyone in the party, from Walter Winterbottom downwards, really felt we could win it. We left London for a World Cup warm-up in Peru hardly bristling with the confidence of men who were to live and play alongside the greatest teams in the world.'

Shortly before leaving England Winterbottom had made a decision which would have enormous significance for a later England squad. On the eve of the FA Cup final in May he collared the new West Ham manager Ron Greenwood and discussed his 21-year-old half-back Bobby Moore. Four days later Moore ambled into Upton Park to collect some kit for West Ham's imminent summer tour of South Africa, and was told to report to Greenwood's office.

'You won't be going to South Africa with us, Bobby,' said Greenwood.

'Why?'

Greenwood grinned. 'You're going to Chile with the World Cup party.'

'You're joking.'

He was not. Moore reported to the Bank of England sports ground at Roehampton for training with the national squad. It took three days for the rest of the squad – captain Johnny Haynes included – to realise that this diffident young man was there not merely to make up the numbers in pre-tournament preparation: he was going with them.

With the Munich disaster in mind, the England squad of 20 footballers, trainer Harold Shepherdson (who had joined up in 1957), assistant manager Jimmy Adamson and Winterbottom flew to Peru in two separate flights. They left on 17 May, a whole two weeks before their first match. Winterbottom had abandoned, without comment, his philosophy that a wifeless player was a lifeless player. The first 'plane appeared to have the favoured team on it; the second carried the reserves. Moore travelled resignedly in the second. At breakfast in Lima Winterbottom approached him and told him he was in the team for that warm-up match against Peru. Bobby Robson had injured an ankle. The 29-year-old Robson would never again play for England.

They beat Peru 4–0. Greaves got three, and Moore staked his claim on the right-half position, as it was still described despite Winterbottom's flirtations with 4–2–4. And then they moved on, with their official translator, the Chilean-born former Newcastle forward, George Robledo, to Chile, to Santiago, and to their training camp.

It was actually a rest camp for executives of the American Braden Copper Company at a place called Coya high in the Andes. The English players boarded a small train in Santiago and sat there for hour after interminable hour as it negotiated one hairpin bend after another, looping around the limitless peaks, finally to evacuate its astounded passengers at a tiny, deserted station where a village band struck up an idiosyncratic version of *God Save The Queen*.

'The trouble was,' Bobby Moore would recall, 'that English footballers are not used to living on mountains.' Half the the squad liked it, enjoyed the isolation and the necessary concentration on training; half came close to rebellion. There was no television at Coya, no pub, no dances. There was a ping-pong table, a torn snooker table, a bowling alley, a tennis court, a tiny cinema which showed Italian films with Spanish sub-titles, and – the saving grace for English professionals – a nine-hole golf course. They were also surrounded by much poverty. Ray Wilson and Jimmy Armfield went for a round of golf one day and were persuaded to employ a child of about eleven who 'looked as though he had not eaten a decent meal for weeks' as caddie. By the 17th hole on their second round of the nine the boy had collapsed. Wilson carried the clubs home, while Armfield carried the caddie.

The talk of football was subdued and apprehensive. 'We knew that Brazil and Russia were two of the fancied teams,' Ray Wilson remembered, 'and that Hungary would present strong opposition in our group. In those days, unconsciously or not, we felt the poor relations. To do reasonably well would satisfy.'

They expected to lose to Hungary in their first match, and they did so by 2–1. Two days later they found themselves up against Argentina, who had done terrible things to the hapless Bulgarians in their first game (there were 69 free-kicks in the match. The Bulgarian dressing-room after their 1–0 defeat looked like a field hospital. One man had stud marks down his spine.). Some English players had watched that battle. 'We left the ground wondering just what we had let ourselves in for,' said Ray Wilson. He soon found out. 'The first tackle I went into [*against Argentina*] I slid with ball and man into touch. He just got up, trod quite firmly on my ankle and walked away. Then, when he could see that I was suitably pained, he returned offering to shake hands on it.'

England responded with spirit and went 2–0 up by half-time. A Greaves goal made it three, and Sanfilippo's consolation strike came too late for the South Americans. It had been England's finest performance yet in a World Cup finals match, but a grudge was formed that afternoon in Rancagua, unpleasant business was left unfinished, which would stir itself again with astonishing consequences four years later.

A draw with Bulgaria put England, for the second time, into the quarter-finals of the World Cup. And as in Switzerland eight years earlier, they faced there the current cup holders.

For Ray Wilson, who was scheduled to mark Brazil's Garrincha, the small forward with the right leg which childhood polio had twisted grotesquely, whom his countrymen had christened 'the little bird', it meant a sleepless night on 9 June. 'I felt as though I was going out to mark a sorcerer; that however brilliant I might be on the day I just would not be good enough. I thought about it hard and long as I lay on my bed the night before the game. If I could hold him we might have a chance, but I had heard so much about his performance in Sweden four years earlier that I knew I was in for a rough time.'

In fact, Wilson did not get too much of a rough time from Garrincha, because Garrincha refused to limit himself to the right wing. The exasperating Brazilians turned out in something resembling a 4–3–3 formation, whatever that was, and Garrincha roamed about the forward line like a palsied elf. He got his first by outjumping Maurice Norman, who stood seven inches taller, at a corner kick. Gerry Hitchens equalised and, thought the optimistic Bobby Moore, 'I seriously began to believe we had a good chance of knocking Brazil out of the competition.'

Eight minutes into the second half Flowers fouled Vava on the edge of the box; Garrincha smashed in a free-kick which Springett failed to hold, and Vava nodded the rebound elegantly home. And six minutes after that Garrincha popped up in the inside-left position, drifted forward, saw Springett off his line and with that bent leg he curled a 25-yard shot around him, if 'curled' is an adequate description of a swerving, dipping drive which did everything but sit on Ron Springett's shoulder and laugh in his face. Brazil were on their way to their second successive World Cup win, and England were on their way home again. 'When I reflect,' says Ray Wilson perceptively, 'on the Chilean proceedings, I can understand why. In the years after that competition football moved with tremendous scientific strides. It had emerged through a revolution by the time the 1966 World Cup came round.

'For the Chile tournament we were in a pretty backward state. There was none of the individual dieting, intensive training and tactics, weekly weighing and pulse-reading and so on that occur now even at club level. We used to laugh at the entourage with the

51

Brazilian team. They always used to have a squad of specialists with their international party and we used to make jokes about them. We ploughed on quite happily with immovable faith in our trainer's magic sponge. We did not even have a doctor with us for the long haul to Peru and Chile.'

That lack of a doctor almost had tragic consequences. The regular centre-half Peter Swan had fallen ill with tonsilitis even before the transatlantic 'plane got into Lima. He was carted up to Coya where he proceeded to contract dysentery. The Braden company doctor mis-diagnosed his complaint and actually prescribed a laxative. Harold Shepherdson grew alarmed and rushed Swan to hospital, where at one stage there were very real fears for his life.

'We returned,' says Wilson, 'realising that the Brazilian method of organising everything down to the finest detail was the wisest.'

They returned also to an announcement from Walter Winterbottom that he was relinquishing the management of England to become general secretary of the Central Council of Physical Recreation. It was a declaration comparable in effect with the resignation of Margaret Thatcher 30 years later. There were young-sters who had never known another England manager. There were England internationals who had not started school in 1947, when Winterbottom first moved on from being Director of Coaching at the Football Association to become part-time manager of the national side.

The Winterbottom era is associated now, and was associated throughout the 1960s, with national footballing stagnation, if not national footballing decline. That is certainly unfair to a loyal, hard-working, knowledgeable and civilised man. Aside from his record of 137 matches played, 78 won, 32 drawn and just 27 lost, it is easily forgotten that he was an intelligent coach who won the respect of most of his players and his fellow managers.

'He was a warm, outgoing man,' remembered Bobby Moore, 'who loved talking about techniques, tactics, skills, attitudes. You could bet your life he knew every good player in every country by his Christian name, knew every individual's strengths and weaknesses. The man was a walking education on football. Walter had impressed me because he knew so much about the game, every aspect of it. I had been with him on youth and coaching courses and he was responsible for getting coaching organised in this country. He made people think about football.'

Walter Winterbottom, said Moore's club boss and a future England manager, Ron Greenwood, was, in his time, the instigator of all new ideas in English football. 'I found him to be a terrific fellow,' adds Ray Wilson. 'Here was a man who knew the game inside out and, what is just as important, he really knew how to handle people. He had the game sewn up tactically and could not be faulted on that score. Perhaps he could conceivably have been a more ruthless, bolder manager. At any event, I maintain that he did English soccer a great service when he was at the helm.'

But Walter Winterbottom carried around his neck two smallish albatrosses, and one so immense that eventually, after 17 years, it dragged him down.

The small birds were, on their own, supportable. One was his background and manner. He had been an undistinguished player, turning out only occasionally for Manchester United at centre-half in order to pay his way through Carnegie College. Thereafter he became a schoolmaster, and he looked and spoke like a schoolmaster. Unlike Alf Ramsey, Winterbottom did not need to affect cultured tones, and to some in the game this made him an effete, ivory-tower snob. Coupled with his carefully prepared dossiers on the opposition – which were 'complete and sweeping', says Bobby Charlton – and gentle, articulately delivered team-talks, which left some players yawning and scratching their heads, Winterbottom's academic demeanour made him seem too much like the maths teacher that many professional footballers had departed early from secondary modern school in order to escape.

All of which segues into his second minor burden: the assertion that he was too tactical. Winterbottom operated, of course, in the last 17 years of the Age of Innocence. In comparison with every one of his successors, he was about as tactical as an 18th-century peasant punting a pigskin towards the next village. But . . .

But: 'There cannot be many men in the game,' says Bobby Charlton, 'who saw the theory, practice and politics of football as clearly as he did. But . . .' But: '. . . he didn't have a professional back-

53

ground and he couldn't put his ideas over because he would never push you hard enough. He was too nice.'

Charlton himself was also too nice to stab Winterbottom fatally in the back. It was left to Saint Stanley Matthews, the emblematic English footballer of the Age of Innocence, to put the boot in with relish (after his international retirement, of course). Stanley was such a child of his gilded age that he even objected to the manager talking to his team before kick-off. His judgement of the failings of Walter Winterbottom illustrate more clearly than anything else the yawning gulf which opened up between the 1950s and the 1970s. It is a manifesto of the Age of Innocence, written in its dying months.

'I noticed,' said Matthews of his return to the post-war England side which happened to be coached by Walter Winterbottom, 'the will to win was sadly lacking in the England team . . . I blame this on the pre-match talks on playing tactics that had been introduced for the first time by our team manager. You just cannot tell star players how they must play and what they must do when they are on the field in an international match. You must let them play their natural game, which has paid big dividends in the past.

'I have noticed that in recent years these pre-match instructions have become more and more long-winded while the playing ability of the players on the field has dwindled. So I say scrap the talks and instruct the players to play their natural game.'

'I have repeatedly insisted,' replied a hurt, defensive Winterbottom, missing the opportunity to explain to Matthews and to the general public the difference between successfully disciplined skills and joyous, impotent anarchy, 'on our players having every opportunity to play as a team before an important match to enable us to cut down on these instructions. Players are always encouraged to play their own game.'

But these were modest loads for a manager of England to bear. The one which broke his back was the Football Association's International Selection Committee. Throughout his long tour of duty, Walter Winterbottom was never once allowed to pick his own side. It would not do to exaggerate the influence of the Selection Committee: certainly towards the end of his regime, Winterbottom occasionally got his own team selection for no-account friendly matches rubber-stamped by the old men of Lancaster Gate. (When their brief had finally been cancelled, one of their number would actually claim that he could hardly recall an occasion on which Walter had been overruled, that Winterbottom had called the tune '99 per cent of the time', which, as well as being untrue, begged the unanswered questions: if you were so redundant, what were you doing on all of those international flights; and why did you not vote yourselves out of office years ago?)

The truth was that throughout Winterbottom's career they were always there – 25 of them in all, responsible for youth teams, under-23s, and a jury of 12 to determine the full England senior squad – looming in the background, lurching to the fore as each World Cup came round, grasping for the junket tickets to exotic locations, filling out the expenses forms, chipping in with their giddy opinions, shamelessly haggling with each other (for most of them were also club directors) to push forward their own favoured players, failing to recognise members of the England team when they walked past them at Wembley. 'For a good many of the early years I spent as England captain,' said Bobby Moore, 'I was addressed as Ron by certain committee men because they thought I was Ron Flowers, who also happened to have fair hair and played at wing-half.'

Stanley Rous, who was FA secretary between 1934 and 1961 and was consequently better placed than most to observe these mastodons in their pomp, offered possibly the best and most scathing description of the International Selection Committee at work. 'They say of the camel,' offered Rous, 'that it looks so weird it could only have been designed by a committee, and some of our international teams were just as ill-balanced as a result of the system. The committee of up to 12 would discuss each position in turn and vote on it if necessary. Invariably personal preferences intruded and positions were considered in isolation rather than thought being given to the team as an entity.

'A typical exchange might start with Major Keys saying: "But you cannot include Ronnie Clayton. The last time I saw him play, our own half-back looked much more impressive." Then another would add: "Yes – when we played Blackburn he wasn't in the same class as ours."

'Walter would point out that they were judging Clayton on one away game, and in away games there is a disdavantage for individuals as well as teams. He would add: "The real reason I want Clayton is that he and Bryan Douglas understand each other so well that we are much stronger down the right when those two play together, even if two other individuals may be as good or better, as individuals."

'But within a few minutes the committee might have ruled out Clayton and be considering the other players of their own nomination. By the time the process was repeated with four or five other players it was a hybrid side that was finally announced to the press.'

'I couldn't understand,' Bobby Moore also said of Walter Winterbottom, 'how he allowed himself to be messed about by the amateurs of the FA Selection Committee. I felt he'd lost the will to fight the system.'

He had, and he would not be rewarded for it. Winterbottom resigned partly because his will had finally failed him, and partly because the FA had refused to make him its secretary – a post to which he would have been perfectly suited – when Stanley Rous moved on to replace Arthur Drewry as president of FIFA following the latter's death in 1961. They gave the job instead to one of their own, Dennis Follows, and Walter Winterbottom, after service and experience which spanned four decades, walked unrecognised and virtually unthanked out of English football. He would not be the last to be so mistreated.

At least one of his older players had a good word to say of him. 'Like everyone in football,' said the Ipswich Town manager Alf Ramsey of his introduction to the international squad back in 1948, incidentally providing the clearest available picture of his predecessor's methods, 'I had heard of Mr Winterbottom's famous pre-match talks . . .

'After a pow-wow of about 90 minutes, I had a great respect not only for Mr Winterbottom's knowledge of the game, but his ability to put over points in a concise and easy-to-understand manner. Before touching on the football the England team manager pointed out to us the importance of everything being correct and the fact that our own soccer prestige was at stake . . . Then he got down to business . . .

'It was clear that the England chief, realising that the best men for the job had been chosen did not waste time trying to sell ideas to footballers who have already proved themselves in an international match. Rather did Walter Winterbottom act as chairman of the meeting at which ideas were pooled with Walter himself explaining just how he thought our opponents would play. Even I, as a new-comer, realised how skilfully Mr Winterbottom, a splendid speaker, contrived to blend together our ideas and to pick out the weak links in our opponents' armour and suggested ways and means of taking advantage of them.'

But Walter Winterbottom went, and it was right that he should go because his will had deserted him, and because 17 years is long enough for any international manager at any time, but especially because by 1962 the Modern Era – to which he was only marginally better suited than was Stanley Matthews – was clearly dawning. The only question left to be asked was: would the Football Association's International Selection Committee operate to form and make entirely the wrong appointment as his successor?

Alf Ramsey was in pole position. When Winterbottom announced his departure Ipswich Town had just become League champions. If Ramsey can do that with no money and a bunch of players that nobody has ever heard of, wondered the press and the public, what could he do with Bobby Charlton, Jimmy Greaves, Johnny Haynes and George Eastham?

He was undoubtedly the people's choice. A *Daily Express* readers' poll declared in August 1962 that 'the 38-year-old Ipswich manager' had collected 17½ per cent of their vote, with the Arsenal manager and former England captain Billy Wright second on 16½ per cent; and Bill Nicholson of Spurs and Stan Cullis of Wolves in joint third place with 15 per cent. (Alfred was actually, at the time, 42 years old. He must have felt occasionally like Dorian Gray: his ageing process spiralling uncontrollably in the wrong direction, his loved ones wide-eyed and wondering how the devil he achieved it.)

Down at the bottom of the *Express*'s poll, with one per cent of the popular vote, was the Football Association's first choice as the new manager of England. Jimmy Adamson had done a good, steady job at Burnley, keeping them in the top half of the First Division most of the time, winning the League in 1959–60, and finishing as runners-up to Ipswich in 1961–62. When Billy Wright, who had been assisting

Winterbottom, took on the Arsenal job and refused to travel to Chile, Adamson had been pulled in as his assistant.

Perhaps that was why he said no. Adamson was certainly approached before anybody else by the Football Association and he turned them down flat. There was no talk, at that stage, of scrapping the International Selection Committee, and Adamson had observed from a ringside seat how the FA treated his friend Walter Winterbottom. When they offered him the same poisoned chalice he shook his head politely and turned away. Burnley might not be the richest or most fashionable club in the land, and its chairman Bob Lord could be – shall we say – difficult at times, but it was still preferable to taking orders from Lancaster Gate. At Turf Moor, at least he got to pick the team. There could be no greater indictment of the organisation which governed English football than that the manager of a worthy, plain, middle-of-the-road Lancashire side should reject its offer to him to manage his national squad in a World Cup series which would be held in England.

So they turned next to the manager of a worthy, plain, middle-of-the-road East Anglian side. Winterbottom had resigned on 31 July, offering the honourable guarantee that he would see the team through its European Championship and Home International games for the remainder of the year, before joining the Council of Physical Recreation on 31 December. The FA wasted August and September in deliberations and the abortive approach to Adamson, and it was not until early in October that John Cobbold received a letter at Portman Road from the FA chairman Graham Doggart. Cobbold called a board meeting and Ipswich Town agreed to release Alf Ramsey for the England job – if Alf Ramsey wished to go.

He took the best part of a month to decide. Ipswich were, after all, in the European Champions Cup, and they had a First Division place – if not a championship title – to protect. On the other hand, England, judging by a desperate 1–1 draw with France at Hillsborough in the home leg of the first round of the European Nations Cup on 3 October, were about to be dismissed from yet another tournament.

Ramsey consulted Arthur Rowe, who told him: 'It's easier to run the England side than Ipswich, when you're picking from the top players in the country. At Ipswich, you're always fighting people

58

with gates twice your size.' But there was more, much more, and it took a long meeting with FA chairman Doggart at Portman Road and a talk with Walter Winterbottom to clear up his precise job description. What was discussed at those meetings would only become apparent on Thursday, 25 October 1962, when the FA announced that Alf Ramsey was to become the new manager of England. He would be paid £4,500 a year. Walter Winterbottom had earned £2,000 a year.

He would take up the position full-time at the end of the 1962–63 League season. That would leave England without a manager between 31 December and May, five months which encompassed the second leg of the Nations Cup tie with France in Paris, the Home Championships game against Scotland at Wembley, and a friendly with world champions Brazil. Those bridges, thought the FA, would just have to crossed at the time.

His duties would be fivefold, FA secretary Denis Follows told the watching world. Alf Ramsey would:

● Produce the general England training programme;
● Arrange training get-togethers for the squad;
● Work with the FA's new Director of Coaching, Allan Wade (that appointment being a tacit admission that for 17 years the FA, the richest sporting body in England, had been employing one man to do its two most important jobs);
● Win the World Cup; and . . .
● Alf Ramsey would be responsible for team selection.

'There are important duties for selectors other than picking teams,' added Graham Doggart absurdly. 'They will support the new team manager.'

After 90 years of English international matches the Selection Committee, the famous 12 good men and true, poor Walter Winterbottom's biggest albatross, was finished; ditched by a man who knew his own mind and who knew the way the world was turning. It might – just might – have those rudderless first five months of 1963 to prove itself at the last, but after that, after May, the FAISC would be history.

His background as a player and an impoverished manager, said

Ramsey, would give him an entirely fresh perspective on the England team. And those who might later complain, could never accuse him of not being honest from the start. 'I have always had to look at expensive players, say Jimmy Greaves, from the standpoint of how to stop them . . .' he said immediately after his appointment.

'I believe that even in the days when England had great players -' and note his implication that the golden years of natural brilliance had passed, that there were no more giants '– like Stan Matthews, Tom Finney, and Raich Carter, the team would have been even better with a rigid plan.'

Not just a pre-match discussion, Stanley, and not just a plan, but a rigid plan . . . 'Any plan must be adapted to the strengths and weaknesses of the players and must be acceptable to them. That is the secret of football planning . . . It is exciting. I want to do it. You see, I believe in England, and Englishmen, as well as English football.'

But the plan came first. Any player, however English he may be, to whom the plan was unacceptable, would himself be unacceptable to Alf Ramsey's England. There would be no more appeals over the manager's head to an International Selection Committee, no more sentimental attachment to the fondly remembered flair of such as Stanley Matthews. In a month in the autumn of 1962, England's Age of Innocence was buried.

It was interred to widespread applause. 'If you looked the whole world over,' Arthur Rowe told the FA, 'you couldn't have found a better man. He is a shining example of what you can make yourself from application and honest effort.'

'Alf's the only man for the job,' echoed John Cobbold. 'Our loss is England's gain.'

'Alf has succeeded because he takes his football seriously,' put in Bill Dodgin. 'He won't try and copy the Brazilians. He'll do for England what he's done for Ipswich, make the best of the material he has. And he'll stick to the English style.'

Few people other than the three quoted above really knew Alf Ramsey. And so he succeeded to the biggest job in English football in a blizzard of received wisdoms and pseudo insights . . . imperturbable, approachable, patient, broadminded, his players' greatest friend and admirer, doesn't smoke and drinks only in moderation, an intense, honest man in smart, sober suits, black shoes, clean collars, and ties with rather large knots, hiding his thoughts behind steady, dark eyes ...

But in two months, he had at least won back two years of the missing four. 'Alf Ramsey was born in Dagenham in 1922,' decided the *Daily Express*. 'Alf Ramsey, 40, has been appointed England team manager,' announced the front page of the *Daily Telegraph*. That was something. The dates may not yet have been quite correct, but at least he was counting once more in 1947 time. Only another two years to gain.

4 ENGLAND

'The simple fact is, Alf never talks about anything other than football or footballers.'

– GEOFF HURST

He took over early, in farcical circumstances. In October 1962, after his appointment to the England job had been announced, he received a 'phone call at Portman Road from his old international room-mate Jackie Milburn.

'Any chance of your job, Alf?'

Milburn would insist later that Ramsey's reply was cautious, that he was warned of the difficulties facing a manager of Ipswich. 'We haven't got much. Not much of a first team, and not much in the reserves.' The League champions were also seventh from the bottom of Division One, with just two wins in 14 games.

That did not matter much at the time to Milburn, who was filling in his days as player-manager of non-League Yiewsley (although after Ipswich's ignominious decline and a few ill-chosen comments from Ramsey to the effect that he had handed over a perfectly good team, Milburn would be stung into insisting that he had been given precious little useful help or advice from his former team-mate). He took over as manager of Ipswich Town on 28 January 1963. Ipswich retained their First Division place that year, but slid inevitably out of the top flight, and out of this story, 12 months later.

Initially Ramsey was to have worked full-time with Milburn at Portman Road until May 1963. On 3 December 1962 the FA's Selection Committee was officially disbanded, and Walter Winterbottom was handed a silver salver at a farewell lunch. The pre-

63

dicament of the England team seemed pressing. Graham Doggart was making noises about a 'possible temporary appointment' to the England job for the first five months of 1963.

Late in January the Football Association made an extraordinary announcement. The International Selection Committee, which had been informed, at Alf Ramsey's request, of its imminent redundancy back in October, and had finally been put out to grass in December, would, just two months later, be reconvened under Joe Richards, the former chairman of the senior squad committee, for the first three games of 1963, with Alf Ramsey as one of its members. Once the committee had picked the England side, Ramsey would work with the players for three days before each match. In between times, he was free to continue introducing Jackie Milburn to Ipswich.

If the committee members were to be believed, never before had they exercised such untrammelled power. Messrs Richards, Follows, Doggart, Mears and Collings (not one of whom had ever played professional football) picked their side and, having left out the brilliant Fulham play-maker and ex-England captain, Johnny Haynes and the great Arsenal schemer, George Eastham, travelled to the Parc des Princes. Ramsey told the squad which had been presented to him to play as they had always played, and after 45 minutes England were 3–1 down. It fell then to Ramsey to give his first half-time talk to an England team. The players, most of whom were still loyal to the memory of Winterbottom and were wary of the new man, expected harsh treatment. He spoke to them quietly and calmly and concluded by saying: 'I don't see why you can't win this match.'

They did not, of course. France swept home by 5–2. England, out of the European Nations Cup, would have no competitive practice between 1963 and the World Cup finals of 1966. What was worse, most of the players felt themselves now to be playing in a very bad international team indeed. That defeat in Paris probably marked the nadir of spirit and expectation in the English international squad. Despite the presence of such as the ageing Raymond Kopa and Just Fontaine, France was a comparatively minor footballing power. In the 26 months before that thrashing of England they had won just one international, drawn five and lost seven. Alf Ramsey emerged from the Parisian changing room to assure the waiting press that he was not disappointed – 'Why should I be disappointed?' But others felt differently. 'England's footballers,' said one player, 'began to get the idea that all continentals were superior beings, just as before the war they were all reckoned to be easy meat for an England side.' It was in this ferment of pessimism and lack of confidence that Alf determined to close his pre-match team-talks with a heartfelt and sincere assurance to the players that they were as good as anybody else in the world. That formula would not change substantially for ten years, although later he would feel justified in suggesting to them that they had graduated into the best in the world – 'the fittest, the strongest' – before they trotted out on to any pitch, anywhere. Belief in themselves, he rightly judged to be nine-tenths of the battle.

On the coach leaving the Parc des Princes Ramsey went to sit beside the 22-year-old half-back Bobby Moore. 'Alf started asking a million things about the way things had been done under Walter,' Moore remembered. 'I was playing a sort of old-fashioned right-half at the time, neither functioning properly in midfield nor in defence. I was falling between two stools and he was obviously going to sort that out.'

The interrogation continued on the 'plane back to England, despite the fact that down the aisle sat the dropped Johnny Haynes, who had travelled with a group of fans to watch the game, and ribald shouts of 'Can't leave him out now, Alf', and 'Alright, John, must be back for the next one', echoed through the aircraft. The imperturbable Ramsey ignored them. He had another playmaker on his mind.

Bobby Moore had been brought up in the West Ham United academy of football. As an apprentice he had been taken under the wing of the established half-back Malcolm Allison. 'Take control of everything around you,' Allison told the teenager. 'Look big, think big. Keep forever asking yourself, if I get the ball now, who will I give it to. That was Di Stefano's secret.' It was a piece of advice which Moore would never forget and for which he would always be in Allison's debt. Hearing those words was, he would say, 'like suddenly looking into the sunshine'.

And when West Ham won a First Division place in 1958, the 17-year-old Moore replaced Allison in the first team. He was tall and strong and able to put himself about. The latter quality came in useful at first because he was also slow and inadequate in the air and blatantly right-footed. Only gradually did those famous compensatory qualities arrive to mask his deficiencies: his reading of the game ('20 minutes before anybody else,' said the Celtic manager, Jock Stein); his impeccable passing over any distance; his well-timed man-trap tackles. With them came the posture: confident, dominating, apparently unruffled, and erect, above all, erect, striding through a match with his head held high in contemptuous, dismissive, arrogant anticipation of every opposing move, and authoritative control of his own side's response. Even at the age of 22, Bobby Moore was a captain of men. By the early 1960s football players and supporters had grown out of calling people 'The General', but that title was on Alf Ramsey's mind as he saw Moore play and as he whiled away the long trip back from France in the young half-back's company.

The Selection Committee lost its second game as well. It was against Scotland at Wembley, which meant that it was by no means unprecedented. But to at least two men it was no more welcome for that.

In common with many Englishmen, Bobby Moore and Alf Ramsey were baffled by the perverse Scottish ability to compensate for a host of humiliations on the international stage by beating England, particularly at Wembley. Although it was, in fact, not dissimilar to the English habit of boastfully defeating foreigners in meaningless friendlies and then collapsing at their feet in real competition, Ramsey and Moore considered that by embracing such tunnel vision the Scots shot themselves in both feet; that if the same passion was to be applied in equal measure against all opposition, instead of being stoked up over a 12-month period to have its valve released in one awesome gush of energy during that one comparatively insignificant game, then Scotland might achieve at least moderate success in such trifling contests as the World and European Nations Cup (which latter competition they would not even bother to enter until 1966).

Unlike some other Englishmen, such as Bobby Charlton, who would shrug off this Scottish atavism with a resigned smile and quip that the worst thing about losing to Scotland was the stick you had to suffer from Anglo-Scots in the dressing-rooms of England for the next 12 months, Moore and Ramsey actually hated the annual replaying of the battle of Bannockburn. Moore was annoyed by the self-proclaimed Scottish 'guts and fire' once the twin towers of Wembley were in their sights, perceiving it as a slight on English pride – 'I'm as patriotic as any blasted Scotsman'.

And Ramsey ... something deep in Ramsey was both frustrated and fired up by the Caledonian assumption that they could always, once the chips were down, outplay eleven Englishmen. It was not unusual for Alf Ramsey to convert through his own interpretation of events a bad England defeat into a moral victory, but his comments after that 2–1 Scottish win at Wembley in April 1963 were particularly graceless. Bobby Smith had crippled the Scottish left-back Eric Caldow, who was carried off with a double fracture of the left leg, and Denis Law was limping for most of the game. In those circumstances it was an outstanding Scottish victory by the remaining nine-and-a-half fit members of an exceptional Scottish team. Jim Baxter scored both goals, and most European managers would have been happy to concede a narrow defeat to a side containing him, Law, Ian St John, John White and Dave Mackay.

But ... 'We missed far too many chances,' said Alf afterwards in a marvellous reprise of his statement after the defeat by Hungary ten years earlier. 'If just two or three of them had been accepted, we could have won.'

'I would not care to comment,' said the Scottish manager Ian McColl when Ramsey's words were read back to him.

It was the beginning of an openly hostile relationship, and possibly the beginning of the end of the Home International Championships, which were finally dumped by the English FA in 1984 on the grounds that they had become too fervent for comfort. 'Welcome to Scotland, Sir Alf,' a Scottish journalist would announce as an England party disembarked at Glasgow Airport in the late 1960s.

'You must be joking,' replied the knight.

On 29 April 1963 Alf Ramsey paid his farewell visit to Ipswich Town's Portman Road ground and received a going-away gift from the players and staff: an automatic brewer of tea, selected by himself, of the brand species 'Teasmaid'. On 8 May England took an unsatisfactory 1–1 draw from Brazil at Wembley, and the International Selection Committee was finally banished from its table of power. After that, Alf Ramsey was on his own.

At first it seemed to suit both Alf and England. A couple of weeks later in May he took his squad away on a tour of Europe. They could not have known it at the time, but that tour would prove to be, if not a false dawn, certainly Alf Ramsey's sunniest spell for a full three years. They won all three games. Jimmy Armfield was injured for the first one, against Czechoslovakia in Bratislava, and Ramsey instantly replaced him as captain with Bobby Moore, making the West Ham half-back England's youngest ever skipper. 'Whatever you do on the field,' he famously told Moore, 'whatever decisions you think are necessary, you'll have my full backing.' (Words which were to be repeated throughout their two interwoven international careers. 'He knows, and the team knows,' Ramsey later repeated in public, 'he's representing me on the field. There is another Alf Ramsey on the field in terms of Bobby Moore.')

'I was thrilled,' said Moore. 'I like being a captain. I like the feeling of responsibility, that if something happens on the field I have to make a decision. I find the job makes you a lot more aware of what is happening inside a football team . . . I loved that first experience of leading England out. The atmosphere was magic. The crowd are fanatical in Bratislava. I decided we'd only get beat over my dead body.'

No corpses were required. It was a satisfactory blooding for the man whom Ron Greenwood would describe as the archetypal big match performer. England beat the Czechs 4–2, went on to a 2–1 defeat of East Germany in Leipzig, and then to Basle and – with Armfield back in the side and Moore by then playing at centre-half – an 8–1 stuffing of Switzerland. There was no disputing Ramsey's tactics at this time. He was employing a straightforward 4–2–4 system: two centre-backs (Moore and one other) inside two full-backs; a variety of partnerships in midfield; and two orthodox wingers (Bobby Charlton, who got five goals on tour, on the left and Terry Paine on the right) outside two orthodox strikers (preferably Greaves and one other).

And it worked. If you had doubts, Alf Ramsey seemed to be

saying on his return, prepare to shed them now. The majority of that touring squad had been England players for years and had shared the depression of Winterbottom's last days in office. On the continent of Europe in the summer of 1963 they seemed rejuvenated, freshly inspired. Nor were the victories confined to the playing field. For the first time since the Second World War England took a doctor – a jovial, popular young medico named Alan Bass – on tour. After the Czechoslovakia game Jimmy Greaves went down with tonsilitis ('I thought I was going to die'). Bass diagnosed accurately, procured penicillin and other drugs, and saved Greaves – as he might 12 months earlier have saved Peter Swan – from suffering in a badly equipped foreign hospital. The organisation on and off the park impressed most observers in 1963 almost as much as did the sight of English internationals joyfully twisting the night away in their Bratislava and Leipzig hotels, to celebrate their first victories on continental soil in two long years. 'England will win the World Cup in 1966,' said Alf Ramsey, back on British turf, and as his team put four past Wales in Cardiff, many fewer people than before were prone to disagree.

England was changing. 'There was a hardening process going on in the England team,' recalled Bobby Moore. 'What it boiled down to was this – neither I nor any of my team-mates cared too much about whether we lived up to a "Good cricket, sir" image. We became very bad losers. Anything but victory was a failure, and the old "Good show, chaps" attitude disappeared.'

Alf also was changing. Upward mobility required constant personal reappraisal and reinvention. An old acquaintance, such as the journalist and Tottenham fan, Ralph Finn who had, in the early '50s, driven Alf and his colleagues to and from White Hart Lane and Manor House Station, was staggered to find himself suddenly and brutally cut: 'Alf ceased to know me. When he was manager of Ipswich I first noticed that his normal aloofness had grown even more distant. And [as] manager of England he did not recognise me . . . I hated being made to feel this way. I hated the thought that this man, now manager of the England team, could make me feel like a grubby little boy.'

When the gifted young Chelsea inside-forward Terry Venables,

69

who was born three streets away from Ramsey's family home in Dagenham, was first called up to train with the senior squad in 1964, a friend of his father's who had lived next door to the Ramseys asked him to say hello to the England manager. 'Sid from Dagenham sends his regards,' said Terry to Alf at the first reasonable opportunity. 'There was a pregnant pause. He looked at me as if he had just stepped in something unpleasant, turned on his heel without a word, and marched off to the other side of the ground. For some reason, I got the feeling that Alf's Dagenham roots were not a subject that he was keen to discuss.'

Bobby Moore, who always liked to see the nobler side of his fellow native of Essex, reckoned that the new Alf was the true Alf, finally planted in his natural environment, and that the Alf of the past, Alf the player and Alf as one of the boys, had been an ersatz Alf: 'I say that the serious, responsible Alf is the real Alf.

'Without trying or meaning to, he fooled everyone. It was in the old days that he wasn't being himself. I've talked to some of the old players he used to knock about with and they'll tell you that although he used to go to the dogs or the pub, it wasn't really his scene. He went because his one or two pals were going but he stood back a bit. They remember him changing, drifting away from them. Well, I'd bet my mortgage that one day he was on the train home and he thought: 'I don't need all that, it's not me.' He took elocution lessons and out came the real Alf who everyone found so baffling.'

Real Alf or invented Alf, a strange and sometimes terrible Alf was born in 1963. The Alf was created then who would walk up to the young Leeds striker Allan Clarke on an aeroplane during Clarke's first tour with England, notice him laughing with team-mates, and suddenly snap: 'Enjoying yourself, Allan?'

'Yes, Alf. Great. Thank you.'

'You don't fucking enjoy yourself with me. Remember that.' And then a bulky turned shoulder, and a frowning five o'clock shadow, and the measured walk back to his seat of an imagined retired colonel of cavalry.

This was the Alf whom Geoff Hurst initially regarded as an extremely odd and cold fish indeed: 'I was darned if I could see how he was going to get his players pulling out the stops for him with this remote approach.' Hurst had first come across Ramsey on Paddington Station in November 1964 when the young West Ham forward was on his way to join the under-23 team. 'The first sight of him was a bit of a shock, he didn't seem like a football man at all. He was so carefully dressed, so quietly spoken he seemed more like a businessman or a bank manager. He had none of that casual air you usually find with ex-players. He ushered us quietly into the compartment he had reserved and even before the train had left the station he was talking – about football. Or not so much talking, as asking. Right away it was: 'Tell me Geoff, how did so-and-so play against you last Saturday . . .?'

This was the Alf of whom another newcomer to his squad commented: 'He's a strange bloke. Personally, I'm never really comfortable chatting to him. It may be my fault. It's just that he's . . . well, so relentless about the game. None of this is a giggle for him in any way.' A fellow ex-professional from the south-east of England found himself sitting opposite to this Alf during a train journey, and having listened in semi-disbelief to the effect that elocution lessons had had on the England manager's Essex accent, cried out more in dismay than anger: 'Bleedin' 'ell, Alf! Leave it out.'

(Those elocution lessons would follow him through life like a criminal record. They were a strange step to take even in the respectable, proper, bourgeois, Churchillian/Eden/Macmillan decade of the 1950s: they smacked of Peter Sellers' insecure shop steward absurdly trying to talk like management in the film *I'm All Right, Jack*. And by the middle of the 1960s it had become positively unfashionable to speak with anything other than a regional accent – all too late for Alf. The implant had taken by then, and the manager of England was condemned for the rest of his days to sound like a Voortrekker struggling to pass himself off as a Broadcasting House newsreader.)

This new Alf was the Alf of Ipswich Town, squared. He was an Alf possessed of an extraordinary sense of duty. During the 40 to 45 weeks in the year when England were not on tour or did not have a home fixture he commuted between Ipswich and London and checked into his tiny third-floor office at 22 Lancaster Gate between 10.00am and 4.30pm on four days a week, taking Friday off in lieu of Saturday, which he would spend watching club fixtures – usually

71

First Division, occasionally Second, rarely Third and never Fourth. ('The top talent, in the main,' he pronounced, 'is in the top drawer.') He began each League season by making up dossiers on about 100 players. The files contained the footballer's medical and playing records, but never his strengths and weaknesses: 'I carry those in my head.' He had no secretary, but used a typist from the Football Association's pool. And every now and again he sat down in that sparsely furnished, pokey little third-floor room (13 feet by eight) to write eleven names on a sheet of paper, telephone the players' clubs, notify the chosen ones by letter, and pass on his selection to the vestigial, atrophying International Committee – not for approval, but as a matter of courtesy.

Like most managers, he always preferred the training pitch. For all his idiosyncrasies, he was a players' man. One of those players, John 'Budgie' Byrne, the West Ham United forward, considers that Alf Ramsey 'didn't hold a candle to [*Ron*] Greenwood on knowledge of the game. Not in the same street. Between them they'd have made a good manager. Ron's knowledge and Alf's way with the players.'

On those rare and precious training days he would hurry down to the Bayswater Hotel which had been chosen as the squad's meeting place, making sure that he was there before the most eager new recruit, who would be greeted with the assurance that Alf – and it was always 'Alf' to his players – wanted him to play for England as he played for his club: 'Perhaps later on you and I can agree on how you can vary your game a bit. For now, just be natural.'

Then on to the hired coach to the Bank of England ground at Roehampton or to the FA's centre at Lilleshall in Shropshire, and six-a-sides or, when the numbers made it possible, full-scale practice matches with Ramsey in his earlier days playing, and as age crept up on him, refereeing and talking constantly. The easy, unembarrassed deferment to experienced players on the finer points of practical tactics; and the careful, dispassionate, unhistrionic briefings which smacked more of Montgomery than Patton (and which owed more to Arthur Rowe and Walter Winterbottom than anybody else); and further reassurance to the new boys – 'You're playing as though you're surprised to be in this company. If you hadn't been as good as anybody on that pitch you wouldn't have been picked. Think about it.'

On 23 October 1963 the Football Association celebrated its centenary year with a friendly match against a 'Rest Of The World' XI at
Wembley. FIFA had been unable to attract Pele and Garrincha from
Brazil or Maldini from Italy, but they assembled a squad containing
the Russian goalkeeper Lev Yashin, the West German defender
Schnellinger, Masopust, Kopa, Law, Di Stefano, Eusebio, Baxter,
Uwe Seeler and Puskas. The friendliness of the event was heavily
diluted 24 hours before kick-off, when FIFA announced that they
intended to use all of their 16-man squad, putting on five of them at
half-time in a pre-arranged series of substitutions. FIFA's own rules
for friendly internationals at the time insisted that only an injured
goalkeeper could be substituted during a game, and one other player
up to the 44th minute. No substitutions whatsoever were allowed in
any competitive match, for any reason.

Ramsey, who believed in doing things by the book, was furious.
'This is a disgraceful statement,' he declared, adding that: 'The FIFA
team have been invited as players with outstanding reputations and
they will have to live up to them or we shall destroy them.' He
himself refused to countenance any substitutions in the England side.
FIFA were, of course, simply trying to give all 16 of their far-flung
squad a kick of the ball and 100,000 people a chance to see all the
stars on offer. Ramsey was angry not because the use of five substitutes would assist his opponents, but contrarily and character-
istically because he believed that the move would further fragment a
team whose players were already unfamiliar with each other, and
would consequently devalue 'a competitive match'.

We who came afterwards can now see that game against the Rest
Of The World in grainy, stuttering monochrome almost as an inter-
lude, as a marker of time, as part of the great watershed . . . as a
distant, dreamy vision of the abandoned past. The England side of
that day was certainly closer to the epoch of Winterbottom and all
who came before him, all of those long-shorted, hoop-shirted,
tackety-booted free spirits of the Golden Age, than it was to the finished Alfian product. Banks was in goal, and Wilson at left-back, and
Moore in central defence, and Bobby Charlton on the left and Jimmy
Greaves in the middle of the forward line . . . but the relaxed genius of
George Eastham prompted them from midfield, and the gentlemanly

Jimmy Armfield captained them from right-back, and the big, brave, bustling and entirely uncerebral Bobby Smith put himself about at centre-forward. There was one small tactical deviation which went almost unnoticed at the time. England, everybody assumed, were still playing 4–2–4. In fact, Bobby Charlton played deep and accepted a free role to move forward from midfield. Alf Ramsey was not quite, not yet using 4–3–3. What he was doing was far more understandable, and in some strange, inexplicable way a little eerie: driven by memories of an assault from East Anglia on the unprepared English League Division One, he was using Charlton as Jimmy Leadbetter. Jimmy Leadbetter with wings.

They were playing against a team which had not travelled to London in order to get injured, a fact which added to the vague unreality of an occasion which began with two ambassadors from the golden past, Armfield and Di Stefano, shaking hands on the centre-spot. As uninterested as ever in losing to England, Denis Law worked feverishly between the gentle artists of the Rest Of The World, but rather than take their lead from him they looked on indulgently, and Djalma Santos practised his exquisite chips into midfield from the full-back position, and Kopa danced elegantly away from tackles, and Eusebio renounced running on goal in favour of long-distance shooting practice.

England won 2–1, and it should have been a clearer margin. Greaves – looking entirely at home in such company and in such an uncommitted contest – weaved through to score brilliantly, only to see play brought back for an ineffective foul on himself. The referee somehow contrived not to see Jim Baxter handle the ball in his own penalty area, nor a momentarily confused Schnellinger immediately place it with his own right hand – thereby committing a second handling offence in the box – and take a non-existent quick free-kick. Bobby Charlton hit the post square on with substitute goalkeeper Soskic beaten. And then Terry Paine scored; Denis Law equalised; and Jimmy Greaves broke the Scot's heart by nipping in for the winner with five minutes left.

It was a wonderful period for English self-deception, and the ability of soccer fans to deceive themselves is timeless; all of which made for an orgy of gleeful, giddy delusion. The Rest Of The World had been beaten: bring on the the rest of the world. The country was sold on Ramsey. The unequivocal, black-and-white response of the football fan was urged to unexplored extremes by the multilingual comments which issued from the visitors' changing room at Wembley on the evening of 23 October. The FIFA team manager Fernando Riera considered: 'It is more than possible that England will win the World Cup in 1966 in their own conditions.' The Czech half-back Svatopluk Pluskal thought, 'England at home are a different side, a much better side, than they are away. They can look forward to 1966.' And the 37-year-old Galloping Major, Ferenc 'Jellyroll' Puskas, whose last memory of Wembley had been ten years earlier when, as the slimline 27-year-old Ferenc Puskas, he and his Hungarian team-mates had packed up England, Alf Ramsey and all, and taken them home as toys, nodded and agreed. 'They are a good side now.' The English football enthusiast rolled over on his back and gurgled.

One month later Northern Ireland were beaten 8–3 at Wembley. England had won six games in a row – effectively the first six games of Ramsey's management, the nation could tell itself – scoring 32 times and conceding just ten, and you couldn't have bought Alf for a solid gold semi-detached on the Ipswich by-pass. Nobody pointed out that, just a year before his resignation, Walter Winterbottom's England had also won six consecutive matches, scoring 40 goals and conceding only nine. Alf, who would know that, did well to enjoy the balmy goodwill. In football, he hopefully philosophised over a glass of sherry in the comfort of his own armchair, in football nothing lasts.

Scotland – who else? – let out the first litre of air. Ramsey tried a new striking duo of Roger Hunt and John 'Budgie' Byrne in place of Smith and Greaves against England's oldest opponents in April '64, but Dundee's Alan Gilzean made the only breakthrough of the game, scoring in the 72nd minute. The nature of the defeat once more irritated Ramsey. Gilzean's goal was headed in directly from a corner, and those things just should not happen in the perfect, predictable world of modern, organised football. 'Scotland,' said Alf churlishly, 'scored with the kind of goal you don't expect in this class of football.'

He would never have held down a job in the diplomatic corps.

The man would not accept defeat. There are just four explanations for these strange, defensive, self-justifying comments which punctuated the press conferences after each England defeat. The first one, that he was simply disappointed, we can dismiss ('Why should I be disappointed?'). All managers and players are disappointed by defeat; virtually all learn to live with it. They have to. The second is that he was in a condition of mild shock. His England of early 1964, like the England of his playing days in 1953, just did not get beaten, particularly by upstart Caledonians, or by anybody visiting Wembley. If they were defeated it could not possibly be on merit: there had to be a fluke, a once in a lifetime occurrence (like Alan Gilzean scoring from, or the England defence sleeping at, a corner; or like Hungary finding the net four times from outside the box!). The third is that he knew full well that his team deserved to lose, but was unwilling to tell them so; he was anxious always to keep their confidence high, even if that meant telling outrageous fibs.

There is much to be said for the third, but the fourth finds most favour. It is that he was absolutely serious. He was certainly possessed of more than a hint of Captain Mainwaringesque blind faith in English invincibility; but it is more than likely that Alf Ramsey, while sounding arrogant and insensitive, was being nothing other than frank when he announced that his players should have closed down the opposition at corner-kicks, or taken their own chances in front of goal. Those are the things that he told the press and the public; but – more importantly to him – they are also what he would say to his players in the privacy of the changing room. You were beaten, but you should not have been. Scotland and Alan Gilzean did not beat you, you beat yourselves. Iron out those deficiencies and nobody will beat you, ever again.

To Alf Ramsey football was a game which – like chess or billiards on a perfect baize – need not be influenced by chance or luck. Football could, with sufficient thought and planning and the right players in the right places, be made entirely predictable; and the team which came closest to such sterile perfection would never lose a match. That belief was central to his philosophy, and an understanding of it is essential to those who would comprehend his influence on the game of soccer.

He did not care much for the opinions of the affronted Scots, but they came anyway, and they hit their target. Bob Kelly, the chairman of Celtic, retired as president of the Scottish FA a month after that 1–0 win at Wembley, and he then felt free to strike. Ramsey, said Kelly, was coaching all of the talent out of the England team. 'They are puppets. Ramsey pulls the strings and the players dance for him. I think he has theorised them out of the game. They mustn't think for themselves. They mustn't deviate from the plan. They have been so brainwashed by tactics and talks that their individual talent has been thrust into the background.'

Kelly's was an absolutely seminal statement. Five months earlier Ramsey had been questioned nervously about his attitude towards the artistic Johnny Haynes, when he failed to invite the Fulham player to winter training. Ramsey had answered charges that Haynes was being punished partly for his innocent association with the Winterbottom years, partly for his preference for passing a ball over tackling an opponent, and partly, crucially, because he was nobody's puppet, by asserting that all of the complaints came from south-west London. It was transparent nonsense: Johnny Haynes was one of the best loved and most admired players in Britain, but the English press, buoyed up by the results of 1963, had been disinclined to pursue the matter. If Alf was winning, who cared how? In years to come others would look back at Bob Kelly's remarks and nod their heads ruefully, in years to come wise men would paraphrase those comments and repeat them as if newly minted, but in 1964 the Celtic chairman was a lonely, perspicacious voice.

He may have hurt Alf Ramsey more than he knew, and a group of England players would shortly afterwards suffer for it. In the middle of May, immediately after Kelly's scathing analysis of Ramsey's methods, the squad was about to set off for a long and gruelling tour of Portugal, Ireland, the USA and a 'Little World Cup' series in Brazil. Their schedule was straightforward. They would train at Roehampton on the Wednesday, fly to Lisbon on the Thursday, train at Estoril on Saturday, and take on Portugal in the Stadium of Light on Sunday.

After the first workout at Roehampton Ramsey ordered his players back to Hendon Hall Hotel in north London for dinner and an early night. After dinner seven players – Bobby Moore, George Eastham, Geoff Hurst, Johnny Byrne, Bobby Charlton, Gordon Banks and Ray Wilson – retired to their rooms, got changed and headed off into the West End. At 11.30pm Ramsey and Harold Shepherdson made a routine examination of the squad's sleeping quarters. When the delinquent seven returned shortly after midnight they found their beds unmade (a curious gesture) and their passports on their pillows.

Alf let them stew. All 15 players caught the 'plane, and nothing was said throughout the following day. On Saturday the whole squad travelled for training at Estoril Stadium. Ramsey ordered a ten-minute warm-up, ten minutes of sprinting and then a five-a-side. 'Out you go, except the seven lads. They know who they are.'

They did, and they waited uncomfortably. The manager approached them coldly. 'I don't admire what you have done,' he said. 'If I had enough members here to make up a team, none of you seven would play. You'd all be on a 'plane on the way home. But I realise I can't do this in the circumstances. Make sure it doesn't happen again.'

He then selected all seven for the match, and England celebrated the 50th anniversary of the Federacao Portuguesa de Futebol by beating their hosts 4–3. Byrne got three – the last of them, the winner two minutes from time, a goal of unrepeatable quality – and Charlton the other.

They flew on to Dublin to beat the Republic of Ireland, to New York to take belated revenge on the USA by winning 10–0, and then to Brazil and the 'Little World Cup' games which almost brought Alf Ramsey down; which reversed in a week all the work of the previous year; which sent English football staggering back into self-disgust; which arguably took 18 months to recover from; and which certainly, had they taken place a year later, would have cost England the official, Big World Cup in 1966.

After 17 hours in the air the team arrived in Rio to take on Brazil at the Maracana Stadium. It would be the first time that any of the squad had faced Pele, who had been unavailable for their World Cup meeting in 1962, for the last friendly at Wembley and for the Rest Of The World anniversary game; and despite all of Ramsey's assurances

– and a warning to look out for a certain free-kick which the Brazilians had practised at Wembley in 1963 – they were apprehensive. 'I suppose,' said Moore, 'I had a subconscious fear of Pele before I went on the field . . . maybe fear isn't the right word. For years I had read about Pele, how he was some kind of superman, how he could run, jump and shoot harder and faster than anyone in the world.'

The Brazilians gave the English nerves plenty of time to procreate. Kick-off was delayed for an hour for a variety of strange excuses (the Brazilian team coach was actually held up in Rio), while the visitors sat in their kit, drumming their studs on the changing room floor. Shortly after the start Moore went out to close down Pele on the by-line. Deciding that the Brazilian was bottled in and would have to come back inside, Moore put in his tackle. 'I found myself a clear two yards away from the man. It was one of the most convincing feints I've ever seen – a dropped shoulder doing all the work, sending me the wrong way entirely and giving him all the room in the world.'

Brazil won 5–1, after a match that lasted more than two hours because of the South American media's insistence on running on to the field to interview and photograph players after each goal. This was a different world. Ramsey was furious, not so much at the result as because Brazil had scored from the very free-kick device against which he had cautioned his squad before the game. Two days later they drew 1–1 with the same Portugal side they had beaten three weeks earlier in Lisbon, and then went down 0–1 to Argentina, who wound up winning the 'Little World Cup' by comfortably defeating the astonishing Pele and Brazil by 3–0 in a bad-tempered match which was refereed by one Gottfried Dienst of Switzerland, who would reach the pinnacle of his career and antagonise millions of his fellow German-speakers at Wembley two years later, and who, in Brazil, missed the game's most notable incident: the holy Pele putting the nut on his marker Mesiano, who was carried off with a broken nose and replaced – under FIFA's 'friendly' rules – by a tall, elegant fellow named Antonio Rattin. Argentina, it was noted, used three different formations in three matches: 4–2–4 against the underdogs Portugal; 4–3–3 against England; and 5–3–2 against Brazil. Argentina, it was also noted, were dab hands at the kind of provocation which was then attributed solely to the hot heads and amorality of the Latin nations.

A different world indeed. England finished bottom of the four-team table at the Little World Cup, and even Alf Ramsey was shaken. 'We came here with a dual purpose,' he announced. 'To win the tournament and to find out the standard of football in the top South American countries. We now know there is a gap in our respective standards of football but it is not one that cannot be bridged.'

Oh no? On the day of the Brazil/Argentina match the England players were given the choice between going along as spectators, or relaxing on Copacabana beach. Predictably, for professional foot-ballers do not often enjoy watching the game but very much enjoy lying in the sun, they unanimously opted for the beach. And as they lay there on the sands they gazed idly at pre-teenaged boys playing football by the sea, a game which required that the ball be kept permanently in the air, and the England party stared in wonderment as the ball was caught on shoulders, allowed to run slowly down backs, flicked up again by heels, bounced from head to knee to instep and back again. The pink-skinned professionals looked at each other wrily, and not one of them volunteered to join in and show the young-sters how it should be done. They were in a different world.

England had a problem and no amount of stubborn dissembling by the manager could disguise the size of it. If the occasional humiliation at the hands of Brazil could be discounted (which of course it could not: Brazil would be arriving in England in 1966 looking for a hat-trick of World Cup wins), the problem lay not in defence. Ramsey understood defence and he was at least halfway to building an effective back line for England. The excellent Gordon Banks had been since the end of 1963 his preferred goalkeeper. Jimmy Armfield was on his way out, but George Cohen seemed a useful enough replacement, and Ramon Wilson was unmovable at left-back. He desperately wanted either Spurs' Maurice Norman or Wolves' Ron Flowers to work as the hard man beside Moore in the middle of defence, but if, as seemed increasingly likely, both of them failed to make the grade, that was no immediate cause for panic. English football had another two years to throw up an effective tradi-tional centre-half – and English football would not let him down.

His problems were in midfield and in the forward line, and although it would take him an excusably long time to realise it (excusable because this was, after all, 1964), they stemmed as much as anything from his rigid adherence to 4–2–4. Bobby Charlton might sometimes work as a roving link-man (and it was only some-times – as often as not Ramsey told him to get out on the left wing and stay there), but unlike Jimmy Leadbetter Charlton was fond of scoring goals, was capable of getting forward to do so from any posi-tion, and he was leaving most of the orthodox midfield work to two colleagues. Ramsey liked the idea of Gordon Milne biting ankles while George Eastham picked up the pieces, but it simply was not working. Too few chances were being created, for which Eastham unfairly got the blame. At that time it was widely accepted that England possessed just one player of genuine indisputable world class in the midfield and forward area, and that was Jimmy Greaves. It was occasionally stated – without much fear of contradiction – that Greaves was the only English footballer who looked at home on an international stage. The striker achieved the unusual feat of being popular with and appreciated by the press, the public and the players (managers would be his problem, but that came later). Jimmy, said one younger footballer, 'impressed by his icy professionalism. Jim is a great kidder. Off the park he laughs it up a lot and appears to take nothing seriously, especially football. It's a false front. He's one of the most calculating pros I know. Just watch him when there's a chance of a goal around. He tingles with alertness . . .'

Bobby Charlton himself had yet to be canonised, but he was accepted as indispensable out wide on the left. Neither Greaves nor Charlton were seriously considered as answers to the midfield problem. And there was more . . . who played beside Greaves, and who played out wide on the right? Between the summer of 1964 and the summer of 1965 Ramsey auditioned 14 forwards for those two places. He tried Terry Paine (for many months his favourite), Peter Thompson, Terry Venables, Alan Ball, John Connelly and even George Eastham on the flanks. He tried 'Budgie' Byrne (the popular, mercurial West Ham forward, so nicknamed – by Johnny Haynes – because of his endless patter, on and off the pitch) beside Greaves, but they were too similar in style. He tried the Liverpool, Everton and

Spurs hitmen Roger Hunt, Fred Pickering and Bobby Smith, but still the most obdurate defences held firm, and to have a hope of winning the World Cup England would have to break down obdurate defences. After a year and a half in the job, the uncomfortable truth was that Alf Ramsey had just two settled players in his front six.

It is an equally disturbing point of fact that although Ramsey was painfully aware of these insufficiencies in 1964, he would not satisfactorily resolve the problem until halfway through the World Cup finals in 1966, by which time he had tested no fewer than 25 forwards and 13 half-backs – and then the solution was thrust upon him, and he should not in honesty have claimed much credit for it. By 1966 he had fortunately switched to a formation which accommodated the changes that were made necessary, and which he should have initiated in a less heated arena some time before.

From the summer of 1964 onwards, one player said, Ramsey was 'probing, adjusting, experimenting . . .' He was, in fact, groping. Confident of too little, he at least fell back on and consolidated the things of which he was sure – which is why Bobby Moore finally replaced Jimmy Armfield as captain of England upon the squad's return from the Little World Cup in South America. Moore had been out of favour, not simply because of the escape from Hendon Hall Hotel in May, but because he had compounded the misdemeanour by popping out for an unauthorised lager in New York, and then by approaching both Doctor Alan Bass and Ramsey to suggest that the extra-curricular disciplines imposed on the squad were too harsh.

Such behaviour in another player would have been, to Alf Ramsey, unforgivable, and it is an indication of the level of his esteem for Moore that it was forgiven. Not only did the actions – freelance drinking – break one of Ramsey's most cherished dictums: that all squad drinking would be done in his company ('Can we have a drink, Alf?' thirsty footballers would inquire, hoping for an evening pass. 'Certainly,' he would smugly reply. 'I shall buy you a drink.' And he would do just that, lining them up on the hotel bar for the whole team if necessary, and sitting watching benignly as the chilled half-pints were demurely sipped by straight-faced, frustrated young athletes); not only was he offended by the indiscipline, but to complain to Alan Bass and to himself smacked horribly of incipient mutiny, and Alf Ramsey was of a similar cast of mind to Captain Bligh when it came to mutineers.

But Moore was different, and both Moore and Ramsey knew it. He regarded the fuss over the Hendon Hall breakout, and the brief foray into Manhattan, as frankly absurd and he was not afraid to let it show. Bobby Moore had come a long way in a short time when Alf Ramsey took him to one side and offered him the permanent captaincy in October 1964. He was outstandingly ambitious, but careful, protective of number one. He knew when to keep his head down. He would be one of the main beneficiaries of his contemporaries' crusade to abolish the maximum wage, but it is difficult to picture Bobby Moore, even if he had been slightly older than 20 and 21 years old when the bloodiest battles of that war were fought, up there waving the flag. He was no George Eastham, and there may lie a clue as to the two men's international fortunes . . .

The domestic politics of English football had passed through some troubled times in recent years. Since the first days of professionalism in 1885 the Football Association had dictated a maximum wage to its clubs and players. It had been £10.00 a week when Alf Ramsey played: more than the average industrial or agricultural wage, but hardly enough to retire to Marbella on. In 1958 the Professional Footballers' Association negotiated it up to £20.00 a week (and £17.00 in the summer). But some young and pushy members of the PFA – notably an articulate former Fulham centre-forward who sported a neat cosmetic beard which was intended to disguise his prominent chin, but which succeeded only in suggesting that he had dipped it in the gravy – wanted the maximum wage abolished altogether, along with restriction of movement from one club to another. Jimmy Hill supported a test case involving a Newcastle player, Queen's Counsel was retained (the QC is reported to have laughed out loud upon his first reading of a typical professional footballer's Victorian contract), the QC, the Newcastle player and Hill took the matter to the High Court, and they won.

The principled Newcastle United player who bravely held out against his bosses – who, in their turn, denied him a kick of a ball in anger for the best part of a year, and who would obviously sooner have seen the young man's career ended than concede their case –

and the abuse of much of the press, was George Eastham. The first big beneficiary of Eastham's struggle was the Fulham captain Johnny Haynes, whose wage was promptly increased by his showbusiness chairman Tommy Trinder to £100.00 a week.

Those two were established England players of indisputable merit, but they were not Ramsey men. He never picked the wonderful Haynes, and he fidgeted over Eastham's equally glorious independent talent before discarding him. Bobby Moore, on the other hand, took the new free-market benefits without publicity, ruthlessly and dispassionately: insisting on top money from West Ham year after year; usually being the last to sign a new contract at Upton Park and the first to insist on a sizeable increment. Bobby Moore, despite his occasional truancy and his willingness to speak his mind to his managers as much as to his colleagues, albeit in gentle tones, was neither a northern rebel nor a West London superstar. Ramsey knew him and his type: he was prototypical Essex man. He was enormously generous and helpful to his fellow professionals, but he could at the same time shrug off the dropping of a good friend from the international team with the words: 'When did nice guys ever win anything?' He would act, at the close of day, always and with instinctive accuracy in his own and his team's best interests. And if those interests could be made to coincide with those of the manager of the England team, Alf Ramsey had a lieutenant for life. They had much in common other than their shared birthplaces. Each had diligently remade himself, both on the field (where, by the end of 1963, Bobby Moore's left foot was beginning to look as educated as his right) and off the field (Moore came from a socialist family but would become, in the 1980s, a supporter and periodical guest of Margaret Thatcher). Each perfected a studied aloofness from many of their contemporaries, and even from their managers. Geoff Hurst's first impressions of Ramsey were of a 'cold fish'; after his debut for England Alan Ball could not convince his uncapped Blackpool team-mates that Moore was a warm-blooded mammal, as sociable as any other footballer. Even Ron Greenwood was driven to exasperation by the contrast between Moore's stiff-backed refusal to approach him in a relaxed manner, as West Ham captain to West Ham manager, and the young man's apparent delight in the company of those much-travelled moneyed fans whom Greenwood regarded as sycophants and leeches. Conversely, Moore could never understand most of the criticism of Ramsey; he felt that he knew and appreciated Alf as well as he needed to and as much as he needed to. In every way that counted, they each knew where the other was coming from.

This marriage made in Essex was formally and finally consummated in a Belfast hotel before England's first game after the disastrous Little World Cup in Brazil. On 2 October 1964, the evening before England's Home Championship game against Northern Ireland, 'Alf asked me to join him for a few minutes,' reported Moore.

'We talked about being ready to commit ourselves to the objective of winning the World Cup in 1966. We sorted out our priorities on and off the pitch and agreed we would back each other up. Alf made it clear he expected the captain as well as the manager to conduct himself in a responsible manner and that was that. No problem as far as I was concerned.

'All the lads felt already that he was a players' man. We were attracted to his loyalty. He shared our desire for success. Really, that's all any players ever want. Success. If you win things and get your rewards for them, you're happy. Alf's first thought was for his players so there was never any problem about getting the players to do what was asked of them. What more can you want from a manager than being successful? What more can a manager want from a player? We both had the same incentives, so we had a deal.'

The Brazilian debacle and its aftermath proved that England's new-found confidence had been paper-thin. Unhappy draws – two of them at Wembley – with teams from the undeveloped world such as Belgium, Holland and Scotland only served to heighten the sense of gloom. The famous promise looked hollow and empty; England's stock slumped so low that John Cobbold, the Ipswich Town chairman, felt able to approach Ramsey to offer him his old job back after Ipswich had been relegated and Jackie Milburn had resigned. Ramsey said that Ipswich was always in his heart, but he could not desert his country.

While one club offered him a job the others were acting up, threatening not to release their players to an England team with such ordinary prospects. The Football Association asked the Football League management committee to twist a few arms, at least in the last full season before the World Cup finals, during which Ramsey planned seven friendly internationals. The FA was comprehensively rebuffed. 'Some time ago,' pronounced one League official, 'the clubs were definite that the maximum number of internationals should be four a season.

'Of course we want to help the World Cup build-up and appreciate the problems, but it is up to our clubs to review the position and make their decision.' On 8 February 1965, just two days after that statement, Ramsey turned up at Lilleshall expecting to train with 22 senior players for three days. He arrived to find Bobby Charlton, Terry Venables, Gordon Banks, Peter Thompson, Gordon Milne and Fred Pickering absent. All were fit, and all but Venables were regular internationalists. But all of their clubs – Manchester United, Chelsea, Leicester City, Liverpool and Everton – had FA Cup ties on the following Saturday.

Alf was unamused. 'Players,' he insisted, 'will have to be available when I want them next season – even before cup ties, if I think it necessary. It is as simple as that.'

Out of that reduced training session came a momentous change of policy. Missing two of his favourite wingers – Charlton and Thompson – Ramsey decided to toy with 4–3–3. He got the under-23 team to put up an eleven and told them to play their normal (4–2–4) game. He then presented them with a full English international side playing an officially mandated 4–3–3 system for the very first time, with Bryan Douglas of Blackburn on the right-hand side of midfield, Johnny Byrne in the middle and George Eastham on the left.

The first team 'ran riot with the young lads,' Ramsey would cheerfully reflect later, 'they didn't know what it was all about. The senior team enjoyed it tremendously. They were full of enthusiasm.'

Full of enthusiasm they may have been – after all, Argentina had in very recent memory beaten them using 4–3–3, and by the early months of 1965 English internationals were willing to put in at any tactical port in a storm – but it was by reverting to 4–2–4 that Alf achieved a result which meant much to him when Hungary, who were rebuilding for '66, visited Wembley in May for the first time since

1953. Before that game Ramsey showed his team the film of the 6–3 rout. After it, when England had won 1–0, he responded with his usual humility: 'This is a better England team than the 1953 one, and I am entitled to say that because I was in it. I am delighted by their victory, but I am not so delighted by the score. I am disappointed that we didn't score as many goals as Hungary scored against us in 1953. We should have taken more of the chances we made. We could have turned that 1953 score right round and beaten Hungary by it.'

In victory: magnaminity . . . forget it. The Hungarian manager Lajos Baroti was more circumspect. 'If they are to go a long way in the World Cup,' he warned, 'England must improve their team as much as Hungary. We too missed chances. We should have drawn.'

Slowly and unremarked, it turned into a significant summer. In April 1965 two men who had previously escaped the eyes of the selectors made their debut for their country against Scotland at Wembley. Twenty-eight-year-old Jack Charlton, Bobby's older brother, who had long since resigned himself to life without international honours, was centre-half with a Leeds United side which had won promotion to the First Division the previous spring, conceding a miserly 34 goals in 42 games, and which was about to finish second only on goal difference to Manchester United at the top of the League. Leeds had just beaten Manchester United in an FA Cup semi-final replay at the City Ground, Nottingham, on 31 March when one of the International Committee edged up to Jack – they may have relinquished their authority, those elderly mandarins, but they would be slow to shuffle out of the limelight – and whispered in his ear that he must not tell a soul but he would be playing for England on 10 April.

Charlton broke the confidence only by telling his brother Bobby. It would be the first time in the 20th century that two brothers had played together in an England team: the Comptons, Denis and Leslie, had done it only in unofficial wartime internationals. And the Charltons came from rather different stock than did the dashing, upper middle-class cricketing Comptons.

They were born in the Northumbrian mining town of Ashington, Jack in 1936 and Bobby 18 months later, two of the four sons of Jackie Milburn's cousin Cissie, who had married a coalminer named

Robert Charlton. Uncle Jack was not the only footballer in the family: Cissie's four brothers also played League soccer (all as full-backs), and the three sisters grew up playing the game with the boys and then – as puberty arrived – avidly supporting them. Cissie Charlton was an unusually football-daft mother. Jack was a tough kid, forever returning home with fingers broken in fights, or fish-hooks embedded in his hand. Bobby, the milder soul, spent much time as a youngster in the neighbouring house of their maternal grandfather, 'Tanner' Milburn, a former goalkeeper with the local side who would take the youngster down to the park where the prize-money sprinters trained, rub embrocation on his little legs, and send him off on sprint bursts against the quick, kindly champions of the local track.

Bobby spent his first holidays away from home in Chesterfield, where his Uncle George was playing for the local team in the post-war years, and he followed the players about from training session to changing room to public house, and he adored them. Unlike Jack, Bobby passed his eleven-plus and got a scholarship to Bedlington Grammar School, but there never would be, there never had been any chance of him staying there to sit his GCEs. When he reached the age of 15 there was just one road beckoning to Bobby Charlton.

He had, of course, been a brilliant footballer from an early age: fast, uncannily skilful, and with a shot so powerful that it was difficult to imagine that it had issued from those scrawny pre-teenaged legs. He was picked up first by East Northumberland Boys when he was just ten years old, then by the full Northern youth side, and then by England Schoolboys, for whom he scored twice and made a third on his debut, and by the time of his 15th birthday every First Division club in the land was scrabbling for his signature.

Manchester United got it because even in the early 1950s there was a rainbow hanging over Old Trafford. Their youth team was the best in the country, and what was more, Matt Busby picked 17- and 18-year-olds for the first team. If they were good enough, they were old enough. So Bobby signed and began playing immediately for United's fifth team in the Altrincham League, and began training with Duncan Edwards, Tommy Taylor, Jackie Blanchflower, Mark Jones, David Pegg . . .

Bobby Charlton survived the aeroplane crash at Munich which destroyed the brightest hopes of English soccer in February 1958, but for a short time afterwards he vowed to give up the game. By then he had been with United for five years, he had progressed effortlessly into that exciting first team, and the dead and injured who haunted his memories had been his friends, his family, his future. But he was just 20 years old and he was persuaded that life, and the game, must go on, and two months after Munich he was picked to play for England against Scotland at Hampden Park. England won 4–0 and Charlton scored, and what would become the most eminent international career of any Englishman was underway. He had always been a quiet, shy boy, respectful and discreet and making no secret of his distaste for the extra-curricular antics of such post-Munich latecomers as George Best. Nobody would ever be able to assess how much of this serious, single-minded diligence was the product of a ghastly winter's night on a German airfield. And only a few would realise the courage which was called upon to enable him to take to the air again for his club and country. That most understanding of team-mates, Ray Wilson, was sitting next to Charlton when their 'plane took off for Madrid for an international against Spain in May 1960. Concerned to say only the right thing, Wilson spotted a golf course beneath the ascending flight path and invited the enthusiastic golfer Bobby Charlton to look down at it. Wilson glanced at Charlton and was struck dumb. His friend and room-mate, a normally 'gay, witty' man, was sitting bolt upright, staring straight ahead. Without looking sideways, let alone down, he forced out a few quiet words: 'It's . . . just like any other golf course.'

Jack's had been a comparatively mundane career. He and Bobby were both playing in a local under-18s League at the respective ages of 15 and 13, when Jack was spotted by a scout for Leeds United. He went almost immediately for a trial at Elland Road, joined the groundstaff there, and at the age of 17 broke into United's Second Division team. His early professional life was broken by two years' National Service in the Horse Guards, and then a career in football which seemed occasionally to be threatened by his outspoken, aggressive manner was harnessed by the arrival of Don Revie as manager at Elland Road. When he selected Jack Charlton to play for

England, Alf Ramsey was gambling on the old, solid virtues of a raw-boned uncompromising centre-half succeeding at the international level, where many said that such qualities had long been redundant.

There was a second newcomer that spring. Norbert 'Nobby' Stiles of Manchester United was just 23 years old. He was a product of Irish Manchester and well valued by the club of his dreams, but his selection for England was equally unexpected. Both Jack Charlton and Stiles were cheerful, charismatic characters, good for changing-room atmosphere; but both men were little more than playstoppers. Despite his ungainly appearance Charlton was a commanding figure with well-honed heading ability in his own or in the opposition's penalty area, a solid, long-legged tackler, but with dubious creative qualities. Stiles was simply a tiny tigerish hard man, a ball-winner, the sort of player whose hallmark was to make the opposition's fancy boys think twice before they pulled any clever tricks around the penalty area; a tenacious, hard-working player whose Manchester United team-mates and manager (Matt Busby) claimed none-the-less to be possessed of considerable footballing vision.

Whatever their virtues, neither Jack Charlton nor Stiles could possibly be vaunted as the players to close that skill deficit between English and South American football, the 'gap' which Ramsey had admitted to, and which he had pledged himself to bridging less than 12 months earlier. In selecting them, Alf Ramsey was clearly taking a different path. Nor were the two new boys popular with the remainder of the country without the environs of Old Trafford and Elland Road. When the rumours that Alf was watching the Leeds defender were first noised about, one First Division manager declared to his players: 'If Jack Charlton ever plays for England I will leap off that skyscraper outside our ground.' After his selection had been announced Charlton received a letter with a Barnsley postmark. Its sender assured Jack that he was the worst centre-half in the land, 'and how you have been picked to play for England I'll never know.' Charlton stuffed it in his pocket and took it along to the international get-together. There, he began to tell fellow debutant Stiles about his poison correspondence. Stiles grinned, pulled an identical letter from his pocket, and said, 'Snap!'

England's defence for that 2–2 draw with Scotland was, for the first time: Gordon Banks in goals, George Cohen and Ramon Wilson at right- and left-back, and Bobby Moore and Jack Charlton in the middle. Nobby Stiles, as the midfield ball-winner, spent much of the afternoon augmenting them. They went 2–0 up within 30 minutes, but then lost two players through injury. Ray Wilson went off with a pulled muscle and 'Budgie' Byrne with a twisted knee. Byrne, who had held down as regular a place as anybody else in the maelstrom of the previous 18 months, and who had seemed more likely than most to feature in the 1966 finals, would never again play for England. Scotland equalised against nine men with 30 minutes to go, and seemed odds-on to win. But this kind of challenge was meat and drink to the likes of Jack and Nobby.

'Some critics disagreed with their selection for England,' Moore would admit. 'Stiles, they said, was too much of a club destructor, and Charlton – well, he didn't seem to look like an England player.

'How wrong these critics were proved. The sleeves-up example of Stiles seemed to affect us all. If a little fellow like that enthusiastically looked for the tackle, we all could. Charlton was totally dominant in the air and tremendously effective on the ground – and, most unusual, he had a flair for going forward and creating attacks.'

England held out; the match finished at 2–2; and barring accidents Alf Ramsey had, after two years, found himself a defence with which he could do business.

Up front things were still pretty clouded. Despite the lesson of Lilleshall in February, Ramsey had reverted to 4–2–4, playing Stiles alongside Byrne in the middle. With Byrne and Bobby Charlton both injured and calling off from the imminent European tour, that would have to change. Ramsey called up a 19-year-old who was making waves at Blackpool, and when England arrived in Belgrade to face Yugoslavia Alan Ball made his debut in the two-man midfield alongside Stiles, in front of the defence which had held out against Scotland, and behind the four front men Terry Paine, Jimmy Greaves, Barry Bridges and John Connelly.

England drew 1–1 that day in the Red Star Stadium, with Ramsey taking most joy from the fact that an old club device had finally paid off for his country. England's first corner was floated unsuccessfully to Jack Charlton at the far post. Come the second corner and there was Charlton again, surrounded by half the Yugoslav defence – only this time Paine thumped a near-post ball to Bridges, who edged in his first international goal. 'That move,' crowed Alf, 'brought Ipswich at least ten goals in one season.'

Three days later in Nuremburg Alf Ramsey picked an English side to play a 4–3–3 formation for the first time in a full international match. He kept the same defence, but as Stiles and John Connelly had left the squad to join Manchester United for an Inter-Cities Fairs Cup game at Strasbourg the midfield became Ron Flowers, Terry Paine and George Eastham, and the forward line was Mick Jones, Derek Temple and Ball. Paine scored in a 1–0 win over West Germany which was more comprehensive than the scoreline suggests (the German crowd was chanting the name of their absent, injured hero Uwe Seeler before the end), but just two of those six men would kick a ball in the 1966 World Cup, and one of them only for 90 minutes.

Ramsey retained 4–3–3 for the next game against Sweden in Gothenburg, bringing back John Connelly for Derek Temple and Nobby Stiles for Ron Flowers, and England won 2–1, Ball scoring his first international goal and Connelly getting the other. But five months later it was back to 4–2–4 for two Home International games against Wales and Northern Ireland (0–0 and 2–1), punctuated by a bad 3–2 defeat at Wembley against a young and experimental Austrian side who had already failed to qualify for the 1966 finals, which had the Austrian manager Rudi Fruhwirth saying: 'Yesterday I thought Mr Ramsey's England team would win the World Cup. Today it is another picture.'

'It was my fault really,' said Alf carefully of his team. 'They were only doing what I told them to do.' He then added that his midfield had been 'brilliant' and England would have won if they had taken their chances . . .

Thirty years later, when there are almost as many tactical variations as there are successful soccer teams, and when the national team itself flits whimsically between 1–3–3–3, 1–4–3–2 and 4–3–2–1, Alf Ramsey's prevarications over the way his sides lined up seem almost incomprehensible. But in 1965 footballers – English footballers especially – had been born and bred into just one system: that famous old 3–2–5. The first elementary break with the past had been towards 4–2–4, which at least involved keeping the wing-halves/inside-forwards (as the middle two, and possibly, like Jimmy Greaves, as one of the strikers in the front four), the wingers and the full-backs doing more or less what their apprenticeships had taught them to do, which was respectively: win the ball and service the striker; hurtle up and down the touchline; tackle and cover.

But as the likes of Stanley Matthews had made clear, even 4–2–4 was regarded as dangerously revolutionary, as stifling the players' natural instincts. Such men not only did not stop to study and learn from foreign sides; they also managed to forget that the old system had itself been a tactical device. Three-two-five had not been ordained by God; it had been invented by the Victorian originators of the organised game. In Great Britain the system had become, over the years, almost as unassailable as Holy Writ. Schoolboys were taught the old positions along with the laws of the game. All coaching manuals were devoted to the old team shape. All childrens' guides to football insisted upon the classical formation. All soccer literature – and there was plenty by the 1950s – celebrated the honourable, mythic duels between full-backs and wingers, centre-halves and centre-forwards, inside-forwards and half-backs. And of course, all football clubs, from the humblest schoolboys' League to the First Division, played that way.

So most of the good players available to Ramsey knew no more than one position, and many would have been dismayed by the suggestion that they play elsewhere. How could he do without wingers when that would surely mean doing without Paine, Connelly and Thompson, three of the best footballers in the land? The 4–2–4 system might be new, but at least it encompassed two attacking flank men.

But to work properly, 4–2–4 demanded of its wingers that they accept extra-curricular duties. They had to drop deeper and help the abbreviated midfield to win the ball – or at least make themselves available to relieve the pressure on the two orthodox middle men. Many could not or would not do that (and as we have seen, even Bobby Charlton initially found it difficult to combine his accustomed left-wing role with the added responsibilities of midfield playmaking – Charlton, in fact, vastly preferred the midfield to the left wing, where Matt Busby had been playing him for three seasons, because as a winger he saw the ball too infrequently, and when picked as an out-and-out flank man he would frequently stray from position, thus negating any intended 4–2–4 or 4–3–3 tactics) which left England, during Ramsey's first experiments, too often dangerously short in the area of the pitch known as the boiler room; and that is why, when he first lined them up in 4–3–3 formation, the relief was instantly felt. Back in the old days (and back at their clubs) the midfield area was effectively covered by three or four players: at least one of the two inside forwards, and the two half-backs. The two men in the middle of 4–2–4 could not alone plug that gap overnight. Three men, however, could and did.

Why then did Ramsey not switch immediately and permanently to 4–3–3 after its success in training against the under-23s and on tour against West Germany and Sweden? Partly because he was still using orthodox wingers like Paine and Connelly in a formation which, if it was to be used to maximum effect, had no real place for orthodox wingers. The players from the old system who were best suited to fit comfortably into the early, 1965 editions of 4–3–3 were inside for-wards and half-backs, and centre-forwards (four of the former and two of the latter), or exceptional wingers like Bobby Charlton with a propensity to cut inside and look for the ball. But Ramsey was not only persisting with an out-and-out winger such as Connelly as one of the front three; he was also using the likes of Paine in the middle three, alongside such practised half-backs and inside-forwards as Flowers and Eastham. He may as well have asked Greaves to play like Nobby Stiles. Despite the overall success of the system, Paine and Connelly often struggled.

There was another drawback. All tactical meddling was seen in many quarters of the British press and public as devious, unneces-sary, and as possibly sacrificing the ancient, strong-boned qualities of the British game on the tinselled altar of innovation. Even 4–2–4, which when used by British players looked at times little different to the old style, was perceived as flashy and foreign and superficially fashionable: like those Zigoni shoes the kids were wearing, or their Italian suits, cappuccino coffee and Lambretta scooters. And although the chance would have been a fine thing, Alf Ramsey could not in truth ignore either the British public or the British press. A large part of the reason for his grudging manner with, and occasional hostility towards, the media was his thorough – indeed, possibly exaggerated – understanding and fear of what they could do to him. But equally, he could not go back to the 1950s. He knew too much about football to countenance that. His captain put it best when he said: 'I still hear people proclaim that the "good old-fashioned style" would put England back on top. They are living in the past. The good old stuff would ensure a slaughter in every game we played.'

So Alf embraced 4–2–4, and if he could have done so he would have stayed in its arms, because there were other – not unjustified – public concerns about the raft of new formations. Essentially, each one of them as they cropped up, invented by some foreign wizard with an 'o' on the end of his name and practised (to English eyes) by Brylcreemed Latins who disliked honest tackling, was perceived in Britain as being more negative and defensive and cynical than the last.

There was something in this. Even 4–2–4 did not always produce the kind of penalty-area warfare which was customary in the British Age of Innocence, when valiant defences tussled in the mud with five-man forward lines. And 4–3–3 was seen as being even more defensive than 4–2–4. And 4–4–2 was – obviously – even more negative than that. Had not Argentina worked their way through that scale of formations as their opposition grew more difficult in the Little World Cup in the summer of 1964? And as for the 'catenaccio' sweeper system of 1–3–4–2, or even 1–4–3–2 (both of which were in international use by 1965) . . . the less that British audiences heard of such things, the better. Highly-qualified men blamed such tactics for the imminent death of the game of football.

Ramsey had to juggle with his players' capabilities and adaptability, with their clubs' conservatism, and with the scepticism of the press and the hostility of the paying public towards the tactical formations of the Modern Age. It was not an easy job. Two years later, after the ultimate success of the new system, Bobby Moore would still feel obliged to plead: 'I can imagine that the ordinary spectator watching on his TV set at home found the whole style of football vastly different from the stuff that attracts the crowds at home – with none of the fast, end-to-end play and goalmouth incidents of our club soccer.

'But this carefully controlled, scientifically thought out soccer is what international football demands today.'

With English club soccer largely isolated from the fluid continental and South American thought on the subject of team formations and tactics, Ramsey was left to herd his flock clumsily from 4–2–4 to 4–3–3, losing more than one lamb along the way. He had proved to himself and to most of his players that 4–3–3 worked, but none of them was sure how well it could work until 8 December 1965, when he employed it again for the first time in seven months, just eight months before England's first game in the World Cup finals which he had vowed to win.

The match was a friendly international against Spain in Madrid. Spain were the holders of the European Nations Cup which England had disappeared from in Ramsey's first game back in 1963; four weeks earlier Spain had qualified for the 1966 finals by beating the Republic of Ireland in a play-off; and England had never beaten Spain in Iberia.

With the exception of Bobby Charlton who, by the end of 1965, was regarded as more of an all-purpose player than anything else, Alf Ramsey did not pick a single winger to face them in the Bernabau Stadium. His team that freezing, blizzard-swept Wednesday night was:

Banks
Cohen   Charlton J   Moore   Wilson
Ball   Stiles   Eastham
Hunt   Baker   Charlton R

Both Roger Hunt and Joe Baker were centre-forwards for their clubs, Liverpool and Arsenal. Baker scored in the tenth minute; Hunt added a second; and England quite outplayed their hosts in coasting to a 2–0 win.

The publicity pendulum swung back again: the England side which had not been worth a dime a year earlier was suddenly touted once more as potential world champions. Ramsey, who had said all along that he wished only to be judged by the results in July 1966, was hailed as a soccer Svengali who had finally achieved his model of perfection. The term 'wingless wonders' was coined not in mockery but in wholehearted, gobsmacked praise of this revelatory performance. The bookies' odds brought England down to 5–1 second favourites. (Brazil were at that time 9–4 favourites, with Argentina at 8–1, Russia 9–1, Italy 10–1, Portugal 14–1, Hungary 16–1, West Germany 20–1, and France and Spain both 25–1. The rest – Uruguay, Mexico, Switzerland, Chile and Bulgaria – hovered between 33s and 66; while the joke side of the championship, the only team from the whole of Africa and Asia which had not withdrawn in protest at FIFA's allocation of just one place to their two continents and Australasia combined, poor, isolated North Korea, stood at 200–1.)

England may even have been that good in Madrid. Jack Charlton remembered it as the turning point, 'just about the greatest morale-booster England could have had . . .

'The scoreline didn't tell the whole story, we could have finished up the victors by a six-goal margin. And it wasn't so much the victory as the way we achieved it, which was a good omen for the future. I don't think we played as well in any game after that, until we kicked off in the World Cup proper.'

'Till then,' according to Bobby Moore, 'there had usually been a recognised winger or two in the side. But that night there was born England's 'wingless wonders', with overlapping from behind and a volume of blind-side running. Here was the modern all-action game which gave Alf what he considered to be the best of both worlds.'

'This was the first time,' Ramsey would accede, usefully forgetting that his tour of Europe in May had come after the epochal training session in February during which he had first experimented with a three-man midfield, 'that I had been able to pick a squad with the idea of playing a 4–3–3 team. It was 4–3–3 at its finest. It was at this time that I realised the system could win the World Cup in 1966.'

'I wish he would let his hair down occasionally and throw his cap over the moon,' Mrs Victoria Ramsey told a journalist. 'It would do him a power of good. There is nothing spectacular ever in his reactions. But in his quiet way he's on top of the world. I can't think of any reason why he shouldn't bring the cup to England. He deserves it.'

5 SCOTLAND, LISBON AND LILLESHALL

'One is all in favour of free thinking and free movement
in a game where the ball can be swept through 180
degrees of the compass. Yet these new methods, which
started so well in Madrid in December, seemed to get
nowhere . . . If England are to persist in the 4–3–3
formation, not only must they have finishing power but
the finesse and ingenuity to go with it.'

– *THE TIMES*, FEBRUARY 1966

Faced with the once-in-a-career opportunity of playing in a World
Cup which was being staged on their doorstep, the neighbouring
countries of Britain and Ireland fought bravely for qualification.

Bravely, but in vain. The Republic of Ireland had, on the face of
it, the most straightforward task. They were initially landed in a peculiarly matched group with Syria and Spain, but Syria had withdrawn
without kicking a ball as part of that Afro-Asian protest against
FIFA's niggardly and racist allocation of one final place in 16 to the
two emerging continents. (Syria had been placed in an otherwise
European qualifying group for geographical reasons: being a
Middle-Eastern country they were actually closer to Europe than to
the Far-Eastern entries from the Koreas and Australasia.) The same
protest reduced the original entry to the 1966 World Cup from 70
teams to 53: as well as Syria, Algeria, Ghana, Guinea, Cameroon,
Sudan, Liberia, Mali, Morrocco, Senegal, Ethiopia, Gabon, Libya,
Nigeria, the United Arab Republic and South Korea also withdrew.

The Republic's task was therefore obvious: they had to beat
Spain, the European champions, over two legs. They cleared the first

99

hurdle with a 1–0 win in Dublin in May 1965, waited five agonising months before going down 4–1 in the Seville stadium which the Spanish traditionally reserved for their most awkward fixtures, and then lost the play-off in Paris by a single goal.

Northern Ireland's was arguably the most agonising departure from all of the qualifying groups. Drawn with Switzerland, Holland and Albania, a team from the province which included Derek Dougan, Willie Irvine and the incomparable young George Best got off to a flyer, sharing the spoils at home and away with Switzerland, taking three points from Holland and hammering Albania 4–1 in Belfast. For most of 1965 they topped their group, but Switzerland came in with a late run – doing the double over Holland – and on 24 November the Northern Irish travelled to Tirana knowing that the obvious win over Albania (who had not a point in the group and had won only one international since 1953) would guarantee them a play-off against the Swiss. They drew 1–1 and missed the finals by a point. His finest opportunity gone at the first attempt, George Best would never play in the World Cup finals.

Wales also finished in second place in the European Group Seven, behind the highly-rated USSR; but it was the fate of Scotland which excited most attention. The Scottish vintage of 1964–65 was probably the most potent to have emerged from that country. Its pool of players may have been shallow, but those available were indisputably strong. Any side, it was suggested, able to draw on Denis Law, Ian St John, Jim Baxter, Jimmy Johnstone, Billy Bremner, Willie Henderson, Alan Gilzean, Pat Crerand, John Greig, Billy MacNeill, Ron Yeats and Willie Johnston, should have little trouble with Poland, Finland and Italy.

And so at first it seemed, as five points were taken from the opening three games (this was, of course, back in the hazy, distant days when just two points were awarded for a win, and one for a draw). The Scottish FA appeared to improve still further their side's chances of qualification when, between the first and second games, Ian McColl was replaced as team manager by the impressive Celtic boss Jock Stein.

In October 1965 107,000 people crowded into Hampden Park to witness the inevitable demolition of Poland. Billy MacNeill gave

100

Scotland the lead and all seemed comfortable until the last six minutes, when Poland scored twice to steal a 2–1 win. Italy arrived a month later and, being a better team than Poland, they were of course beaten, which left the Scots in a classical Caledonian fix: they needed a draw in the volcanic atmosphere of Naples in December to force a play-off with the Italians. Both Matt Busby and Bill Shankly refused to release their players from Manchester United and Liverpool for squad training before that game; Denis Law and Billy Stevenson were injured on the Saturday; goalkeeper Bill Brown, Billy MacNeill and Willie Henderson all failed fitness tests; and Scotland collapsed out of the 1966 World Cup qualifying Group Eight by 3–0. 'Most roads are paved with good intentions,' said Jock Stein, 'but this one was littered with obstacles.'

Englishmen shed crocodile tears and uttered weasel words of regret at the absence of their neighbours from the English World Cup finals but, in truth, the players and the manager were more relieved than distressed. The last thing any of them wanted was a quarter-final at Wembley against a Scottish side spitting blood and breathing fire and seeking vengeance for the events on Culloden Moor 220 years earlier.

So, Alf Ramsey and his men continued on their wingless way unencumbered by fears of what mayhem their Scottish and Irish colleagues from the First Division might wreak in the shirts of the Celtic fringe in July 1966. And suddenly, after the revelation in Spain, England had a fresh objective. Alf Ramsey had to find new and talented forwards who were not wingers.

On the Monday morning of the last week in December 1965, Geoff Hurst was training with his West Ham United team-mates on the (thawed) skating rink at Forest Gate. Come the five-a-sides, and nothing was going right for Geoff – 'I was passing like a blind man'. Manager Ron Greenwood appeared on the sidelines, stood watching for a while, and then called Hurst across. The centre-forward trotted reluctantly over.

'Not going too well this morning, are we?' asked Greenwood rhetorically.

'No.'

There was a silence.

'Well, perhaps this will liven you up. I've just had a call from Alf Ramsey. You're in the England party to play Poland at Everton next week.'

Hurst was astonished. He had played off-and-on for the West Ham first team since 1958, he had held down a position in the forward line since 1962 and he was, in the midwinter of 1965–66, the leading goalscorer in the First Division. But in all of that time, while forwards had been in and out of Ramsey's team like a rally of fiddlers' elbows, Geoff Hurst had never once been tipped for an international cap. Not by the maddest pundit in the most desperate newspaper on Fleet Street. Everybody else who had been within ten yards of the penalty area in a First Division game had been suggested as an England striker by one paper or another, and most of them had been picked. But not Geoff, and he thought he knew why.

Geoff Hurst had been born in Lancashire but brought up from the age of six in Chelmsford, which made him yet another soccer alumnus from Essex, the county which had already provided the England team of the 1960s with Ramsey, Moore, Venables and Greaves. The son of Charlie Hurst, a centre-half with Oldham Athletic, Bristol Rovers, Rochdale and Chelmsford (a short-statured centre-half who assured his son that challenges in the air were none-the-less not a problem: 'If I can't get my head to the ball, I can always get my head to the back of his head. So I head the centre-forward, he heads the ball, and we're both happy.'), Geoff had been himself an unexceptional player as a boy and had never made the Essex County schools' side. But in 1956 he joined the West Ham ground staff at the age of 15, and he spent two years in the juniors and the reserves and painting the stadium before signing professional forms in 1958. Painting the stadium, and learning the game . . .

Hurst the junior player was standing a few yards from his adored first-team players at training one afternoon, trying to catch their conversation, when one of them called him over.

'Here, Geoff, come and mark me tight while Jack takes a throw-in.'

Hurst jogged proudly into position. 'Clearly I had been picked to take part in the demonstration because they had spotted what a tough baby I was; they wanted a man who knew how to mark tight. I

102

marked tight all right, but suddenly the bloke I was behind ducked just as the man with the ball threw it in as hard as he could from about five feet away. I didn't have time to move. The ball smacked me full in the face, making my nose bleed and my eyes water. Without so much as a glance or a word to me as I staggered about, the first teamers walked away. I heard one of them say: "See, it works ..."'

Having picked up a few elementary lessons in self-preservation, Hurst was selected for West Ham's First Division side as a half-back until Ron Greenwood, in need of a forward who was 'big and strong and not afraid of work' to take some of the weight off Johnny 'Budgie' Byrne, picked him in the front line. And there he stayed: hardly, in his own assessment, a forward possessed of the international-class skills of a Greaves or a Byrne, but one who studied his own game and attempted to improve it, one who laboured selflessly for others, one who was in his own words 'happy to be the bread and butter side' of the partnership with Byrne, one who wasn't afraid to take a pot at goal, and one who was ... well, big, and strong, and not afraid of work. Were they qualifications for an England cap?

Under Alf Ramsey, the answer was yes. Byrne was injured and would never return to the national side. But Hurst was worth a trial. The only problem was that Hurst himself did not wholeheartedly agree. He spent the first training sessions scarcely able to wish his fellow internationals good morning, let alone shout at them to pass him the ball. In the end Ramsey called him over.

'Geoff, I've picked you because I believe you can play. But there's nothing more I can do for you. It's up to you: you've got to go the rest of the way towards becoming an England player by yourself. You've got to open your mouth and let yourself be heard.'

To nobody's surprise, least of all his own, Hurst was not picked from the squad of 22 for England's 1–1 draw with Poland at Goodison Park, a game which was distinguished chiefly by the fact that it featured an England goal which would have been almost unthinkable four years earlier: an open-play cross from an over-lapping full-back, George Cohen, was headed in by a central defender, Bobby Moore.

Within a week of that uninspired result the squad was given a sharp reminder of the imminence of judgement day when FIFA made the draw for the 1966 World Cup finals. England, all of whose Group One games would be at Wembley, was to be served, in this order, with Uruguay, Mexico and France. The bookies quickly calculated it to be a gentle passage to the quarter-finals for the host country (on their last visits to Wembley, in 1964, 1961 and 1958 respectively, the three opponents had each lost, by 2–1, 8–0, and 4–0) and shortened England's odds to 9–2. More peculiarly, the odds on Brazil, who had been thrust into the lions' den at Everton with formidable European opposition in the shape of Hungary, Portugal and Bulgaria, also shortened to 2–1.

And on 23 February, a month after his disappointment in Liverpool – a month which he had spent assuring himself that he had never been in with a realistic chance of selection, and now never would be – Geoff Hurst finally gained his first cap. For the first time in 12 years, West Germany visited London for a friendly. With hindsight, it was an absolutely seminal friendly fixture; one of those games which changed the whole course of future events. At the time, for players and fans alike, it was the strangest and most unpleasant of contests.

Helmut Shoen's West Germany was missing three key players who would certainly be there in July: the AC Milan defender Karl Schnellinger and the forwards Uwe Seeler and Horst Haller. Alf Ramsey was burdened by no such problems, but he chose to ignore the claims of Jimmy Greaves, who was recovering from a seriously debilitating attack of jaundice. Instead he gave Blackburn Rovers' Keith Newton a (remote) chance to replace Ray Wilson at left-back and he put Norman Hunter of Leeds United (a player whose tyke supporters had fondly nicknamed him 'Bite-Yer-Legs', and one whose fellow profesionals made no bones about describing him as an 'assassin') into the middle of defence alongside Jack Charlton, shifting Bobby Moore into midfield with Nobby Stiles and Alan Ball. Considering that Hunter, Jack Charlton, Stiles, Roger Hunt and Geoff Hurst, none of whom was exactly a ball-juggling will o' the wisp, consequently dominated the centre of the pitch from one penalty area to the other, with only Bobby Charlton assigned to provide some wan artistic relief on the left-hand side of the front three, it seemed to many that Alf was rather over-egging the pudding.

The country was happy to go along with a physical contest if it could still pretend to itself that it was watching football, and if England was winning, but did we have to make it this obvious?

And so, despite the fact that England led by 1–0 from three minutes before half-time, when Stiles of all people followed up to scramble home a Hunt header which had been blocked on the line, until the final whistle, the crowd hated the game and 75,000 of them made their feelings known.

For England to be jeered at Wembley was, by early 1966, not a unique occurrence; many of these same players had been heckled off the pitch after the defeat by Austria just four months earlier. But for England to be booed at Wembley when they were winning was entirely new. And if the crowd hated this laborious trudge to victory, this slow, clumsy, tackle-and-lose-the-ball-and-tackle-again festival of bad passing, the players detested it even more.

Geoff Hurst remembered telling himself before his debut that he would reward Ramsey by giving the manager what he obviously desired: maximum workrate. 'And that's just about all that happened – I ran, I ran, I ran. I felt like the bandsman who had been given the music for last week's concert: I did all the things I had been doing with West Ham – just as Alf had insisted I do – but either the ball came too late for me or it didn't come at all. I covered miles of that turf keeping my promise to myself. The Wembley crowd were very shirty. I could hear them jeering and slow hand-clapping during the match, and we certainly got the bird as we trotted off, a bit grim-faced, towards the tunnel.'

Inside the dressing-room at the end of the game the players could still hear the fans' bitter, heckling chants. 'Listen to them moan,' said Alf Ramsey to his men. 'But I'll tell you this: they'll go mad if we beat West Germany by one goal in the World Cup final.' Then he left them to tell the press that he was proud of his players – 'They ran their guts out.'

For all his prescience concerning narrow victories over West Germany in the World Cup final, Ramsey was skewered on a dilemma. There could be no going back to 4–2–4. Four-three-three worked – England had won four and drawn one of their five games employing the system – but it only seemed to work at full capacity without classical, touchline-hugging, dip-the-shoulder-one-way-and-go-the-other wingers. Jaunts down the wing, and crosses from the by-line, should henceforth be the part-time job of two extremely fit and willing overlapping full-backs. Yet without wingers, and when the full-backs failed even occasionally to get forward and the game was left in the control of gut-wrenching hard men like Hunter, Stiles and Hunt assisted by willing gophers like Ball and Hurst, 4–3–3 could be unutterably tedious. And unutterably tedious football got the Wembley crowd jeering England instead of gratefully chanting them through a series of 1–0 wins all the way to the World Cup final. It was enough to make you spit, but it was true.

Ramsey was not entirely deaf to the catcalls of the world outside. He compromised and searched desperately to find playing room for a winger. He would continue to do so until fate, injury and sheer necessity forced his hand, five months to the day after that ominous, traumatic win over West Germany at Wembley.

His hand may have been, if not forced, nudged in that direction by a game which was broadcast on British television from Lisbon on 9 March, 1966. It came in such contrast to the Wembley fixture against West Germany that it broke like the sun through the barren grey clouds which lowered over English football, and the country could not help but draw comparisons. It was just Alf Ramsey's luck to field his most sterile, unappealing national side just two weeks before the most glorious performance of Matt Busby's Manchester United.

United had travelled to Lisbon in the quarter-finals of the European Cup to protect an extremely fragile 3–2 lead from the first leg over Benfica, the Portuguese champions and European Cup finalists for four of the previous five seasons, who were widely regarded as the best club side in Europe. The Benfica eleven which lined up against Matt Busby's hopefuls in the Stadium of Light contained eight of the Portuguese World Cup squad, including the fearsome European Footballer Of The Year, the striker Eusebio, his tall, powerful partner up front Jose Torres, and their brilliant provider Antonio Simoes.

Before the match Busby told his players to 'play it tight' for 20 minutes or so, 'until we get their measure'. He could not believe what was then unveiled before his eyes. Suddenly, Manchester United began to play like the greatest football team in the world. Within 12 minutes George Best had scored twice – the second after a breathtaking ghostly drift past three players and the goalkeeper – and one of those rejected England wingers, John Connelly, playing on the left-hand flank of what was effectively a five-man forward line, added a third before half-time. Pat Crerand and Bobby Charlton scored two more, and United had beaten the supposedly unassailable Benfica in their own backyard by a simply unbelievable 5–1 on the night; by 8–3 on aggregate; and by an inspired display of carefree, attacking, innocent football.

It was the British club performance of the decade and it obviously was not repeatable at the snap of thumb and finger. United knew that it was just one of those nights: after five minutes of the game Best caught Crerand's eye 'and he started laughing because he knew we were going to look a great team and he's laughing like a lunatic at the thought. All of us played that night like we never wanted it to stop. We could have gone on forever.'

United did not even win the European Cup that season, but such awkward details could not dim the light which beckoned from Lisbon over the months to come. Aside from Charlton and Connelly, Nobby Stiles had been in Busby's side. Why couldn't England do that?

Part of the answer was, of course, that George Best and Denis Law were not English. But that was only part of it. There was a philosophy at work at Old Trafford which clearly had little in common with the deliberations on the third floor of number 22 Lancaster Gate. Matt Busby's Manchester United might only be able to produce a show of that calibre once in a decade, but the kind of England team which Ramsey had fielded against West Germany could play from 1966 until eternity and never come within touching distance of the sparkling, exhilarating display which had been broadcast from the Stadium of Light. There was unease abroad in England of a most unusual kind. No longer did people only wonder out loud whether or not England had a chance of winning the tournament: they began to question the manager's apparently ruthless manner of doing so. The team which just two months earlier had been the wingless wonders was now publicly caricatured as Ramsey's Robots. Alf had been right: for his team to win the World Cup playing as they had played against West Germany would be palatable to the great majority of British people. But if they failed playing that way . . .

Alf Ramsey was only human: if you pricked him, he bled. If you jeered at him, he fretted deep inside. He had five weeks to reconsider his team before the next friendly. While he thought, the World Cup itself disappeared. The Jules Rimet trophy, which was insured for £30,000, was being exhibited along with three million pounds worth of rare postage stamps at Westminster Central Hall. On Sunday, 20 March 1966, it was stolen from a locked cabinet within the hall. A massive police hunt lasted for eight days until a dog named Pickles unearthed the trophy from beneath a bush in the front garden of a house in Norwood, South London. The dog's owner collected £6,000 reward money, and a man who had demanded £15,000 for the return of the figurine was jailed for two years.

Two days after the cup had been mysteriously lifted, Alf Ramsey named a very different English side to play Scotland at Hampden Park on 2 April. He reverted to his favourite defence of Banks, Cohen, Moore, Jack Charlton and Wilson (although the Everton full-back withdrew injured within a week, and Keith Newton was given another forlorn chance to stake his claim); he put Bobby Charlton in midfield with Ball and Stiles; and he picked John Connelly to play on the wing outside a striking duo of Hurst and Hunt. The changes of personnel may have seemed trivial, but slight as they were the whole make-up of the side changed. There were playmakers – Moore and Bobby Charlton – calling the tune both in defence and in midfield. The team would not have attracted so much as a round of applause in Rio de Janeiro. England still lacked what the South Americans dubbed 'fantasy', but they would satisfy the modest expectations of their own spectators, who assumed – as did the players, the press and Alf himself – that the absence of the one other magician available to Ramsey, Jimmy Greaves, was a temporary fault, soon to be corrected when he recovered full fitness and replaced the least successful of the terrible twins Hurst and Hunt. They were right, up to a point.

By April 1966, just three months from the big kick-off, England's games were of course all crucial games, but this one achieved an almost artifical level of importance which led many to feel that it would have been better not to play the damned thing at all. It was a Home Championship decider, England having taken three points and Scotland two from Northern Ireland and Wales. North of the border, however, it was much more than that: it was Scotland's first game since they had been knocked out of their World Cup qualifying group by Italy in Naples, and it was consequently their last chance to prove to themselves and to the watching world which of the warring tribes of Ultima Thule should really have been in the finals. 'The Scots,' wrote that most knowledgeable of their compatriots, Hugh McIlvaney in *The Observer*, 'look on this fixture as the supreme challenge. They are embittered by the frustration of their own World Cup ambitions, and the only acceptable balm is English blood . . . if they win this one, all the crowing they have done since 1961 will seem to have been mere rehearsal.'

It was Geoff Hurst's first visit to Hampden, and he found it to be unforgettable. 'The Scottish newspapers were incredible, you couldn't believe grown men could be so biased. Reading them you got the funny feeling that the match was already over . . . Scotland couldn't possibly lose; and in any case you couldn't even be sure who they would be playing, for there was hardly a mention of any member of the opposing team.

'The hotel staff, kind as they were, were just as bad; you got pro-Scotland propaganda with your porridge, you were sent to bed with a pitying smile as though you were getting up next morning for a date with the hangman, not Hampden. I even heard one Scotsman in the lounge pursuing the argument with lunatic logic that the dark blues were about to win the title, World Champions. It seemed to him that as Scotland had been somehow connived out of the World Cup by Italy, there was nothing left to stop England winning; and therefore so long as we were beaten next day, Scotland could be said to have lifted a title from us that we hadn't yet won . . .'

In the event Scotland lifted nothing but the ball from the back of their own net. Hurst, who had shaken off his shyness in training and begun to demand the ball instead of behaving 'like an anxious-to-please puppy', scored the first and Roger Hunt the second. Law pulled one back, but Hunt made it 3–1. Jimmy Johnstone again reduced the deficit before Bobby Charlton fired home a screamer from the edge of the box. At that point, Billy Bremner later admitted, 'We should have been murdered. It could have been six for England.' Instead Johnstone – who spent most of the afternoon hammering nails into poor Keith Newton's coffin – got a third for Scotland to leave the final scoreline as 4–3 to England.

Five days later Alf Ramsey released a 'provisional' list of 40 players who were most likely to make up his World Cup squad. FIFA's rules insisted that each national side provided the governing body first with 40 names before the end of May, which should then be pared down to a final 22 players – who, peculiarly, need not all have been in the first 40 – by 3 July, eight days before the tournament began. Ramsey offered up his 40 men earlier than required in order to give their recalcitrant clubs notice that they may be called upon for international preparation. The 40 were: Gordon Banks (Leicester City), Ron Springett (Sheffield Wednesday), Peter Bonetti (Chelsea), Gordon West (Everton), Tony Waiters (Blackpool); Jimmy Armfield (Blackpool), George Cohen (Fulham), Ray Wilson (Everton), Keith Newton (Blackburn Rovers), Chris Lawler (Liverpool), Paul Reaney (Leeds United), Gerry Byrne (Liverpool), Nobby Stiles (Manchester United), Jack Charlton (Leeds United), Bobby Moore (West Ham United), Martin Peters (West Ham United), Gordon Milne (Liverpool), Marvin Hinton (Chelsea), Ron Flowers (Wolverhampton Wanderers), Norman Hunter (Leeds United), John Hollins (Chelsea), Tommy Smith (Liverpool), Terry Venables (Chelsea, on his way to Tottenham Hotspur), Terry Paine (Southampton), Ian Callaghan (Liverpool), Jimmy Greaves (Tottenham), Roger Hunt (Liverpool), Geoff Hurst (West Ham), Barry Bridges (Chelsea), Bobby Charlton (Manchester United), Alan Ball (Everton), George Eastham (Arsenal), Peter Thompson (Liverpool), John Connelly (Manchester United), Peter Osgood (Chelsea), Derek Temple (Everton), John Kaye (West Bromwich Albion), Fred Pickering (Everton), Joe Baker (Nottingham Forest) and Gordon Harris (Burnley).

It was most commented upon because of the absence of one of Alf Ramsey's early favourites, 'Budgie' Byrne of West Ham. But it was possibly most deserving of comment because despite his use of almost 50 players since 1963, several of the above – most notably

110

Martin Peters, Peter Osgood, Paul Reaney and Ian Callaghan – had never once pulled on an England shirt for a senior international match. So he quickly gave Martin Peters his first cap in the next Wembley friendly, and the last before the final run-in, the gathering at Lilleshall and a gruelling four-match tour of Europe which would take them right up to the starting line of the World Cup finals.

That last home friendly was against Yugoslavia on 4 May, and Alf Ramsey kicked off the traces. He not only gave the 22-year-old West Ham midfielder Peters (who curiously also came from south-west Essex) his opportunity; he also used two wingers – Terry Paine and Chelsea's Bobby Tambling, who had not only never been capped before, but extraordinarily had not even been in the list of 40 players released by Ramsey a month earlier – on either side of Geoff Hurst and the suddenly recalled Jimmy Greaves, although in lip-service to 4–3–3 Paine once more played deep. This was almost a reversal of recent trends: it was certainly as different as was imaginable from the side which had been jeered off the pitch three months before. It was almost as if Alf had brainstormed, or as though he was gambling on flair to fail and thereby justify his true intentions – 'Oh Alf,' the crowd would sigh, 'forgive our frailty. Hang wingers and fancy-boy inside-rights; bring back the Robots.' If such it was, it failed. England beat Yugoslavia 2–0 with goals from Greaves and Bobby Charlton, and Paine, Tambling and Peters all looked promising. Only Norman Hunter, whom Ramsey had fought a last-ditch battle with Leeds United to claim – along with Jack Charlton – for his England squad ahead of United's Fairs Cup semi-final play-off with Zaragoza, which had originally been scheduled for 3 May; only Norman The Assassin, slipped into the defence in place of Bobby Moore, who was in contractual dispute with West Ham United and therefore supposedly preoccupied, failed to prove his point.

Alf had not brainstormed. He had left things a bit late, and was now simply filling in some last-minute options. The team which faced Yugoslavia was never intended to play together again in England shirts, and it never would. When talking of that game later he would single out just one moment and just one player: Bobby Charlton, whom Ramsey spotted at one stage moving away from the ball in midfield to cover a Yugoslavian who was drifting down the blind side of England's defence – 'At that moment I thought he [*Charlton*] became a great player,' he said in an expression of Ramseyite perfectionism which was so typically arcane that it was almost snobbish. (It is also illuminating to note that before he could properly identify Bobby Charlton – who was that day playing in his 65th international – as a 'great' player, Alf Ramsey had to see him tracking back to help the defence.) There would be no unnecessary compliments to the extras, to the players who were extraneous to the grand scheme of things. There would be not much more Mr Nice Guy.

Two days after Yugoslavia, on 6 May, he made another squad announcement. This time it was to nominate 28 players who should report for training at Lilleshall for two weeks on 6 June, and thereafter prepare to travel to play Finland, Norway, Denmark and Poland. That 28, from which the final World Cup 22 would be selected, included three replacements: Bobby Tambling came in for Barry Bridges; John 'Budgie' Byrne was after all recalled to the squad in place of Fred Pickering; and Everton's Brian Labone replaced Marvin Hinton. The remaining 12 who had not made the cut were told to be on stand-by. They included Paul Reaney, John Hollins, Tommy Smith, Joe Baker, Peter Osgood and Terry Venables. Most of them would never again (or just simply never) play for England.

Only 27 of the chosen 28 arrived at Lilleshall on 6 June, Brian Labone having experienced the most upside-down World Cup career of any half-back: he was no sooner selected as a latecomer than he had to withdraw with an injury. It may have been a blessing in disguise for the Everton player: Labone may have simply been saved further disappointment; for Alf Ramsey already knew to within two players what his preferred World Cup eleven would be. It was pretty close to the team which had beaten Scotland at Hampden in April. Barring accidents he would field Cohen, Moore, Jack Charlton and Wilson in front of Banks in defence. Alan Ball, Stiles and Bobby Charlton would make up the midfield, with Stiles working as an auxiliary defender (indeed, by the early summer of 1966 most of the rest of the squad significantly referred to 'half-back' Nobby as a member of their defence). Despite the fact that 25 of the 50 players whom Ramsey had selected as manager had been forwards, he had still to determine a forward line, although it would certainly have to include

Jimmy Greaves, playing in the middle alongside either Hunt or Hurst, and flanked by one winger chosen from Paine, Callaghan or Connelly. It was almost but not quite a purely Ramseyite formation: the forward line contained at least one and possibly two deferences to the press and public opinion – and, to be honest, to the vestigial fantasies of the Alf Ramsey of old, Alf Ramsey the player who had found his most delirious moment in drifting forward in place of a crippled winger to score a goal against Second Division Grimsby Town, the Alf Ramsey who had not been burdened by promises of winning the World Cup, the Alf who might in his buried heart have liked nothing more than to win the World Cup final 6–3 in a dazzling dreamscape of graceful runs and smoothly stroked passes and volleys which curled through the sky like comets . . . But this Alf was not that Alf. This was a new Alf, an Alf who had in the interests of his country tried to divest himself of fantasy. This was the Alf who was 'not a dreamer', and the team of his practical intelligence would have to wait for seven long weeks and seven matches before it appeared, delivered to him by fate and a couple of raking French studs.

The apprehensive 27, who knew that their number was shortly to be culled down to a final 22, soon christened their training camp Stalag Lilleshall. They would be there for just over two weeks and during that brief spell of concentrated effort their World Cup destiny would be decided. You are here to work, Ramsey told them on that first day in Shropshire, and to work hard. This is not Butlins. Anybody found malingering or taking leave of absence for an unauthorised drink will be immediately dropped. Anybody who does not appreciate those conditions should say so now and go home. There will be no hard feelings.

His offer found no takers. The 27 settled down to a routine of intensive morning training, afternoon badminton, basketball, tennis, indoor cricket and other supposedly non-contact sports, and evening dinner, film and bed. Some squad members were four or five to a room, which they had to tidy themselves. They shared most menial duties and queued for food at a self-service counter. Their weight was checked daily and they were subjected to exhaustive medical examinations. After a few days some players formed a semi-serious 'escape committee' to formulate ways of breaking out and making it through the woods to the nearby golf club for a drink. Word of this reached the camp commandant, and one morning before training Ramsey called his entire squad together.

'We are here for a purpose,' he said. 'I just want to say that if anyone did get the idea of popping out for a pint, then they would be finished with this squad for ever.'

There was complete silence in the room. The escape committee never met again. Alf Ramsey had been, it should be recalled, a Company Quarter-Master Sergeant between 1940 and 1946.

'As soon as we had been ushered inside the portals,' recalled Jack Charlton, 'the gates were closed and locked. Although we had a two-week break from the end of the season, we had been warned to keep ourselves in trim. Conscientiously, we all did this, and it was a good job we did.

'Normally a player gets down to the ground at his club around 10.00am, goes out for a two-hour training, and relaxes the rest of the day. This wasn't the pattern Alf Ramsey had set for us at Lilleshall. Our day began at nine and finished at nine at night. Mornings were reserved for virtual non-stop training sessions; and after lunch we were split into groups to play badminton, tennis and indoor cricket. Tea-time was the signal for us to have a bath, then come down for dinner, after which we would see a film, play cards or dominoes, have a nine o'clock cup of tea – and toddle off to bed . . .

'At times I felt it seemed just like an exercise in pushing the human mind and frame to the utmost level of endurance – and then some. This was a test of stamina, skill and mental ability to cope with things. In other words, temperament had to be tested, before we went out into the heat of battle. But while we called Lilleshall 'the prison', I do not recall ever hearing one word of complaint about the rigid discipline Alf Ramsey and his backroom boys enforced during the whole time we were there. We realised that this was no picnic, that 15 other World Cup squads meant grim business . . .'

'That was work all right at Lilleshall,' Jimmy Greaves would echo later. 'There were guards on the gates up there. Alf said they were to keep people out. That's his story.'

There were two early medical concerns. The first was extraordinary. Many of the players (who, it turned out, often did not know how

114

to cut their own toenails) were discovered to be suffering from contagious ringworm of the feet, commonly known as athlete's foot. It was treated, but had only been reduced by three-quarters by the time they left Lilleshall.

The second was even more worrying. Halfway through the first day's training Ray Wilson, who was carrying another player around the training pitch at the time, felt his back go with a 'ping'. For four days he lay immobilised in the room which he shared with Bobby Charlton, being fed tablets by the doctor and being shaved and fed food by Charlton. Wilson was convinced that he would certainly now be one of the five rejects, when he was told to start training again and was delivered into the loving hands of Les Cocker, the famously hard Leeds United trainer who along with Manchester United's Wilf McGuiness had been co-opted on to Ramsey's team. Cocker's influence on England's World Cup performances has, perhaps, been understated . . .

There was, said Wilson, 'no rest, warmth or comfort under that man's wing. I can only assume he had been told to take me to breaking point so that when he had finished with me there could be no possible further doubt about my fitness. He really put me through it. When he was finished with me I felt fitter than I had ever been before . . . I knew the reason for the fitness and stamina of the Leeds United players.'

The workrate and the growing tension told on the players. Not long into the fortnight Jack Charlton and Nobby Stiles began to bicker at each other, and the bickering turned gangrenous, and suddenly, halfway through the first period of a training match, Stiles turned on Charlton and screeched abuse at the big centre-half.

Other players got the game underway once more, but the moment the half-time whistle sounded Charlton and Stiles were at it again: Charlton goading Stiles at full volume about the latter's performance when Manchester United had been knocked out of the European Cup semi-finals by the unknowns of Partizan Belgrade; Stiles responding by telling Charlton how pathetic he had been against the Zaragossan forward line. Ramsey stood quietly by and watched, saying nothing, waiting for the geyser of insults to subside; but it did not falter, and only when the same disparagements came round – according to one observer – 'for the third time' did the manager step forward and say: 'Right, that's enough. Let's get this sorted out.'

And he did. Alf Ramsey was nothing if he was not a players' man. Point by point he went over the areas of disagreement with Stiles and Charlton and the other defenders, articulating them quietly and sensibly, creating clarity out of confusion: 'Nobby was right, Jack should have gone in for that tackle there . . . Nobby was wrong, it was his job to pick up that opponent . . .'.

Some members of the squad felt that they had actually been strengthened by the explosion and by Ramsey's conversion of a verbally brutal incident into a positive piece of teamwork which helped to cement a defence made up of potentially awkward, uncompromising individuals. 'It was, I now realise, a great piece of man-management,' said Geoff Hurst. 'If he had cut them off short the feelings would have bubbled along beneath the surface, resentment would have taken the place of reasoning. I go so far as to say that if this squabble had not arisen and been allowed to blow itself out, England would not have won the World Cup six weeks later . . . Nobby and Jack continued to argue all the way through to the final, but there was never again any malice in what they said.'

Hurst was himself to discover the wild side of Nobby Stiles during a basketball game one afternoon which produced what the West Ham forward would call 'the most frightening ten minutes of my sporting career.' Hurst's basketball team contained Jack Charlton and Jimmy Armfield. It was, therefore, a tall outfit playing a tall man's game. It was also extremely plausible: referee Ramsey knew nothing whatsoever about the rules of basketball, and Jimmy Armfield was able suavely to manipulate the manager into giving him all the calls, and the opposition nothing. Most of the opposition accepted this with good grace, until Armfield, Charlton and Hurst came up against Stiles, and Nobby took no more than a minute or two of Armfield's artistry before cracking.

'Every time I went for the ball,' recalled Hurst, 'I was clattered. If I jumped I came down winded with an elbow in my stomach; if I tried to dodge I was tripped; if I stood still I was hammered into the sidewalls. All our team got the same treatment, and Stiles was doing it all. The rest of his team was falling about with laughter. Nobby didn't need them . . .'

The players instituted an award of the Yellow Jersey, which was handed over 'with ceremony and biting insults' to the worst performer in each five-a-side practice match. Stiles had practically to be held down to receive it when his turn came around. Geoff Hurst accepted it with resignation after delivering a pass straight to the opposition's George Eastham, hearing the shouts of 'The Jersey!', blundering after Eastham to try and save the day and watching the Arsenal midfielder slide the ball between his legs and cruise around Hurst just as he crashed helplessly to the ground – 'There was no point in arguing.' And Bobby Charlton – serious, painstaking, accomplished Bobby Charlton, who seemed actually to be enjoying the severe disciplines of the training camp – was determined never to receive the Yellow Jersey, so his brother Jack had to predetermine the result of an 'impromptu' show of hands which gave it finally to Bobby by 26 votes to one.

Throughout the middle of June the hard-working days slipped by, and at times it seemed to them that they had never known a world outside Lilleshall. Jack Charlton walked down to the gates of the grounds one day and saw with something like relief a county omnibus go by, and a small child pointed at him and shouted: 'Look, there's one! Look at that one!', and he laughed all the way back up the long driveway. They had church on Sunday and cocoa at night. They played tennis for five shillings a set, with George Eastham up on the umpire's chair mimicking a 1960s Wimbledon umpire ('Miss Wilson to sairve'); they played in seasonal thunderstorms while the hail came down like golfballs and summer lightning flashed across the Shropshire countryside; they laughed easily together at court jester 'Budgie' Byrne's endless quips and patter; and slowly they achieved that elusive dream of every international team manager: they became as clannish and familiar as the squad of a professional League club. They knew each other's strengths and weaknesses on and off the playing field. They adopted nicknames and played practical jokes and frolicked like the children that they were in Never-Never Land, a place where those favoured not ever to grow old were being paid to play a game they loved on the biggest stage of all, and possibly, just possibly, to win at the end of all of this the acclaim of the entire world. 'Suddenly,' said Ray Wilson, 'we realised that we could win the World Cup.'

But for five of them the dream would soon be over. Before they left Lilleshall Alf Ramsey would reduce his squad to 22 players. On the last full day before the players separated to take a brief time-out at home before flying off on the pre-tournament tour of Europe they trained as usual. And then, as they were collecting their gear and trailing back through the woods to the mansion house at Lilleshall, with all of the squad glancing nervously over their shoulders Alf Ramsey approached – one after the other – Peter Thompson, Gordon Milne, Keith Newton, Bobby Tambling and 'Budgie' Byrne, and he spoke quietly to each of them in turn, and they nodded and then looked ahead with a strained and desperate sadness in their eyes.

By the time that he had finished asking the fifth player if he would mind keeping in training at his club's facilities in case an emergency arose, the other 22 knew that they had made it to the final stage. They all reached the showers in silence; five footballers crushed and despondent, another 22 torn between elation and a terrible pity for their comrades. 'I knew I was in,' said Geoff Hurst. 'I knew I was part of the final party, and that whatever happened to me and to the team in the coming month, I would always be able to say, "I was in that 22." But the five knew that within weeks the world would have forgotten how very near each came to being publicly acknowledged as one of the best 22 players in England.' At dinner that night Hurst could not stop himself glancing across the table at his friend and West Ham team-mate 'Budgie' Byrne, an unusually subdued 'Budgie' Byrne, and thinking: 'There but for the grace of God . . .'

Everton's Ray Wilson had previously arranged to travel back home to Merseyside on the following day with the Liverpool player Gordon Milne. They got a bus from Lilleshall into Stafford, and there Pat Wilson met them and drove them home, and throughout the long journey Milne sat in silence. 'I could imagine,' considered Wilson, 'the emptiness I would have felt.'

6 SCANDINAVIA, POLAND AND HENDON

'Keep on working hard and playing well, and you have a chance of being chosen.'

— ALF RAMSEY, 1966

Alf Ramsey had, in fact, another ten days before he was obliged to inform FIFA of his final 22 players on 3 July, and he took the time. He had told the five cast-offs that they had not been selected earlier than he needed to have done so, for two reasons. One was his sense of fairness: he did not wish to keep them hanging on any longer than was necessary. And the other was plain, brutal practicality: he wanted to give all of the favoured 22 a run-out during the four-match European tour; it would not assist his or anybody else's cause to have tagging along five men who had, in the manager's own mind, already been dismissed from active service.

Ramsey had planned this tour with care. The point of it, he told his players, was to get them to the peak of fitness at precisely the right time, rather than to fiddle about with tactical niceties. It would begin in Helsinki against Finland (who had three wins and one draw in nine matches since the start of 1965); it would progress to Oslo to encounter Norway (four wins – two of them against Thailand and Luxembourg – and three draws in ten games); to Copenhagen and Denmark (three wins and three draws in 12); and conclude, just nine days after the Finnish match, in Chorzow with England's last match before the World Cup finals against the stuffiest opposition of the tour: Poland (two wins and eight draws in 14 games since January 1965).

He ran through his players recklessly. In the first two matches he

119

used all but two of his 22 (and it is worth recalling that although a pair of substitutions were allowed in friendly internationals at that time, Ramsey – preparing for World Cup conditions – abjured them), and those two, George Eastham and the Chelsea goalkeeper Peter Bonetti, were on the field at the start of the third game in Copenhagen. Two players in England's World Cup squad of 22 – Bonetti and the Liverpool winger Ian Callaghan, who were each 24 years old – actually made their international debuts on this warm-up tour, eight days and 15 days respectively before England's kick-off in the World Cup finals.

But there was no arguing with results. A Bobby Moore-less side took the field against Finland, which surprised the erstwhile captain as much as anybody else. 'Everyone thought the writing was on the wall for R. Moore. It made me sit up,' he would say. 'From that day on I never expected to be in an England squad until the letter from the FA dropped through the letter-box, never took it for granted I would be in the team until I saw my name on the sheet or heard Alf call it out.'

He need not have fretted. Once more Norman Hunter, although paired with his Leeds United team-mate Jack Charlton, failed to impress as England bustled to a 3–0 win in the 80 degree heat of a Finnish midsummer, with one winger, Ian Callaghan, playing outside Hurst and Hunt. Callaghan in fact crossed for Hunt to score; Martin Peters scored in only his second international; Alan Ball missed a penalty; and Jack Charlton thundered upfield to register his first goal for England. It was, in Ray Wilson's words, 'a laboured, hard-slogging match', but England had won it without conceding a goal.

Moore was back in the starting line-up three days later in Oslo, and so was Jimmy Greaves, and so were two wingers: Paine on the right and Connelly on the left. For 20 minutes England struggled desperately against Norway. Ron Flowers delivered a dreadful back-pass wide of Springett and Sunde nipped in to put the home side one ahead. In making that error the Wolves defender whom many doddering England selectors had in happier days confused with Bobby Moore, and who was winning his 49th cap at the age of 31, sounded the death knell of his England career and confirmed what most already knew, that a central defence of Moore and Jack Charlton was carved on Ramsey's heart as if on stone.

Then Greaves struck, not once but four times in what *The Times* described as 'as complete an example of forward play as one could find anywhere'. The first was a powerful header – never the little striker's most celebrated skill – from a sharp Hunt cross; the second a run half the length of the pitch which concluded with him steering the ball artfully past Andersen in goals; the third a razor-edged piece of poaching after Andersen and Connelly collided and the ball ran free; and the fourth a neat angled finish to Paine and Connelly's build-up. They were his 40th, 41st, 42nd and 43rd goals in 49 internationals. (No England player of his time or any later period would come close to equalling that ratio. Bobby Charlton, for example, would finish his career with 49 goals from 106 games, and Gary Lineker concluded his with 48 from 80 appearances. Only the legendary Nat Lofthouse, who scored 30 times in 33 internationals in the 1950s, would ever be comparable to Greaves.) Connelly and Moore added two more to make the final score 6–1, but everybody left talking of Greaves's complete recovery from jaundice, of Greaves's return to electrifying form, of Greaves as a potential winner of the World Cup. Even Ramsey was pleased: so pleased that the England players were allowed, that night in Oslo, to stay up for a beer. It would be almost their last taste of alcohol for five weeks. Please, Mr Ramsey, a Danish journalist begged the manager of England afterwards, please play Greaves against Denmark in Copenhagen – 'Our crowd would be overjoyed to see him!'

Greaves was played against Denmark, but Bobby Charlton was dropped. Ramsey was worried about Charlton, as he had been worried about Moore. Moore had lost the West Ham captaincy as a result of his contractual dispute with Ron Greenwood, and until the Norway game it was widely rumoured that he had also lost his form. Bobby Charlton's malady was less easily identified. To most, in fact, the softly spoken, introverted grand master of Ramsey's midfield appeared to have little or nothing wrong with him. But Ramsey became deeply anxious and approached big brother Jack to ask if Bobby had something on his mind.

'Haven't a clue,' said Jack.

Alf was not to be deflected. For half an hour he worried answers out of Jack Charlton. It was common knowledge that Bobby's daughter Suzanne had dislocated a hip and was in plaster back in Manchester . . . could it be that?

'Obviously,' Jack Charlton reflected later, 'Bobby was concerned about the health of his daughter, and the fact that he was hundreds of miles away from home. But I genuinely felt that this was not preying on his mind to the extent that it was affecting his football. But however strongly I said this, I felt I hadn't quite convinced the boss . . . Alf seemed to worry about various other players at odd times during the competition. He would go around having quiet little chats to put people at their ease . . . he lived from day to day, trying to solve the pressing problems and leaving tomorrow to show whether new ones would arise.'

The Denmark game was, in comparison with the last 70 minutes of the match in Norway, inconclusive. Jack Charlton got his second goal in three matches – a typical header from a corner – and George Eastham scored to make it 2–0, but only Alan Ball's limitless workrate made much of an impression. The game left Ray Wilson 'feeling a shade flat' – 'England ran into a few problems here. In the desire to impress we seemed to involve ourselves in more dangerous situations than was necessary. Greaves and Hurst seemed almost incompatible although it was not for lack of trying, and it seemed we were not going to blend well enough to get among the goals.'

Greaves, after having apparently confirmed his World Cup place at the goal-festival in Oslo, was actually described as 'insolent and indolent' by one paper. It was of no account. He was, at that time, actually undroppable.

Immediately before the match in Copenhagen Alf Ramsey announced his final, official selection of 22 players to FIFA and to the press. They were to play in squad numbers, and they were:

No.	Name	Club	Age	Caps
			(on eve of World Cup)	
1	Gordon Banks	Leicester	28	17
2	George Cohen	Fulham	26	24
3	Ramon Wilson	Everton	31	45
4	Nobby Stiles	Man. Utd.	24	14
5	Jack Charlton	Leeds Utd.	30	16
6	Bobby Moore	West Ham	25	41

122

			Age	*Caps*
No.	*Name*	*Club*	(on eve of World Cup)	
7	Alan Ball	Blackpool	21	10
8	Jimmy Greaves	Spurs	26	51
9	Bobby Charlton	Man. Utd.	28	68
10	Geoff Hurst	West Ham	24	5
11	John Connelly	Man. Utd.	27	19
12	Ron Springett	Sheff. Wed.	30	33
13	Peter Bonetti	Chelsea	24	1
14	Jimmy Armfield	Blackpool	30	43
15	Gerry Byrne	Liverpool	28	2
16	Martin Peters	West Ham	22	3
17	Ron Flowers	Wolves	31	49
18	Norman Hunter	Leeds Utd.	22	4
19	Terry Paine	Southampton	27	18
20	Ian Callaghan	Liverpool	24	1
21	Roger Hunt	Liverpool	27	13
22	George Eastham	Arsenal	29	19

Noting the fact that the second- and third-choice goalkeepers were numbered 12 and 13, and the replacement full-backs 14 and 15, and that the first eleven names made up a logical Ramseyite side, almost everybody assumed that, as Bobby Moore put it, 'those who were numbered from one to eleven were going to be the World Cup team'. They were wrong, but not far wrong. On 3 July 1966 Alf Ramsey had just watched Geoff Hurst and Jimmy Greaves fail to work together with any understanding whatsoever. Ramsey considered, in fact, that he had never seen a worse display than that of Hurst from any England forward, and he briefly thought about sending the West Ham forward home and changing his 22 at the last minute. But there was one bonus: of the three orthodox wingers in the squad, John Connelly had filled that tiresome flankman's place most effectively. Had Alf Ramsey picked a World Cup team before the game on 3 July it would almost certainly have lined up as:

Banks

Cohen Moore Charlton J Wilson

Ball Stiles Charlton R

Hurst Greaves Connelly

But Hurst's shocking performance against Denmark relegated him, within hours, from being a favoured son to being one upon whom Alf Ramsey looked with anxiety; one to whom he could not speak in the changing room (a silence which, at the time, Hurst was thankful for). On 5 July he chose a side to play the last pre-tournament friendly against Poland in front of 80,000 people at Chorzow, and he dispensed with all wingers, bringing Peters in for Connelly, and picking Hunt to play alongside Greaves. It may not have been the team which, under the stern eyes of the press and public, he would have sent into a World Cup game, but it was closer to his preferred team. There was always a difference between the two. And in humouring himself and his deepest convictions, he gave Hunt what looked to everybody – Hunt included – like the chance to write his name indelibly on the World Cup teamsheet. And to the delight of manager and striker alike, Hunt seized it.

The Polish game was a fraught affair both before and during the match itself. Ramsey had designed it that way: to test the mettle of his players in the least appealing of environments; and from the moment the English squad crossed the border the Polish authorities obliged. They insisted that the game be played not in Warsaw, where the party had arrived, but far away in Chorzow, a township a few miles from Katowice among the smoke-stacks and slag-heaps and steeply sloping terraces packed with the fiercely partisan soccer fans of the industrial south. Reluctantly, Ramsey agreed, on the condition that his team could fly to Katowice. That was not possible, but they were assured that a flight from Warsaw to Cracow, 60 crow's miles from the ground at Chorzow, would leave them only an hour's coach drive from their destination.

It turned into a nightmarish ten-hour journey towards a trial by fire. Poland anywhere, any time would be a difficult game. Poland in Chorzow six days before the World Cup finals could, many people thought, prove to be a serious, even a disastrous mistake. England needed to go into those finals preferably on the back of a good victory, and certainly with all limbs intact. Neither could be guaranteed at Chorzow. 'Poland were far from being a pushover,' Jack Charlton reflected later. 'They had beaten Scotland at Hampden in the qualifying rounds, and given such an impressive display that they were rated highly unlucky to fail to reach the final stages . . . We were just the sort of team Poland wanted to meet – after all, if they could nail us and score another impressive victory, their stock would be boosted – and ours would slump.'

The English players made their tortuous way towards Chorzow with apprehensive preconceptions of a 'hard, militant, Iron Curtain' opposition, of soldiers and students 'who were to all intents and purposes full-time professionals who spent far more time in their training camps than any British player would ever dream about'. As they flew from Warsaw to Cracow in a nerve-racking twin-engined aeroplane some of them convinced themselves that the eleven to play in Poland would be the preferred World Cup team.

'We knew that our match against them,' said Ray Wilson, 'would be regarded by Alf Ramsey and the watching world as the final dress rehearsal before the big competition. We knew, deep down in our hearts, that he would be picking the eleven which he saw as his first team.' Wilson was almost right. Almost right.

The 'one-hour' coach journey from from Cracow to Katowice turned into a seven-hour haul on a rumbling, broken-down old bus which meandered 'through small villages, seemingly on a voyage to nowhere'. The Polish interpreter, keenly aware of English irritation, made the mistake after five hours on the bus of brightly asking Alf Ramsey what he planned to do later that evening. Ramsey fixed him with a long, cold stare.

'Get to Katowice – I hope,' he replied.

But the match was a triumph for England, and it was played without a single English winger on the field. The Polish players and supporters proved to be as intimidating as anyone had pre-supposed: the former contesting 'every kick, every tackle right to the bitter end', in Ray Wilson's words; and the latter whistling and howling every England move and every disappointing verdict from a frightened referee. 'It was a hard game,' said Jack Charlton, 'but I thought we acquitted ourselves extremely well.'

They did. Moore was all steely authority, Jack Charlton and Stiles were in their element, Wilson looked like one of the best full-backs in Europe, and the rest moved forward from there. It took 15 minutes for England to take the lead with a glorious strike, Bobby Charlton curling over a deep centre which Roger Hunt collected 25 yards from goal and half-volleyed into the top corner of the net. ('This thing of splendour,' reported the *Daily Express*, 'brought only a vicious scream from the crowd.')

England could have had more: Stiles shot into the side-netting after Hunt had put him through, and Greaves beat three men before being pulled down from behind four yards from the goal-line. No penalty was awarded. With the exception of one scare following a rash back-pass from Moore, the defence looked untroubled and sailed through the last 15 minutes as calmly as if they were holding off schoolboys in a practice match . . . or dismissing the under-23s in a training session at Lilleshall when they first experimented with the wingless 4–3–3, just 17 months earlier.

'What we set out to do, we have done,' said a terse Alf Ramsey afterwards. He then repeated in a television interview that England would win the World Cup.

'Among the England team,' said Jack Charlton, 'there was a tremendous spirit of confidence as the aircraft skimmed through the skies towards home, and the real thing at Wembley. Way back, when Alf Ramsey had made his famous prediction that England would win the World Cup, I had believed him implicitly. Then I had a few nagging doubts, when I considered how many slips there could be 'twixt cup and lip; and now I was back to that abounding confidence which the boss had publicly proclaimed in us.'

They returned to a press which was, once more, fawning upon them, and to a country which was as ready as it would ever be to host the World Cup. There were lingering fears of hooliganism. In 1965 some Liverpool supporters had, during a visit to Manchester, smashed the windows of the boardroom, the guestroom and Matt Busby's office at Old Trafford, and thrown missiles at United players on the field; and the fans of Leicester City had been told by British Rail that no more cheap excursions would be provided to them because of the damage done to their football specials. The Football Association subsequently announced that all drinks at World Cup matches would be served in cardboard containers or in paper cups, rather than in glass beakers or bottles. Those were still the days when football hooliganism was seen as a Latin phenomenon rather than an

Anglo-Saxon vice; when hilarious, half-credible stories were told in English pubs of referees being shot in South American cup-ties and of wars breaking out over foreign football matches. There was some truth to the popular conception: Pele said that when he first saw an English ground – Hillsborough in 1962 for a Santos friendly with Sheffield Wednesday – he was surprised by the lack of moats and fences. 'It struck me that only in an extremely civilised country could the devotees of a game be trusted to remain in their seats and not rush out on to the field without a 15-feet deep concrete ditch being interposed to force them to behave themselves. I have played in countries,' said the great man back in those happy times, 'where a moat, a fence, and a battalion of crack troops could not prevent a crowd from expressing its personal opinion of a referee's decision in physical fashion, and Britain was a pleasant exception to those experiences.'

And as the England squad prepared to re-assemble at Hendon Hall Hotel, their north London headquarters for the campaign ahead, as they prepared for training sessions at Highbury and at Wembley before their opening match against Uruguay on Monday, 11 July, the opposition was arriving. The English press, still gloating over a four-game European tour in which 12 goals had been scored and only one conceded, hardly noticed, but those other teams' pre-tournament records helped to put that of England into perspective.

West Germany, for example, almost outsiders at 20–1, had played five matches since that stultifying defeat by England in February and won them all, scoring 13 goals and conceding just two, with Uwe Seeler netting four times and a young midfield player from Bayern Munich named Franz Beckenbauer getting three. Portugal, a country which the English seemed always to have firmly under the hex and consequently dismissed too often as an international force (which would be of no small psychological advantage whenever they met), had also played five and won five since the start of 1966. Since drawing with France in Paris in March, Italy had played four home games and won them all, dismissing Bulgaria 6–1, Mexico 5–0 and Argentina 3–0. Only Argentina out of all of the favourites had been through a sloppy, disorganised run-in. They had not played a game in 1966 until June, when in the space of 11 days they drew with Poland in Buenos Aires, beat Denmark in Copenhagen and lost to Italy in Turin.

But the eyes of Britain and of the world, as the MovieTone announcers put it, were on the reigning champions and favourites, Brazil, and nobody could accuse them of haphazard preparation. Ever since the early 1950s, when the Confederacao Brasileira de Futebol had discovered that international fixtures delivered a guaranteed income to their impecunious association, the commitments of Brazil's national side had been extraordinary. In 1956, for example, they played no fewer than 24 international matches, not one of which was a World Cup qualifying or finals contest. (In the same year England played nine games, West Germany eight, Portugal four, and Italy six.) By the time they arrived in England early in July 1966, Brazil had played 12 friendlies in six weeks. They had won nine of them and drawn three.

The Brazilian squad was not, however, a happy unit. Its huge managerial team was, according to Pele, complacent – as far as they were concerned 'it was simply a matter of appearing at the various stadiums in England where the cup games were being held, accepting the trophy when it was presented by the Queen after we had won it, politely thanking her and bringing it back to Brazil without, if possible, scratching it. I believe we began to lose the title at that point, well before we even began our training and months before we set foot on English soil.'

Their preparation had been bizarre. Forty-four players were initially called up, which was not too dissimilar to Alf Ramsey's first 40 – but the Brazilian managers had divided the 44 into four separate teams and then proceeded to train them apart from each other in a rolling roadshow around the country which covered a dozen different locations. When they did come together for a two-match tour of Scotland and Sweden immediately before the championships, friction was caused by the managers' (and there were many of them) habit of asking senior players such as Garrincha, Gilmar, Djalma Santos and Pele which of the others should be kept and which sent home. In not one of their immense itinerary of warm-up friendly matches was the same side retained, and some players were actually given a game on tour and then put on an aeroplane the following morning and despatched back to Rio.

And like the other South Americans they were nervous about the referees. A hugely disproportionate number of British officials had been allocated by Stanley Rous's FIFA to the English World Cup. There were seven Englishmen, one apiece from Scotland, Wales and Northern Ireland, and another five from Northern Europe, as opposed to just five from South and Latin America and three from the Latin countries of Europe. Rumours swept the training camps of the southern squads, rumours that Stanley Rous, the English president of FIFA who had himself been a referee back in the 1920s and '30s, had instructed the referees of the 1966 World Cup to go easy on the virile, hard-tackling northern style.

Rous denied it, of course, but those rumours gained in credibility as the tournament wore on, and they were to bear a fruit so bitter that the FIFA president would later reluctantly concede that a mistake had been made. 'How desirable it is,' he equivocated in 1979, 'for referees not only to be just but to be seen to be just was well illustrated in the 1966 World Cup. The pool of referees for the finals was heavily weighted with Europeans . . . With hindsight this may appear an obvious error.'

The fact that it appeared as an obvious error at the time to at least eight of the 16 national teams which arrived in England in 1966 would not disturb the even tenor of Alf Ramsey's preparations. He took his players up to the placid panelled corridors of Hendon Hall Hotel in north London on Thursday 7 July, four days before their kick-off at the Empire Stadium, Wembley, on Monday, 11 July. They were all given smart grey suits and a metal badge. Geoff Hurst felt that the badge spoiled the cut of the suit, and so he removed it. Almost immediately he passed Alf Ramsey on the hotel stairs.

'Where's your badge, Geoff?'

'I seem to have lost it, Alf. Sorry.'

Expressionless, Ramsey reached into his pocket, pulled out a handful of spares, attached one to Hurst's lapel, and murmured: 'There you are. Don't lose that one, will you.'

They would watch a specially commissioned film in the evening – Ramsey himself preferred westerns, but he was amenable to a popular vote on the subject – and then at 10.30pm sharp he would wander into the TV lounge and say: 'Good evening, gentlemen', and the squad would trot obediently upstairs to bed. There was no deviating from this 10.30 rule. On one occasion some of the players' League colleagues arrived at Hendon Hall to congratulate them on a win and help to pass the time. At 10.30 Ramsey walked into the lounge and expressed delight at seeing the visitors there – 'Hello, John, nice to see you . . . Hello, Ronnie, how are things . . . Hello Peter, you're looking well . . .' and then he turned to Hurst and continued without pausing for breath: 'Good night, Geoff.'

After all of the bombastic headlines, and all of the newspaper articles which likened the forthcoming contest to another World War, the English players' expectations were comparatively modest. They felt, in those few days before the start of the competition, not that they were certain to win the trophy, but that it would be unwise to bet against them. 'It was only a feeling,' said Bobby Moore. 'But after our powerful preparations and a successful tour, we felt that we had as good a chance as anyone, and perhaps better than most. Our victory in Poland at the end of that tour had particularly satisfied us. It was a good result fashioned out of difficult conditions.'

Moore himself almost failed to qualify to play for England in unusual circumstances. His contractual dispute with West Ham had dragged on throughout the summer, and his current engagement with them had expired on 30 June. That meant that from the start of July the England captain was not associated to any club, and was therefore unaffiliated to the Football Association . . . and was consequently ineligible to perform for the FA's national team. There was a lather of uncertainty. Moore – who was aware of other clubs' interest in him, and was particularly inclined to join his neighbour Terry Venables at Tottenham – was in no hurry to return to Upton Park, not least because he regarded West Ham's position to be intransigent, and because he regarded as dishonourable their leaking of a biased version of the dispute to the newspapers. But without a contract with one club or another, he could not play for England. On Thursday 7th Ron Greenwood was asked up to Hendon. He arrived with a temporary contract which covered the month of July. Ramsey directed Moore and Greenwood into a private room and asked them to re-emerge within 60 seconds. They did so, Moore having become once more an eligible, recognised England footballer.

As far as Jack Charlton was concerned, the only opposition that

England had to fear came from South America. 'I genuinely believed that European teams need cause us little or no loss of sleep. We had met – and beaten – the vast majority of them on our own ground, as we regarded Wembley. So far as European opponents were concerned, I was more worried whether they would receive greater support than ourselves. Because Wembley – up to the World Cup, at any rate – had become notorious as being a cold home for England footballers . . . which left the South Americans, and, despite some heartbreaking stories I had read concerning player trouble, money trouble and every other kind of trouble, I felt that when the chips were really down this facade of frailty would suddenly be whisked away, and we would see revealed some very live candidates for the trophy.'

'I wouldn't say you felt that you were going to win the World Cup,' said Geoff Hurst. 'But certainly the attitude was: we had a great squad of players and tremendous determination and character. Every game you played you never felt you were going to be beaten. That was one of the overriding facets of the squad and of the team that played – you never felt you were going to lose a game.'

The 22 footballers who went upstairs to bed at Hendon Hall Hotel at 10.30pm on Sunday. 10 July, 1966, did not yet know what the team would be for the following day's match against Uruguay. Alf Ramsey never notified his eleven until the morning of the game. He would break that rule just once in the month to come. And some players, even among those who were confident of selection, would sleep better than others.

'I felt that England were on a hiding to nothing,' said Ray Wilson. 'That was my impression, although it was something I attempted to bury in a wave of optimism in those palpitating minutes immediately before the start of the competition proper.

'Outside, however, I knew there was a certain cynicism among fans and critics alike at this early stage. Not a lot of people gave us any great chance of winning. And in those heart-searching moments when I was being honest with myself back at the hotel I knew that my own biggest hope and ambition was totally negative and defensive . . . simply that we would not disgrace ourselves. I reckoned that if we could reach the semi-finals I, and most other people, would feel satisfied.'

7 URUGUAY, MEXICO AND FRANCE

'Until recently England tried to play like an Imperial
power: an extrovert game based on individual brilliance.
Forwards like Mannion, Lawton, Carter, Finney and
Matthews were the soccer equivalents of adventurous
colonisers like Lugard, Rhodes, Warren Hastings and
Clive. As a result of trying to live above our means –
using tactics which we no longer had the talent to support
– a series of humiliating defeats followed. Then came the
appointment of Alf Ramsey as England's team manager.
Now England play a game concentrating on team work
and defence.'

– A SOCIOLOGIST, QUOTED IN *THE OBSERVER*, JULY 1966.

He picked a winger, John Connelly, who had played his first international against Uruguay in that 2–1 win at Wembley in May 1964, and
he picked Jimmy Greaves. He picked, in fact, the first listed eleven
names and numbers in his squad of 22 with the exception of Geoff
Hurst, who was still in disgrace after the stinker in Copenhagen.
Hunt, instead, was retained.

It was a compromised Ramsey side. He held on to Greaves despite
the forward's obvious unease within Alf's 4–3–3, because to lose the
opening game without the presence of the most famous goalscorer in
the country would be unsupportable – and because Jimmy Greaves
did score goals out of nowhere; maverick goals which had nothing to
do with coaching and team selection, nothing to do with planning and
preparation, nothing, in fact, to do with the manager. But they still,
unaccountably, won football matches. And he picked Connelly

because a defeat in the absence of wingers would cause him little less grief – and because, who knows, a nippy little flankman might just have picked holes in the South American sweeper system. He was not cynically giving those players the rope with which to hang themselves; it just worked out that way. Had Greaves, or Connelly, or any of the other poor, soon-to-be-abandoned souls picked up the odd hat-trick, their positions would have been unassailable.

They would be asked on Monday, 11 July 1966, to break down what was reputedly one of the toughest defences in the 1966 World Cup. While they were generally accepted to have declined since their two World Championships in 1930 and 1950 – and they had never been at their best outside South America – Uruguay had qualified for the 1966 finals with four straight wins in their group, scoring eleven goals and conceding just two.

An anxious, belligerent British tabloid press had none-the-less caricatured the Uruguayans as early cannon-fodder for the hosts, largely on the grounds that their eight matches since qualifying had gained them just two wins and two draws, and had featured particularly disappointing defeats in Portugal and Romania.

This made Ramsey nervous, and he spent a good deal of time warning his squad against the Uruguayans. 'We were supposed to have two points in the bag before we had even kicked off,' Jack Charlton recalled. 'But the boss didn't think so. In addition to the advice which Alf Ramsey gave us, I asked our kid what he thought of the South Americans [*like John Connelly, Bobby Charlton had played against Uruguay in 1964*]. He emphasised what good all-rounders they were and the fact that they packed a lot of skill into their football.'

A lengthy opening ceremony, hateful to the players, preceded the kick-off. The Empire Stadium at Wembley was paraded with the flags of 16 nations, and then the teams from Uruguay and England were presented to HM Queen Elizabeth II. Bobby Moore had earlier been given a bouquet to hand over to his monarch. As he was about to do so he noticed absently that the flowers were all in a design of red, white and blue. He bowed and passed them on.

'How happy,' said Elizabeth II. 'Those are the right colours. I hope they bring you luck.'

Then the band of the Brigade of Guards and the flagbearers from schools in Middlesex and London marched off, with the two teams kicking in almost between their departing legs, and the crowd's previously relentless clap-clap, clap-clap-clap, clap-clap-clap-clap, 'ENGLAND!' paused momentarily, and Troche won the toss and the sides switched ends, and the referee's whistle shrieked, and Bobby Charlton rolled the ball to Greaves, who pulled it back to Moore, who played it wide to Wilson, and England won two early corners . . . and the game slowly died on its feet.

'Are you satisfied with the result?' the Uruguayan manager Ondine Viera was asked afterwards.

'Yes.'

'Did you play for a draw?'

'No.'

The first reply probably contained more truth than the second, even disregarding the immediate English assumption that any side fielding so accomplished a footballer as Horacio Troche in the sweeper position must have abandoned any ambition other than that of successful defence.

'The game itself,' said Jack Charlton, 'made me feel more frustrated than in any other game I had played. An early goal for us would have brought this game to life. It would have seen us with our tails up, it would have forced the opposition to come out of their defensive shell and go looking for at least an equaliser. But unfortunately for us, the longer the game went on, the more determined became the Uruguayans to keep the scoreline at a standstill. England nil, Uruguay nil looked very well to them as they came out for the kick-off, and it would look better still, in their eyes, if it remained like that until they were taking their final bow.'

In fact, Uruguay had England's number, and plenty in the English camp acknowledged the fact. After a brief flurry in the opening minutes during which he hurtled in on a through ball and forced Ladislao Mazurkieviez to concede a corner when the Uruguayan 'keeper had been odds-on to collect the ball safely, and then laid on a crowd-pleasing bit of trickery out on the right a few minutes later, Jimmy Greaves lapsed into a familiar, perplexing condition of what appeared to be sullen dejection, but what was, in fact, the striker's natural instinct for retreating from an unprofitable situation and warily saving himself for a more appropriate time.

Poor John Connelly worked harder, which only served to make his redundancy the more obvious. He switched from wing to wing, he took almost every one of his country's 16 corners, and time and again he ran into the contemptuous defensive authority of Horacio Troche. And behind him, England ran out of ideas. The most emblematic moment of the match occurred ten minutes before the end. Reduced to huffing and puffing and swinging over optimistic crosses to Hunt and Greaves (high crosses to Greaves?), the famous 4–3–3 secret weapon of overlapping full-backs was wheeled out for a final time that day when George Cohen went a-chasing down the right wing. Omar Caetano strolled gracefully out ahead of him, controlled the ball, stood and waited for Cohen to arrive like the 6.45 at Platform Nine, pushed it against the Englishman's flailing legs, and wandered back upfield to await the Uruguayan goal-kick.

It was the first time that England had failed to score in a Wembley international since 1938. That evening the odds on their winning the World Cup lengthened to 6–1. There had been some consolations – the host nation might actually have lost, had not Nobby Stiles climbed all over the likes of Pedro Rocha (while restricting himself to whacking just one foreigner, Hector Silva, in the face). Jack Charlton had been determined and authoritative, Roger Hunt had been busy . . . busy? Busy! Shopkeepers are busy. This was the World Cup . . .

'I suppose we were a disappointment,' said Ray Wilson, looking back. 'While all the spirit and endeavour was there we seemed to lack the football that had been shown on tour, especially against Poland . . . In our efforts to swamp them, in our determination to be a roaring success straight off we went at the task too wildly. From England that night there came 100mph, bull-at-a-gate football and for all the energy that was extended the goalless draw left us with a feeling that we simply hadn't got started.'

If Ramsey was concerned, he was not about to show it. As the players trooped back into the changing room at full time, 'a little apprehensive, a little disappointed', and prepared themselves for a beautifully articulated bollocking, their manager instead – to their great astonishment and even greater appreciation – stood in the middle of the floor and proceeded to congratulate them on not conceding a goal. 'You may not have won, but you didn't lose,' said the former full-back. 'And you didn't give away a goal, either. Wonderful, we didn't give them a kick. How many shots did you have to take, Gordon? Two? That's the stuff. Whatever anyone says, remember that you can still qualify, provided you keep a clean sheet and don't lose a game. We can win this cup without conceding a goal.'

'We can still win it,' Ramsey was quoted as telling the press.

'I was mistaken,' he complained the following day. 'I said: we will win it.'

It was and is known as man-management. 'These were the words we wanted to hear,' said Ray Wilson, 'the sentiments that really counted. The fans and critics could talk all day. Our faith was with the manager.'

None-the-less, at training 48 hours later perceptibly more emphasis was put on breaking down defences and scoring goals, rather than shutting the opposition out. It was all very well failing to be knocked out of the World Cup by refusing to concede a goal (and, to be finicky, Alf's analysis was strictly incorrect. Had England finished their group with three points from three 0–0 draws, they could and probably would have been eliminated in favour of two sides with three or more points and a positive goal average), but somewhere along the line one or two would have to be scored.

It was all vaguely unsatisfactory. Despite Ramsey's sterling and successful rallying of their spirits, the England players knew, as experienced professionals, that they had lost the first round, that Uruguay had called the opening shots – in the words of one of them, 'Uruguay got their way'.

'I sensed,' said Jack Charlton, 'that our supporters were going home to wonder and worry. Was the build-up going to be so much ballyhoo? When the chips were really down, would England once more be unable to display the attacking enterprise and initiative so necessary to reach even the final stages of the tournament? These thoughts were on everyone's minds as Uruguay – rightly so – hailed this scoreless draw as a triumph of tactics for them.'

The next morning the squad was taken down to Pinewood Studios to watch the making of the James Bond film *Thunderball* (one of whose scenes had consequently to be re-shot because Ray Wilson, off-camera a few yards from Sean Connery, fell from his chair with a resounding crash) and a couple of pot-boilers featuring Britt Ekland, Norman Wisdom and Cliff Richard, followed by small glasses of wine, champagne and a studio lunch party. They left feeling at one with the British celebrities of their day. That, surely, was their natural level. Come back when you've won it, said the Pinewood boys, we'll have a real party then, and the footballers glowed, and laughed, and got back down to their own business.

On the morning of Wednesday 13 July, two days after the draw with Uruguay and three days before their second match, against Mexico, they trained in the morning, giving forward play that extra bit of emphasis, and then they travelled to Wembley in the evening to watch Mexico play France in their fellow group members' first fixture. It would be the only game that the England players would attend as spectators throughout the World Cup, and it was a reasonably satisfactory experience. They were looking for a draw, and for evidence that France – who had been widely touted as the biggest threat to England in Group One – were no longer the power of the 1950s, or for that matter the power which had knocked England out of the European Nations' Cup in 1963, and they got both.

But it was nerve-wracking. Professional footballers, we have already noted, routinely dislike observing other professional footballers at work. 'Watching them play,' said Ray Wilson, 'was almost as harassing and frustrating as taking them on ourselves. I was trying to sway the result. Ideally we wanted them to draw, since we believed we could defeat the pair of them. As we were due to take them on we felt sure we would be able to qualify for the quarter-finals.'

France and Mexico drew 1–1 after Mexico had first captivated the neutral fans with their exuberance, and then scored first. The days of Fontaine and Kopa were plainly gone. France had technique but too little genius and a seriously questionable level of confidence. The England squad returned to training with their spirits almost fully restored.

And as they gathered around the television set at Hendon Hall (a set which had been privately piped in by the BBC so that the England players could tune into any match they wished to see, rather than whichever game was scheduled to be broadcast) in the five long days between their first and their second matches, they saw little to reduce those spirits. All across England old reputations were toppling and new ones were being made. At Hillsborough West Germany murdered Switzerland 5–0, with two of their goals coming from that young midfielder from Bayern Munich, Franz Beckenbauer, and their odds were instantly shortened from 20–1 outsiders to 6–1: the same as the post-Uruguay odds on England. At Old Trafford Hungary collapsed 1–3 to Portugal, and Eusebio did not even score. On Friday, 15 July, Uruguay beat France 2–1 to confirm the Gallic decline and stress – to English relief – their own good South American pedigree. And at Ayresome Park Pak Seung Zin scored to give North Korea their first goal and their first point in the finals of the World Cup, in a 1–1 draw with Chile.

But the noisiest shock-waves echoed out of Lancashire. In beating Bulgaria 2–0 at Goodison Park on 12 July, thanks to two direct free-kicks from Pele and Garrincha, Brazil had looked unduly troubled. Their camp, already dismayed by that curious pre-tournament preparation, was on the edge of revolt. The Brazilian team's ruling body, its 'technical commission', was largely untried and widely mistrusted by the players, not least as the result of deciding to reject an offer by the Beatles to play for the World Champions while they were in Liverpool, on the grounds that the Fab Four represented – in 1966, it should be marked – long-haired decadence and 'a serious threat to the peace and security of the impressionable young men in their charge'.

The cup holders were also increasingly disturbed by the preponderantly European approach to refereeing. During the Bulgarian game Dobromir Zhechev had paid such fond attentions to Pele – without, the wounded star considered, referee Jim Finney doing anything about it – that the directors of the Brazilian technical commission decided to rest their best player (who considered himself bruised but fit enough to play) for their next game, on Friday, 15 July, against those Hungarians whom the Portuguese had already proven to be well over the top.

139

It was an error of enormous proportions, and one which no Brazilian should ever have made. They had not lost a game in the World Cup for better than 12 years, since 27 June 1954 when they were beaten 4–2 in Berne, by Hungary. Incredibly the two best sides in the world, the Brazilians of South America and the Brazilians of Europe, had not met once between that day and this cold dark night in the north of England.

Many, particularly Liverpudlians, would later swear that Hungary were not only better than Brazil, they were comfortably the best side in the 1966 World Cup. Certainly, they provided the best single display over 90 minutes. Florian Albert (whose surname, properly pronounced with an aspirate 't', was being delightedly chanted like a British Christian name by the Liverpool crowd after 30 minutes, and thereafter long into the Merseyside night) produced a performance of such wizardry that no Brazilian could match it, although his own team-mate Ferenc Bene came close, and Hungary won by an astonishing 3–1 margin – a 'slaughter', as the watching Pele described it.

Brazil, the champions and erstwhile favourites, would be left having to beat the unbeaten Portugal by at least three clear goals in order to qualify for the quarter-finals. As England went into their second match against Mexico, their own difficulties seemed trifling by comparison.

John Connelly was dropped. He learned that he had been replaced by Terry Paine on the morning of the game, at the same time that Alan Ball discovered that he would make way for Martin Peters. 'I'm going to have to leave out Ballie,' Ramsey had confided in his captain, Moore. 'I know he'll be sick, but I need a winger.' The formation consequently changed hardly at all: the immutable Banks, Cohen, Moore, Jack Charlton and Wilson defence remained constant, while a three-man midfield (this time, Stiles, Bobby Charlton and Peters) worked behind one orthodox winger and two strikers: respectively, Paine, Greaves and Hunt.

Having grabbed their point from France by going slaphappily on the offensive, and thereby playing merry hell with the opposition's composure, Mexico – who, the press was keen to stress, had been defeated in recent months both by Israel and by Tottenham Hotspur –

reverted to more orthodox tactics against England. Uruguay had beaten France on the previous night, and so another draw would put the Mexicans in with an unlikely outside chance of qualifying. The dour, depressing spectacles which were England's first four games in the 1966 World Cup were not entirely, not always, the host nation's own doing . . .

'They erected a penalty area barrier of four full-backs, two centre-halfs and two defensive wing-halfs,' recalled Ray Wilson, 'and as good as said: 'Beat that!' They left just two men in striking positions and we went powering on after the goal we needed so badly. There was every danger of the old frustrations taking over.'

Every danger. While Kenneth Wolstenholme's neo-colonial commentary assured his television audience upon every Mexican passback to goalkeeper Calderon that 'the crowd may not like that, but there's precious little Mexico can do against England . . . we may not know much about them, such a colourful people', the evidence accumulated onfield that England could do precious little against Mexico. Isidoro Diaz whacked the ball down the pitch into Banks's hands straight from the kick-off, and while the puzzled England goalkeeper collected it first bounce, stepped forward and booted it back, Diaz's midfield and extended defence slotted dutifully into position, rolled up its sleeves and set about containing a less than terrifying English assault. Terry Paine got concussed early in the match and spent the remainder of it as little more than a passenger on the right wing, while it was looking increasingly as though Greaves's sure touch had deserted him – transmigrated, perhaps, to Albert, or Bene . . . or Troche, or Diaz.

After 36 minutes, and from their hundredth optimistic long cross in the first two hours of the tournament, when all seemed bleak and vain and pointless and the cold Wembley crowd was shuffling its feet and beginning to look embarrassed, and chants of 'Meh-hee-coh' were sounding louder than those for the home team in the Empire Stadium, England suddenly scored. Bobby Charlton, who had never ceased to seek out the ball all across the flagging midfield, crossed from the right; Peters rose cleanly, and in an onside position, to head it down to Hunt, who in turn headed powerfully past Calderon into the roof of the net.

And the Italian referee Carlo Lobello disallowed it. He was wrong. Peters was neither offside nor did he obstruct a defender, and Roger Hunt was plainly onside and two yards clear of any other player, but Lobello disallowed it. That may have been the spark which lit the fuse on England's best goal of the tournament. Two minutes later, with the crowd still whistling furiously at the referee, Hunt picked the ball up inside his own half, played it square to Bobby Charlton at the English perimeter of the centre circle, and then peeled off on what was to prove to be a useful decoy run to the right.

Charlton accelerated forward, shifted left, then swerved to the right and, before the Mexican defence could think about regrouping, thumped his right foot shot past Calderon's dive from 30 yards. The ball's 70-yard progress, from Charlton's first possession to crossing the line wide of Calderon's grasping right hand, had taken seven seconds. The Korean linesman Choi Duk Ryong raised his flag, presumably because Jimmy Greaves had raced (from the edge of his own penalty area!) into an extremely dubious position on the left-hand side of the Mexican box just as Charlton shot, but Signor Lobello ignored it. In order to be offside, Greaves would have had to be interfering with play, and short of sitting on Ignacio Calderon's head it was difficult to see how he could advantageously have interfered with Charlton's goal.

'You can barely imagine the relief that overwhelmed us all,' remembered Ray Wilson. 'I could have turned cartwheels. I can see the move and the goal so sweetly even now that you would think I had scored it myself.'

The goal, thought the scorer's brother Jack, was 'of double significance . . . It was the first time England had found their opponents' net in the World Cup tournament, and it showed the way to rifle through those retreating defences. It was also a great relief to every man in the England team, let alone the scorer. From then on I was certain that we would chalk up our first victory. And three points out of four didn't look bad, from where I was standing.'

It took England a further 40 minutes to sink Mexico with a second goal: 40 minutes of pedestrian build-up and terrible finishing which were finally, thankfully crowned with a goal which would prove almost as significant as any other scored by England in the tournament, if only because of whose name would be attached to it, and whose name would not.

Bobby Charlton slid a through ball into the path of Greaves, who then scurried down the inside-left channel and released a low left-foot shot towards Calderon's far post. The 'keeper dived and pushed it clear – but Hunt, following through, scored. It was the Liverpool striker's first goal in the championships, and his 13th in 15 games for his country. Jimmy Greaves, by contrast, was still to open his account.

The Mexican match was England's 16th game in the World Cup finals overall, and only their fourth win. In the days that followed a variety of different warning shots were being fired across the land. Argentina and West Germany were drawing 0–0 at Villa Park in a bad-tempered contest which saw Jose Albrecht sent off, and his coach Carlos Lorenzo invade the pitch to gesture and shout at his players and, apparently, the referee. Lorenzo also was ordered from the field.

Uruguay and Mexico drew 0–0 to put the former in the quarter-finals and the latter on the 'plane home. Both Argentina and West Germany went on to victory in their last group games, but the Germans topped the group on goal average thanks to their spanking of Switzerland, which meant that the runners-up, Argentina, would face the winners of Group One: a position which England needed only to draw with France to attain.

And Brazil went out. Portugal, who had already qualified, displayed no familial fondness of their American offspring in a 3–1 win which featured the brilliance of Eusebio and the final, brutal nobbling of Pele, who was left limping after a series of fouls midway through the first half and thereafter tottered ineffectually, tragically about on the wing.

Italy, another double World Cup winner, disappeared on the same day in the most extraordinary and unpredicted of circumstances. The Italians were enjoying a typically laboured start to the tournament, having gone down 1–0 to the Soviets and beaten Chile by 2–0, when they wandered into Ayresome Park to face North Korea requiring just the formality of a single point. Four minutes from half-time Pak Seung Zin slid the ball inside to Pak Doo Ik, who scored from 15 yards. North Korea held on to their lead, and Pak Doo Ik was rewarded with a bear-hug at full-time from a pitch-invading Middlesbrough matelot and a tie in the quarters against Portugal, while the Italians flew home to be pelted with surplus agricultural produce.

So England, for all of their occasional self-doubt and the reluctance of many of their fans to accept that they had been watching the performances of world champions in waiting, approached their final group match with feelings of comparative equanimity. Despite the numbing mundanity of their first two matches, England had effectively qualified before they faced France. Mexico were out, and France had just one point: the chaps from over the channel would, as Kenneth Wolstenholme stunningly articulated it, 'be allez-ing back home' unless they managed to beat England at Wembley by two clear goals.

'The pressure was on them,' reflected Jack Charlton. 'We knew we couldn't afford to lose, for our own slip would have been showing in that case, but we never felt really worried about this game. I was certainly confident that if we could contain the Uruguayans and the Mexicans and come through with a draw and a win, then we wouldn't let France pull off what would have been an utterly unexpected win against us. I felt the French, knowing they must attack, would be vulnerable to our own forward thrusts. And there was no doubt that the French defence was no Iron Curtain.'

Ramsey's caution, and the luck of the draw, and a stroke of genius from Bobby Charlton ten minutes before half-time against Mexico, had delivered England into pole position in their group. They could almost decide who to play in the quarters: West Germany (as runners-up after a one-goal defeat by France) or Argentina (as group leaders after beating or drawing with France). It was a time for consolidation, for archetypically Alfite talks and warnings to his players: 'We want to win and please people the way we play, but winning comes first. If it needs eleven men back in defence to stop them, let's have eleven men back there. Let the crowds boo if they want to. They'll cheer all right when we win . . . I have never kicked anyone deliberately, and I am not asking you to kick anyone either. But if the ball can be won in a fair tackle, then you have got to go and get it. And if that means

going in with everything, giving the tackle everything you've got –
then do it.'

Some players, the next 90 minutes would reveal, took the last
sentence more closely to their hearts than others.

Ramsey made just one change: his third orthodox winger,
Liverpool's Ian Callaghan (who actually performed most of his club
duties in midfield, but no matter) was given Buggin's Turn out on the
flanks. It was Callaghan's second international cap.

The opening whistle blew, Nobby Stiles rushed forward, the ball
evaded him, he collided clumsily with referee Arturo Yamasaki, and
the Manchester United half-back fell down clutching his left shin.
The muttered multilingual prayers of skilful footballers all over
England were shortly silenced again as Stiles rose and hobbled off to
resume his duties. Many would later suggest that the incident was
responsible for a misplaced degree of leniency on the part of Mr
Yamasaki an hour or so afterwards.

After just four minutes France were effectively cut down to ten
men. Robert Herbin twisted his knee in a 50/50 challenge with Bobby
Moore and limped through the rest of the game. Strangely, their
World Cup did not immediately look to be over. The reduced French
proceeded to play with a shaming amount of flair and fluency which
twice came close to giving them a goal, and which contrasted
wonderfully with such English tactics as the 25-yard direct free-kick
(put the ball down and stand sharply back as Jack Charlton comes
lumbering up at the end of a 50-yard sprint to thump it at the scoreboard), or the overlapping full-back (watch George Cohen make his
way to the corner flag before flighting a cross towards the hindmost
photographer), or the direct route to goal (look for Jimmy Greaves
making his run, let him go, give him time to get comfortably offside,
and then punt the ball in his direction).

'We did not play well,' admitted Ray Wilson, who described the
final result as 'that hollow victory'. 'For some reason which I am not
able to explain we were not at our best in midfield, and had a couple
of shaky patches in defence.'

But on the half-hour, England seemed to have taken the lead. Stiles
sliced a long-range shot which Callaghan prevented from going for a
throw-in out on the right wing; the Liverpool player's cross was

headed down by Peters and Greaves put it in from close range – only to find himself, once again, being penalised for offside. Ten minutes later a similar goal was allowed to stand. Greaves crossed nicely to the back post, where Jack Charlton headed the ball down. It bounced and flicked against the upright, and made its way along the line behind the hapless Marcel Arbour. It would still not have gone in had not Roger Hunt, standing in a blatantly offside position, finished the job. Referee Yamasaki ignored French protests and allowed it.

The game degenerated, if degeneration was possible, into a sorry confusion, a caricature of the worst of European football. Greaves spent more time offside than on, and Callaghan was mimicking perfectly his anxious predecessors in his unenviable efforts to carve out a winger's place in Alf Ramsey's England. Twenty minutes into the second half some natural justice was restored when Bobby Charlton had a goal disallowed for offside (Artelesa was plainly playing him on), and then with 15 minutes to go Nobby Stiles narrowly escaped a second booking in the match, and promptly celebrated by assaulting Jacques Simon – who had just been inches from equalising when his fine header forced Banks to save acrobatically – from behind, after the ball had long ago disappeared from the vicinity, on the halfway line directly in front of the referee, who bizarrely waved play on.

With Simon writhing in pain in the centre-circle Bobby Charlton switched the play to Callaghan, who crossed towards Hunt, whose header downward through the drizzle seemed to be covered by Arbour, until the French 'keeper fumbled the greasy ball and watched it roll behind him for Roger Hunt's 15th goal in 16 internationals.

Simon was carried off. France, with the bandaged Herbin hirpling uselessly about the halfway line, were down to nine fit players. They were out, and England's 'hollow victory' was complete.

For me, commented the Irishman Danny Blanchflower afterwards, the Stiles foul on the artistic Simon 'ruined the game'. It was genuinely difficult for anybody, not least some of his England teammates, to understand how Nobby had been allowed to remain on the pitch. But the incident had its advantages. It offered a further marvellous opportunity for Alf Ramsey to demonstrate to his players that qualities such as loyalty were, in his interpretation, indivisible.

There was a noisy outcry. Many other national sides, and most surviving representatives of the Age of Innocence, had long since found it difficult to accept that Norbert Stiles was picked for the English national side for any reason other than his propensity for putting himself about. The assault on Simon was therefore not, in their opinion, an aberration, but was rather the logical and entirely predictable result of putting the letters 'Stiles, N' on a team-sheet. And being logical and predictable, it was naturally bound to recur. Stiles, protested the French press, was a brute and a beast. (Their English equivalents responded by protesting that Nobby had himself come to within an ace of being nobbled by the referee in that early accidental collision. As the result of that clash, claimed Fleet Street, our half-back lost his edge for a good five minutes.)

Ramsey said not a word in public to Nobby Stiles. He had not been happy with his side's performance, but he made no mention of the injury to Simon. Instead, back in the changing room, he singled out the off-form but mild-mannered and comparatively innocent figure of Ray Wilson. Fixing Wilson with his eye, the England manager loudly pronounced: 'There were one or two people tonight who thought they were good players. And you were one of them.'

Then Ramsey turned away and was silent. Wilson looked after him angrily, upset, and wondered about 'having a go back at him'. Wisely he did not do so, but the comments hurt all the way back on the coach to the hotel, as the full-back replayed in his mind every little bump and niggle of that unsatisfactory match, 'every move and every switch of play', and finally Wilson decided that it had been no more than Alf's manner of dealing with perceived complacency, and he tried to forget all about it.

The Nobby Stiles storm broke quickly. The disciplinary committee of FIFA immediately made it public that they had passed a note on to the Football Association, informing them that 'if this player were reported to them again by a referee, or other official, they would take serious action'. Certain members of the FA's vestigial international committee then suggested to Ramsey that for the good of all concerned it might be better to drop Stiles at least for the next game, the flashpoint quarter-final against Argentina.

Ramsey refused outright. His half-back had, after all, picked up

147

just one booking in three competitive World Cup games. And he was, in Ramsey's view, an absolutely crucial figure. 'Basically,' Alf would muse later, 'our game in defence before 1966 was not based on a sweeper as used in most European countries. We had little experience of how to utilise a defender behind our four defenders.

'What I preferred in the case of Nobby Stiles was that instead of a sweeper at the back I would have a winner of the ball in front. I would have a man who would remain sitting in the centre of the field to win possession before any ball reached the back defence. In this way I changed Nobby Stiles's method of playing to meet the needs of the team.

'He was the central figure of our defensive set-up. But at the same time he had to be aware of what was coming down the right and the left. He had to be prepared to support players on either side of the field . . .'

So Stiles stayed, and the manager told the FA that if any similar pressure was put on him again he would resign. He then had a long talk with Stiles in private while the rest of the squad was training, in the course of which Stiles convinced Ramsey that his intentions towards Jacques Simon had been entirely honourable ('He explained what he had tried to do,' Alf would say. 'I am convinced that he was right, that his main objective was to win possession. Simon was too clever for him, but by that time Nobby had already committed himself to the tackle.' Needless to say, film of the incident does not support the Stiles version of events.) Ramsey then called the 22 players together and announced that, no matter what they might have heard or read, Nobby was not to be dismissed from the camp. 'If Nobby Stiles doesn't play,' he said, 'England don't play.'

'Everyone felt that was great,' said Bobby Moore. 'All right, we were biased. All right, Nobby was there first and foremost to spoil, to mark people, to niggle and upset people. But he could still play the game. Nobby did a great job for Alf. Nobby was there to get the ball and give it to Bobby Charlton to go and do something constructive for us.'

'I can tell you,' said Jack Charlton, 'that morale in the side must have been affected had Nobby been deposed – we were all on Alf Ramsey's side when he revealed the decision that Nobby stayed.'

With two 2–0 wins and a 0–0 draw, England finished on top of Group One. But they had been, in their individual ways, deeply unsatisfactory matches. 'Those first three games that England played,' said Geoff Hurst, who had been on the sidelines throughout, 'were a torture to watch, let's be honest about it.'

Hurst had found himself, during the France game, almost picking a fight with a fellow spectator who was freely 'indulging his right to criticise the players and the play – he had to bear the brunt of my depression that had built up during the first three matches. But I knew that the frustration of the fans was nothing compared to the desperation of the England players: this was their home pitch, their greatest test . . . don't you think they wanted to turn on the flowing artistic stuff?

'But they hadn't a hope in hell of making those matches real entertainment. Uruguay, a very much better side than they had been given credit for in advance, made not the slightest attempt to win. The way they leapt about at the final whistle showed just how much they had been planning to get that goal-less draw. Mexico were not much better, again, a team quite prepared to trudge through 90 minutes without making a chance, so long as they could stop the opposition from doing any better. And France were hardly in an adventurous mood. They had already lost their chance of achieving anything in the series and would rather go home boasting they'd drawn with England than risk another defeat.'

That was the mood in the England camp as the quarter-finals approached: that if there had been an absence of entertainment, it had been wished upon, rather than delivered by, England. It had nothing to do with a sterile insistence on pumping high balls in towards Jimmy Greaves and Roger Hunt, and everything to do with cynical Latin manoeuvring.

'We in this country,' considered Geoff Hurst, 'had never before known such a coldly realistic attitude to a game we have always played with an instinctive sense of adventure. Even our more defensive sides had been wildly rash compared to the stuff we were seeing now.

'My heart bled for my team-mates down there. I knew what they must be going through, desperately trying to put on a show against

149

opponents who just shrugged as you tried to lure them into a tackle, and instead drifted away to join the masses packing the area in front of goal.

'Like all professionals, I tend to watch matches with an especially keen eye on the men who were doing my job. I watched the games, but mostly I watched Roger Hunt and Jimmy Greaves – noted their efforts to find spaces to work in, felt for them when they did the right thing and found that it turned out wrong because of the skill and caution of the opposition. I hardly twitched a muscle, but I played every match in my mind from high up in the stands. And when the whistle ended each game I got up feeling as drained and tired as those blokes drifting away in their white shirts towards the bath.

'Listening to the comments around me certainly had not helped. Hearing spectators having a go at Roger or Jim, and utterly ignoring the size of the problem they were wrestling with, made me simmer with rage. Finally, as I say, I blew up. I'd made the odd cutting remark earlier in the series, but this time – near the end of the game with France – I started on the bloke sitting just in front of me.

'I remember my wife Judith tugging at my sleeve trying to get me to shut up and sit down, because I was really causing a scene. But I just had to let this bloke have it, and any other critic who happened to be listening.

'I feel a bit sorry for him now, he had to carry the can for how I was feeling. Because building up inside me, apart from the despair that England weren't getting either the rewards or the praise the players deserved, was the certain feeling that I was not going to be in a position to help.'

Geoff Hurst left Wembley after the game against France that Wednesday evening, and made his way back to Hendon Hall Hotel still nursing the 'certain feeling' that he would not be able to help his side's cause. He arrived at Hendon 'to find Greaves sitting staring at an ugly great hole in his shin. I knew at once that I would play against Argentina in the quarter-finals. I didn't know whether to laugh or cry.'

8 ARGENTINA

'Before Mr Ramsey publicly insults a small but friendly
nation represented by a visiting football team, he should
remember that, quite apart from Latin temperament,
language difficulties and the different way a game is
played in South America, the British side was penalised
no less than 33 times against the 19 fouls perpetrated by
the Argentinians.'
                    – LORD LOVAT, LETTER TO *THE TIMES*, 26 JULY 1966

The wound to Jimmy Greaves's shin, which had been caused by the
raking studs of a French defender, needed four stitches. He would
clearly not be available to play against Argentina in three days' time.
His World Cup, indeed, his entire career – and that of Geoff Hurst,
and of their country – was at a turning point.

Alf Ramsey said, many years later, that he had been on the point
of dropping Greaves anyway after his ineffectual first three showings
at Wembley. 'As he was injured,' suggested the manager, 'the question of his selection for the next match had to be considered very
carefully.

'Remember he had played in three matches and had not scored.
You might say that he almost scored against France [*Ramsey presumably meant Mexico*] but the goalkeeper stopped it and Roger Hunt
was there to force the ball home. Roger had scored three up to this
stage of the competition. This was important.

'Apart from that, Jimmy Greaves had not shown his true form to
substantiate his position in the England team and would not have
been selected for the Argentina match.'

It was not quite the end of the little striker's international career. That came two years later in Rome, when he learned that he had been dropped yet again from a fixture with the Soviet Union. In a fit of pique he approached Ramsey and requested that he should not be included in any further England squads unless he was going to get a game. 'I cannot consider players who wish to impose special conditions on their playing for England,' pronounced the manager, and that was it: the most accomplished goalscorer to wear an England shirt in modern times (and some would argue, in any times) saw his dreams of international glory finally dissolve. It was the conclusive torching of all that had begun on the night of Wednesday, 20 July, 1966 in Hendon Hall Hotel. 'Greavsie was sick at being out,' remembered his captain, Bobby Moore. 'He was to be a lot sicker by the end of the tournament.'

And on to the same bonfire went the last weak lip-service to wingers. Like Greaves, they had not delivered, and like Greaves they were ditched. Ramsey had tried all of them in his squad, and now he must stiffen his upper lip, adjust his collar and announce the divorce.

'The sad part for Alf,' considered Bobby Moore, 'looking back, is that he wanted to play wingers but he was crucified for doing away with them. Paine, Connelly, Callaghan . . . they all had their opportunities but Alf got no success with any of them. He wanted wingers because they give you a way to get round behind defences, create chances and win games. But the ones who were available didn't have the right attitude, the right temperament . . . the right something.

'What do you do if the people you play aren't good enough and aren't doing the job for you and you've got other people you can utilise in a different way? I'll tell you. You use Ballie and Martin Peters.'

There were many reasons for the failure of England's experiments with 4–3–3, and the wingers should not be scapegoated. In a three-man forward line the solitary winger's role was ambiguous. Did he stick to running riot down one flank, or did he try to pop up on both? Should he even stay out wide all of the time, or should he be in the middle with the other front men waiting for the crosses from the overlapping full-backs? Even when he did so, those crosses – particularly when delivered by that excellent stopper George Cohen – were as likely as not to end up among the photographers. What should the winger do? Dispossess Cohen? By switching to 4–4–2, which effectively he did, Ramsey introduced a simpler system to unsophisticated players. Two strikers stayed unquestionably up front, and two wide midfield men worked down the flanks.

So Ballie and Martin Peters and Geoff Hurst it was. Ramsey may have allowed himself a few sad reflections on what might have been as Greaves and the wingers passed out of his squad, but they were more than compensated for by the fact that now, at last, he had a team in which he was able to believe with all of his being: a strong, hard-running, consistent eleven, with two big boys up front, a doughty foursome in midfield, and that solid defence behind them. He had a team, in short, which would be extremely difficult to beat, a team which exemplified the old adage about the British Army to which the manager had once belonged: they may not always have been absolutely the best in the world, but nowhere else in the world would individual members of a unit have such powerful faith in the stolid, unbreakable will of their colleagues. It was a team which would not wilt under fire, and those qualities were presupposed to be essential against Argentina.

The British relationship with Argentinian football had been for many years a schizophrenic affair. Neither country could forget that Britain had introduced the game – not unusually – to Argentina. Club names such as River (not Rio) Plate and Newell's Old Boys still bore witness to the influence of British tradesmen and railway workers, who first formed the Buenos Aires Football Club in 1865; and the founder of the Argentine Association Football League in 1891 had been one Alexander Hutton, the director of the country's English High School.

At times the Argentines had had occasion to turn back for help and support to the game's mother country. In the 1930s, when match-fixing threatened the very existence of professional soccer as a valid sport in Buenos Aires, the Argentine FA turned in desperation to Britain and paid for a number of uncorruptible referees to cross the Atlantic to officiate at key fixtures until the stables had been swabbed out.

But by the '50s and '60s colonial gratitude was a thing of the past.

In the eyes of Argentines, Great Britain was a spent imperial force living on past glories, and in particular the English national football team was a collection of top-heavy Stone Age cloggers who would only ever win a tournament if the referees were partial to their idiosyncratic style of play.

And to the English, Argentina came quickly to receive the brunt of the prejudice which was traditionally reserved for Hispanic Latin Americans. Uruguay and Mexico were condescended to and solemnly rebuked for petty infringements of Anglo-Saxon codes of fair and open play, but they were ultimately too unthreatening to occupy much space in the British press. The lovable lighthearted samba-merchants of Brazil were, of course, beyond criticism. Argentina were the real bad boys: good enough at the game to be truly worrying, and possessed of an undeniable black streak, tempers as quick as a flick-knife, and carrying with them everywhere a whole semi-mythological repertoire of dirty tricks involving finger-nails, eyes, noses, hair and spittle.

Luckily, Argentina had in large part lived up to their advance billing. After their evil-tempered contest with West Germany they turned on the form against Switzerland at Hillsborough, but to no avail. The Sheffield crowd booed them on to the pitch, jeered them whenever they got possession, howled at the remotest suspicion of a foul (although in fact Argentina committed only eight offences, and the Swiss 14) and cheered their defeated opponents to the echo. The Argentines travelled to face England at Wembley with a fair idea of the reception which would be prepared for them at the Empire Stadium.

Both sides took the pitch in an almost intolerable condition of suspense. Every player expected trouble. Ramsey was not a manager to indulge in what one player described as 'that "go out and die for the old red white and blue" stuff' in his pre-match talks, preferring instead to dwell upon finer points of tactics and performance. The opposition was usually dignified by no more than a passing, dismissive reference to 'those people' or 'them'.

But before the Argentine match he warned his team in untypically melodramatic fashion: 'Well, gentlemen, you know the sort of game you have on your hands this afternoon.'

It was an auspicious comment. 'That was,' remembered Bobby Moore, 'enough. The players didn't say anything or admit anything publicly or even among ourselves, but deep down we all had secret fears about Argentina.

'We accepted in our guts it was going to be hard. Maybe brutal. We hadn't conceded a goal in the tournament so we didn't feel that they ought to beat us on overall quality. The problem was that this was a sudden death, knock-out quarter-final, and that while we were going for the win they might upset us, frustrate us and catch us unawares. We even knew the public doubted we could do it, because we hadn't looked like scoring goals.'

'The atmosphere was wrong even before the start,' said Geoff Hurst. 'As we stood in the tunnel waiting to walk out into the Wembley sunshine I watched this giant man Rattin lecturing his team. There was a look of sneering arrogance about him, you didn't have to speak Spanish to understand from his voice and his gestures towards the England squad that he was saying that the game was as good as decided already.'

The game had no chance. Soon after kick-off Alan Ball took an acrobatic dive at the edge of the box; no penalty was given, but the crowd took its cue and bayed for vengeance. Stiles had a stand-up row with Ferreiro, who then fell over. Perfumo was booked, and the Argentine captain, a pampas aristocrat named Antonio Rattin who was possessed of enough skill and grace to adorn any international stage, stuck out an unworthy late foot as Bobby Charlton swept past him. Charlton regained his balance and went on to shoot and miss, but the German referee Herr Rudolf Kreitlein booked Rattin none-the-less.

In between the whistles, England had started well, forcing a number of corners and keeping Argentina on the back foot. But this game was never going to be won and lost on footballing merit . . .

'I've been involved in the odd fracas in my time,' recalled Geoff Hurst. 'You can't play through season after season in the English League and FA Cup – much less European competition – without knowing what it is to be hammered about a bit; without meeting teams with the odd 'killer' in their midst.

'But I have never known anything like this Argentinian team.

There was an air of cold, calculated hostility about the side that I have never met before, or want to again. Most teams have a hard man or two in the eleven. They had about eight. Even the forwards went about the business of putting opponents away with a sort of frozen detachment that was far, far worse than honest, impulsive rage.

'In most games a player knows the moments when he might get kicked: going for a 50/50 ball you are tensed against the possibility of a foul tackle; chasing a pass you can hear or sense someone at your shoulder who might hack you down. These things you accept and are ready for.

'But in this match with Argentina there was never a moment's peace of mind. If you have ever walked down a dark alley late at night in a strange town, and felt yourself suddenly swinging round to peer into a doorway not knowing quite why you are edgy, you will know the feeling of being on that pitch. At any moment, for no reason, you felt you might be fallen upon from behind. At least twice when the ball was nowhere near – once, indeed, while I waited for a player to get the ball for a throw-in – I felt a sudden stunning kick on the ankle. Each time I swung round to stare at a ring of blank faces. I never knew who had kicked me.'

Shortly after his booking, Rattin blatantly up-ended Hurst out on the left wing. The free-kick was given, but the Argentine captain might have escaped further censure – and the game might have rolled on to a comparatively unremarkable conclusion – if it had not been for his extraordinary volubility.

Simply, Antonio Rattin could not stop talking. 'They had some brilliant footballers,' thought Ray Wilson, 'Rattin included, but all their tactics were forgotten as they went on a bender of wrecking. Whenever the referee intervened with free-kicks for us Rattin would argue. He wanted to referee the match.'

So, he fouled Ball, he was duly penalised and he shouted at Herr Kreitlein. He was booked for an attempted trip on Charlton and he shouted at Herr Kreitlein. He up-ended Hurst and 'instead of being grateful that he had got away with a terrible foul, he stood there yelling at the referee'. It was truly self-destructive behaviour. Rudolf Kreitlein clearly had no desire to involve himself in a World Cup quarter-final controversy, but it was equally clear that the time was quickly approaching when his desire to be rid of Antonio Rattin would outweigh his fondness of a quiet life.

That moment arrived in the 36th minute of the game. Following the foul on Hurst and its resultant free-kick, Perfumo tripped Hunt at the edge of the Argentine penalty area. Bobby Charlton had just shot wide, so referee Kreitlein gave nothing, but on his way back to the halfway line he paused to book Luis Artime for some obscure dissent.

Immediately Rattin was on him again, leaning over the tiny referee and talking urgently in his ear, plucking at his own captain's armband and stabbing his forefinger furiously at Kreitlein. 'They were foreign words to me,' said Ray Wilson, 'but the tone, delivery and gesticulations that went with them left no one in any doubt that this was dissent – that seems a mild word somehow – of the worst possible type.' The referee waved the Argentine captain brusquely away once, and then he snapped. His right arm went directly up into the air, he glared at Rattin and he pointed to the touchline.

Rattin was off! The crowd, which had just finished buzzing over the news that North Korea were beating Portugal 3–0 at Goodison Park, was suddenly stilled, and then broke into a cacophony of delighted whoops. Antonio Rattin had become the first player ever to be sent off in a football match at Wembley – and he was an Argentine, and he was captaining his side against England in a World Cup quarter-final, and he had just chopped Ball, Charlton and Hurst, and he had a surname which was in the English language so horribly evocative of vicious behaviour that the whole wonderful occasion seemed to have been scripted by a benevolent English god!

'As I had been detailed to harass him – he was the starting point of most of their great football – I suppose I was in a better position than most to say what happened,' said Geoff Hurst.

'I was surprised when he was sent off. Not because he didn't deserve to go, but because I just didn't think this little bloke Kreitlein would have had the courage to take such a decision in a match of such importance. I know many, many referees who would have lacked the nerve to do their duty.

'Rattin's protest [*which was made later*] that he had only been asking for an interpreter was just nonsense. I was there, right there, and I know that his attitude changed like somebody switching off a tap when he knew he'd been sent off. Until that moment his whole attitude towards the official had been one of obvious contempt. He was snarling and sneering, giving a false laugh every time a foul was given against Argentina, spitting at the ground when Mr Kreitlein walked near and patting his pocket and pointing perhaps to suggest the referee had been bribed.

'But when he was booked and ordered off, Rattin was all amazement. Then he started pointing to his captain's armband, then he started pointing to the sidelines and asking something, then he started speaking softly and with great humility. It was quite a change, but too obviously phoney.'

Rattin at first refused to go. For eight extraordinary minutes the match was held up while a ruck of Argentine players surrounded the referee and at one point all left the field themselves in apparent sympathy with their captain, who became briefly the only Argentine left on the pitch. Ken Aston of the FIFA referee's committee jostled for order with the match commissar Harry Cavan and a host of interested police officers, while Ray Wilson sat on the ball in the sun and commented: 'Let him off, ref, and let's get on with the shambles.' 'It might have been a match on Hackney marshes,' thought Bobby Moore.

Just when it seemed as if the game must be abandoned, a form of peace broke out. Ten Argentines strolled reluctantly back on to the field, Herr Kreitlein blew his whistle once more, and the game resumed.

'As he [*Rattin*] went down the tunnel,' Bobby Moore knew, 'he left the door open for us. Just a crack. Even with ten men they still put up a hell of a struggle.

'The South Americans play the game by a different code. They were sure as hell not very pleasant to play against. They did do nasty things. They did tug your hair, spit at you, poke you in the eyes, and kick you when the ball was miles away and nobody was looking.

'It wasn't nice, but it wasn't worth losing the game over. I managed not to get involved. Around and about me I could see lads like Ballie and Nobby Stiles and big Jack Charlton getting steamed up and finding it difficult to get on with the game.

'I just said that the only way to deal with them was to beat the bastards. That was what would hurt them. Because their attitude was simply not to lose. Not at any cost. Off the pitch they were supposed to be charmers. I just said that off the pitch we didn't even have to look at them. Just beat them out here.'

It was brilliant captaincy, and it was needed. Instantly after the restart a furious and frustrated Geoff Hurst left a trailing leg for Roberto Ferreiro to run into. Ferreiro made the most of it, rolling and writhing as though Hurst had castrated him with blunt pliers (before getting to his feet and resuming normal play). Beyond giving a free-kick, referee Kreitlein chose to ignore the offence, but he might not do so a second time . . .

'Argentina would retreat and retreat and retreat,' recalled Jack Charlton, 'hoping to contain us until the end, hoping that they would hold out even in extra time, and win through to the semi-finals on the toss of a coin. They were also hoping, I'm sure, to even the score numerically, by reducing England to ten men. Twice I went into tackles – each time I was scrupulously fair – and twice my opponents went down on the ground, writhing in seeming agony, holding their legs as if they would fall off should a gust of wind blow.'

Argentina also played on the unlikelihood of Herr Kreitlein sending off a second South American. Early in the second half Jack Charlton collided with goalkeeper Antonio Roma as they both challenged for a high ball. Both men fell badly and needed treatment, but before Charlton could receive attention an Argentine boot had lifted him off the ground, driven him three feet sideways and winded him severely. Bobby Charlton saw the incident and raced, enraged, to the scene, to be manhandled away by cooler team-mates. Herr Kreitlein booked both Charltons for 'ungentlemanly behaviour', although neither were aware of the fact until they received the official FIFA written warning on the following day. ('A bit of a facer,' thought Jack, 'to say the least – we had all so consciously been striving to keep out of trouble.')

By then it no longer seemed to matter because England had won the game. They did so after a spell of Argentine pressure which denied the fact that they had lost their captain and playmaker, and which eclipsed momentarily all that had gone before. 'They played the ball out with an unruffled composure that had me completely baffled,' said Ray Wilson. 'I felt that if they had only abandoned their destructive spoiling much earlier they would have given us a far greater fright by the use of their pure skills, which were completely abandoned amid all the excitement.'

And so Mas found himself free on goal but shot wide of Banks, and then, with 15 minutes left, Wilson broke up another attack and pushed the ball short down the left wing to Peters. Peters's West Ham team-mate Geoff Hurst was drifting through the middle, but he says: 'At the moment he [*Peters*] collected the ball out near the left touch-line, he did not know where I was; and because he had a defender almost on his toes, I could not see him at all. We acted together out of habit, nothing more.

'There are few better players in the game at curving a ball than my mate Martin. Without hesitation he let go with his left foot, sending the ball swinging around the defender facing him and out on a wide arc to a point just short of the post nearest to him. It was there. Just before it crossed the line, I met it with my head after running 15 yards. The timing was perfect. I was able to get up without opposition and flick the ball back . . .'

And it bounced across the face of the stranded, wrong-footed Roma and rolled into the side netting just inside the far post, and Hurst and 88,000 people inside Wembley Stadium sent a deafening roar up to the clear skies above north London. There was no doubt that Rattin's dismissal had contributed to the goal which sunk his side, not least because it was effectively the first time that his erstwhile marker, Hurst, had a free jump at a high ball: 'I was getting clouted from the moment I took the first step towards meeting a centre. If I ever got near the ball it was with an Argentinian clinging to my arm or my shirt; I felt I was trailing defenders behind me like bits of bunting on a kite as I jumped.'

'I knew,' said Bobby Moore, 'and the rest of us seemed to know: "This is it!" We took it from there.'

But the controversy was not ended by Herr Kreitlein's final whistle 15 minutes later. George Cohen took off his shirt and was in the process of ritually exchanging it for an Argentine jersey when Alf Ramsey came storming over and, grabbing at Cohen's arm, stopped the exchange. ('There is no dignity,' the England manager would explain unconvincingly in calmer times, 'in bare-chested footballers parading on the pitch.') Down in the tunnel, bedlam was breaking out. One Argentine player spat on a FIFA official's blazer; another urinated on the concrete tunnel wall; the Argentine coach Carlos Lorenzo went up to the English team doctor Alan Bass and rubbed his forefinger and thumb together meaningfully; and Argentine players hammered on the locked doors of the England changing room, shouting insults and accusations, while others began to trash their own changing room. Rudolf Kreitlein, his black referee's shirt torn away at the shoulder, revealing a sweet little undervest, was escorted from the ground by a phalanx of police officers.

An hour later Alf Ramsey emerged for a television interview. The England manager had just seen his side amass ten wins and one draw in eleven matches, its best international record since 1912, and reach the World Cup semi-finals for the first time. But he was desperately aware of the criticisms, of the comments that since Mexico England had failed to beat eleven players, of the absence of goals of any kind, let alone great goals. And he was still seething from the exhibition at Wembley.

'We have still to produce our best football,' he told the television cameras. 'It will come against the right type of opposition, a team which comes out to play football and not act as animals.'

Relationships between the two great soccer civilisations of Europe and South America had never before been, and never again would be, at a lower ebb than on that night of 23 July 1966. The word 'animals', which was quickly broadcast around the world, was a bad enough insult to a northern European: Latin Americans were shocked, humiliated, horrified and dismayed. 'The reaction in Latin America to calling the Argentinians "animals",' in the judgement of Pele, 'remained to plague England in future World Cup matches anywhere in Latin America. All Latin Americans resented it, especially in view of the poor judging they faced from English referees in those games.'

Pele had a personal axe to grind: he blamed Messrs Jim Finney and George MacCabe for allowing Bulgaria and Portugal to kick him out of the competition. But just as Rudolf Kreitlein was losing his patience with Antonio Rattin, up at Hillsborough an English referee –

Jim Finney again – was sending off two Uruguayans, the brilliant Horacio Troche and Hector Silva, in that country's quarter-final with West Germany, which the Europeans went on to win 4–0.

The tantalising notion of a European conspiracy to do down the delicate artisans of the New World spread like an infection. FIFA acted quickly in an effort to mend fraying relationships. The news of the Charltons' bookings was made public; Argentina was fined a total of 1,000 Swiss francs (which was, in 1966, about £80.00); Antonio Rattin was suspended for four matches; Ferreiro and Onega for three matches each; the two Uruguayans Troche and Silva were also suspended for three games; and Uruguay's Julio Cortes, who had actually kicked Jim Finney after the final whistle, was given a six-match ban.

The disciplinary committee also asked the English FA to censure Alf Ramsey for 'the unfortunate remarks made by Mr Ramsey in a television interview. In the opinion of the committee such remarks do not foster good international relations in football and desire the FA to take appropriate disciplinary measures.' Denis Follows had a quiet chat with his manager, which could have been construed as anything from a dressing-down to an endorsement of his actions (and was certainly closer to the latter than the former), Ramsey made a clipped statement avowing that no insult had been intended, which was massively underreported in the British media, and then nothing more, needless to say, was done.

Turning its attention back to Argentina, the disciplinary committee suggested that that country should be refused entry to the next World Cup in 1970 unless an assurance was received concerning the good behaviour of its players. 'We cannot accept entry on such a condition,' said the president of the Argentine FA, Dr Menendez Behety. 'I do not approve of the conduct of our players and officials yesterday, but they were provoked by the referee. He was absolutely biased in favour of England. The referee and those who selected him were, in my view, responsible for the trouble.'

Whoever was responsible, the plain fact remained that the semi-finals of the 1966 World Cup consisted entirely of European teams. West Germany, as we have seen, had dismissed Uruguay; the much-fancied Hungary had gone down 2–1 to the Soviet Union; and

Portugal and Eusebio had come back from that 3–0 deficit against North Korea to win 5–3.

The South American sides so feared by the English had all gone. (Not that all of them felt an overwhelming sense of failure. 'Why should I resign?' asked Carlos Lorenzo. 'We have done very well. Better than Brazil.') Only the Europeans, none of whom was held in much awe by English footballers, remained. Portugal first, in the semi-finals, and then either the Soviets or West Germany . . .

But a vague and cloying sense of injustice also remained; a feeling which was not confined to South America that the odds had been stacked in favour of the undeserving sides of Europe; and that out of the undeserving sides of Europe, the odds had chiefly been stacked in favour of England. It may not have been precisely the kind of open financial corruption implied by the Argentine players and coach; but it was there and it would smear and reduce any achievement of Alf Ramsey's team. It may have been a post-imperial backlash, it may have been a response to England's unadventurous football ('If England reach the World Cup final,' said a Prague newspaper after the Argentina quarter-final, 'football will go back a hundred years.'), but it was in large part an intimation that some sort of a fix was in operation.

Once hinted at, such a sense of bias would not disappear. There had been an understanding in the north of England, which was widespread, which was supported by all of the pre-tournament literature, and which had never been either confirmed or denied by FIFA or by the Football Association, that if England qualified for the closing stages of the competition they would play at least one game outside of Wembley. Indeed, the publicity material all suggested that this particular semi-final would take place at Everton's ground. By the time it became apparent that England would face Portugal, Liverpudlians and most of the rest of the world were convinced that Goodison Park would host that semi-final.

And Liverpudlians and foreigners were not the only ones labouring under this belief. The England players had also been told that they would play at Goodison. 'There was a bit of confusion about it [*the semi-final*],' said Bobby Moore afterwards. 'We understood originally that we would have to go to Goodison Park for the game.

163

Frankly, that didn't worry us one way or the other. We didn't care where we played.

'But Alf's main concern was not to give up our headquarters at Hendon Hall which had become our home and where everything was geared to our smallest requirement. His problem was to decide whether to go up to Liverpool on the Sunday for a three-night stop, or merely for the Tuesday with an overnight bag for the game the following day. As it happened the FIFA committee decided that we should play at Wembley, and at once people began to write and to ask how lucky could England get. . .?'

Goodison Park had been, of course, Portugal's early home. FIFA claimed that it had all along reserved for itself the right to announce the semi-final venues once the quarter-finals had been completed, and that Wembley should host the England/Portugal game on the grounds of greater capacity. A sense of grievance in the north of England only compounded the feelings from abroad that niggling injustices were being enacted in London. Those feelings could not be hidden from the England players, who reacted with dismayed disbelief.

'Apparently quite a few foreign observers,' reflected Jack Charlton later, 'especially those from Latin American countries, were convinced that the 1966 World Cup was a carve-up. They said, and it was in complete seriousness, that the draw and the venues had been arranged in such a way that the countries like Brazil, Uruguay and the Argentine would be eliminated before the final stages, and that England would win the trophy.

'The only point on which they disagreed, it seemed, was the choice of England's opponents in the final itself. Some plumped for Russia, others for West Germany. But on one thing they were adamant: "It has all been arranged that a European country will win the World Cup, and that country will be England."

'Referees came in for some stick too, for upon them was thrust the blame for the exit of teams like Brazil – "Those referees made sure that the best footballing countries were not protected against opponents who used brawn more than skill." How ridiculous can you be?'

9 PORTUGAL

'We entered Wembley Stadium for the semi-final against the Portuguese in a frame of mind we had not known before. We knew that if we were knocked out we could still face the world with a smile. We had reached the last four.'

— RAY WILSON

At least one contented man walked off the Wembley turf at the end of the Argentina game. All was well with Geoff Hurst. 'I don't care any more,' the cheerful, honest West Ham striker was telling everybody about him, 'I don't care, now. I don't care if I never get another game. I reckon with that goal I've done my bit towards the World Cup.'

Hurst could not believe that he was not living on borrowed time. The stitches in Greaves's shin were healing fast and by the time the semi-final was played with Portugal three days later Greaves could well be available for reselection. Convinced, even after his match-winning goal, that his chances were no better than 50/50, Hurst worried about his training routine.

He had always been accustomed to training in a tracksuit. A big man at 13 st 7 lb, he liked to sweat in midweek so that he felt lighter during the match. 'Probably this is mostly a difference in the mind, but I feel it was important.' The essentially shy Hurst had been sure that Ramsey would not allow him to do this. There was a fixed routine of players wearing red and white bibs at training: one player kitted out in a full tracksuit would disturb the symmetry. While he had not been playing, and while he had considered himself to be out of the manager's plans, Hurst had made no issue of this. But suddenly he felt it to be urgently important. He approached Ramsey and asked him for permission to train in a tracksuit.

'He looked at me for what seemed ages, then said quietly: 'All right, Geoff. If this matters to you, go ahead.'

So Hurst trained in a tracksuit, and felt instantly 50 per cent fitter, and cursed the residue of his own reticence – 'I should have trusted Alf to know the difference between someone just trying to be awkward and someone genuinely worried about breaking an old habit.'

He should indeed have trusted Alf. Ramsey's famous sense of propriety – which would certainly in normal circumstances have rebelled at the notion of an unbalanced colour scheme at training – did not extend so far as disrupting the well being of key players. That might have got in the way of a stronger managerial instinct: the will to win.

Nor should Hurst have worried about team selection. Ramsey stuck to the eleven who had beaten Argentina. He was never likely to change. He had finally arrived at his wingless wonders: a 4–4–2 formation with Hunt and Hurst harrying up front, Ball and Peters getting forward from midfield down the right and the left (which in its turn had the advantage of taking a lot of weight off the dubious forward runs of the full-backs, Wilson and Cohen – runs which, even when successfully accomplished, ended too often in wasted crosses), Stiles destroying and Bobby Charlton creating, and that solid, thus-far unbroken defensive five. Greaves's unexpected barren period, compounded by his injury, and the failure of the three wingers to deliver any kind of penetrating form had – whatever the reasons for those disappointments – given the manager the chance to play not only a better balanced side, but also one which accorded most closely with his own natural inclinations. Once that side had achieved an important result it was unlikely to be disbanded for reasons other than injury.

By the time they played Portugal, England knew who the winners of their semi-final would meet in the final. West Germany and the Soviet Union had met in the Goodison Park fixture the previous night. It had been a sad match. West Germany won 2–1, but the Soviets had lost Sabo through injury after 15 minutes, and Chislenko had been sent off before half-time. Not many people were making the point that West Germany, like England, were thriving on reduced opposition. But plenty suggested that the Germans had much in reserve.

With this and other things in mind, English squad superstitions were adhered to even more strictly as the semi-final approached. Room-mates Bobby Charlton and Ray Wilson diligently packed and unpacked their kit-bags in the same fixed order (first this boot, then that one, then this pad . . .) and Ramsey looked indulgently upon the quirks and idiosyncrasies of professional footballers approaching the biggest games in their lives. 'Ramsey made a point,' said Wilson, 'of being sure that every member of the squad was completely at ease with life. We were more like a club side than an international team. Anyone who had anything to say was encouraged to say it. Humour blossomed, and those days in the tranquil suburb of Hendon go down as among the happiest in my life.'

Certainly the days between 23 July and Tuesday, 26 July, when they were due to play England's first ever World Cup semi-final, were not unduly troubled by fear of the opposition. Historically, England had it over Portugal. The Portuguese might have been ranked as one of Europe's better sides, but they had only beaten England once, and that back in 1955; they had never got so much as a draw in England, and many of the current squads of both teams could remember from their boyhoods hearing of England's biggest post-war win, a 10–0 thrashing of the Portuguese at Estoril in 1947.

The Portugal of 1966 had one undoubted asset: the big Mozambican striker Eusebio, the European Footballer of the Year whose scintillating goals against Bulgaria, Brazil and North Korea (seven in total so far, building in an ominous pyramid from no goals in his first game, to one in his second, to two in his third, to four against North Korea in the quarters) had led many to suggest that Eusebio had overtaken Pele to become the greatest footballer in the world. Bobby Moore, who 'always felt we had the edge on the Portuguese', who remembered watching England beat Portugal at Wembley by 2–0 in 1961, also remembered from that game 'two searing shots from Eusebio which made our cross bars quiver'. But the English players felt that they had a not-so-secret weapon to

167

deploy against Eusebio. Its name was Nobby Stiles. Stiles had, it was widely agreed, marked Eusebio out of both games during Manchester United's double win in the European Cup over Benfica. In the same way that England were believed to have an insuperable psychological advantage over Portugal, Nobby, they assured themselves, 'had the Indian sign on Eusebio'.

There were other reasons for increased optimism. The Wembley crowd, which had been previously considered as a cold set of home supporters (and that is part of the reason why the players were being no less than honest when they said that they wouldn't have minded playing a game or two in Liverpool – 'Most of us have played more games for our clubs at Goodison,' as Bobby Moore put it later, 'than we've played at Wembley. No English critic has ever before suggested that Wembley is a good home venue for England teams: the opposite in fact.') was showing signs of thawing. Early in the competition even the gates had been comparatively disappointing. Only 75,000 had turned up to watch Uruguay, and 85,000 for the Mexico game. 92,500 had seen the crunch match against France, but it was back down to 88,000 against Argentina. All 93,000 tickets had been sold, so it was clear that either a large number of complimentaries had been dispensed to people who were not particularly interested in football, or that some folk had block-bought books of tickets and were skipping the early, boring games. And those who had attended, the Wembley faithful which Jack Charlton had earlier thought capable of giving continental opposition warmer support than England, had indeed been restless at times, frustrated by England's dour, inhibited football.

After the Argentina game something seemed to change. It was partly the presence of a palpably malevolent comic-book South American enemy, and the subsequent sense of England *contra mundum*; and it was partly the realisation that after everything that had occurred, after all of the criticism and the carping and the slow hand-claps, the national side was just 90 minutes' football away from a place in the World Cup final. But whatever the manifold reasons . . .

'For the first time that Wednesday,' thought Bobby Moore, 'we felt the country was getting behind us. The morning papers at last looked as if they thought we could win the thing.

'I had no doubts by then. I never felt that Portugal could beat any England team. They were the sort of side I would think about playing against with England the way many League clubs thought about playing West Ham – that it would be a good game, but not a hard fight, and we would probably win in the end.

'They had a lot of good players: Torres, Coluna, Augusto, that terrific winger Simoes. Their top club side, Benfica, were having a great run, and this was probably their best side ever. Yet they had needed Eusebio to pull them out of trouble against North Korea, of all people. And Eusebio didn't have the stomach for Nobby Stiles.

'For the first time we felt the crowd rising, sensing we were all on the verge of a World Cup final. Thank God we finally thrilled them, gave them something to cheer. Portugal were a good team who wanted to come forward, not physical at all. It was a good, open game, and we were the only winners.'

Ramsey was, as ever, having no truck with complacency. He assured his team that Portugal would be difficult to knock out. And alerted by the direct, fast, free front-running of Eusebio and Simoes, he took the unusual step of coaching Gordon Banks in the specific task of saving Eusebio's penalty kicks. This was not as difficult a practice as it might have seemed. Eusebio had taken a lot of penalties for club and country, many of them had been captured by the television and newsreel cameras, and careful study of the archive film proved beyond dispute that Eusebio almost always hit his penalties the same way: he hit them hard, with his right instep, at about waist-height, a yard or two inside the post to the goalkeeper's right. They were struck with numbing force but they were not, the England party agreed, clustered around the projector at Hendon Hall, unstoppable, if the goalkeeper chose to dive the right way . . .

Straight from kick-off, the England players loved the Portugal game. Their visitors had been plainly unnerved by the intense criticism that they had received for supposedly hacking Pele out of the World Cup, and by the shock that they had received from little North Korea, and they were cautious to the point of maidenly modesty.

For once, everything seemed right . . . 'The weather suited us that evening,' said Ray Wilson. 'It had been raining heavily earlier in the day and the air was cool. We set off in such swift, splendid style that my first thoughts during those early minutes of settling down were that we could give them a complete hammering.'

'Every man played it hard but fair,' concurred Jack Charlton. 'There was none of this massed defence business, none of the niggling incidents which go a long way towards marring a game. The ball flashed around the field with breathtaking speed.'

It has often been commented of the England/Portugal 1966 semi-final that it was 23 minutes old before the French referee Pierre Schwinte blew for a foul, an obstruction of Eusebio by Peters. Schwinte could have held up the game earlier: Eusebio, subjected to the tight man-to-man marking of Stiles, was obliged to do a lot of hopping and skipping ('Nobby hardly tackled him,' Geoff Hurst would say, 'just showed himself to be there ready and waiting every time Eusebio collected a pass. It was enough to keep his great skill completely in check'); and Hurst himself felt one tackle from Mario Coluna which 'shook my teeth'. But Schwinte let the game flow, and the football benefited.

Any false assurance which may have still been felt by England was dispelled by the quality of their opponents' play. Eusebio may indeed, as had been predicted, have been wilting under the attentions of Stiles; but Portugal was no one-man team. That very Antonio Coluna, whom some England players had been expecting to show his advancing years, almost had Hurst applauding when he 'took a ball on the volley that had been flying at him, and dropped it neatly over an opponent's head to stop dead, waiting for him to collect, two yards away. That takes some doing.'

'If I had to pick a player on the Portuguese team,' echoed Jack Charlton, 'who stamped the game with a complete air of authority it was Coluna, who – when the going was tough for his side – drove his players ever forward in a bid to score goals. Coluna was a giant both in attack and defence.'

Charlton was not doing too badly himself: up against the towering Jose Torres (both men were in fact six feet four inches tall), the Geordie had the better of the earlier exchanges. But it was Jack's brother who would stamp his inimitable mark on the match. Bobby, thought Jack, 'played what I consider to have been his finest game for his country'. It was Bobby who, on the half-hour, made the breakthrough.

'With Portugal playing minus an effective right-winger,' recalled Ray Wilson, 'I had plenty of spare room in front of me. Early on I just missed Roger Hunt with a through ball, but I was being left with so much time and space that I could afford to persist with this kind of pass. Soon afterwards I laid one at his feet. With that hunched, commanding style Hunt swept the ball before him. Pereira, the Portuguese goalkeeper, raced out to the edge of the area and threw himself at Roger's shot. The ball rebounded straight into Bobby Charlton's path . . .'

Charlton met it at the edge of the box and side-footed it, low and sure, past the sprawling Jose Pereira and three Portuguese defenders and into the back of the net. 'As far as I was concerned,' said Wilson, 'we had won the match. Roll on the final.'

Not yet. Banks had to dirty his shorts parrying a Eusebio shot round the post, and Torres began to win high balls for Portugal, and England were happy to hear the half-time whistle. But for some, even as the second half got underway with Portugal resuming a series of threatening attacks, the evening had a gilt-edged, haunted, mystical air about it, an unreal aura of invincibility. Footballers know that feeling, and it seldom betrays them. It just felt like England's night . . .

'It was still possible to stroll about there in the soft Wembley evening,' said Geoff Hurst, 'simply taking pleasure from what you were doing. The ball and the players were never still as the pattern and flow of the game swung and twisted on the skill of this pass, the cunning and speed of that dribble. England's steady teamwork and composure against Portugal's wary defence and swift and deadly individual forwards.'

'The whole game,' said Jack Charlton, 'was made up of moments that are magical in soccer. From the start both teams set out to win by enterprising, imaginative attacking football, without resorting to the rough stuff with which we had become so disenchanted in earlier games. If as some people suggested, Portugal had brushed Brazil from the World Cup trail by physical endeavour, this accusation could certainly not be laid at their door in the semi-final against us.'

Indeed not. The game was 57 minutes old before Portugal conceded their first foul. But the Portuguese were not the only side on the pitch that night who were resurrecting a reputation. It came as an enormous relief to every Englishman in the country to observe proof that their own team could play football, winning football, against eleven fit men. And the performance of Norbert Stiles was little less than a revelation.

Stiles had walked on to the pitch to hear most of the 90,000 crowd, which had been whipped into a petty fever of xenophobic anti-FIFA, anti-foreigner indignation by the governing body's crude attempts to have the half-back censured or dropped, chanting his name. ('The crowd rose,' said Hurst, encapsulating the feelings of most Englishmen, 'to back an honest little bloke in danger of being railroaded.') He rewarded them, and his cleverly loyal manager, and his affronted team-mates, by doing what everybody had prayed he would do. He marked Eusebio out of the game. 'Not once did Stiles lay a boot on his opponent,' said Geoff Hurst, 'he relied entirely on the speed of his interceptions and the cunning positioning that lured Eusebio into positions where he could be robbed.'

Pele, who was watching this game between the unworthy English and the Portuguese who had clogged him into submission in an agony of uncertain loyalties, chose to credit Stiles with England's victory. 'Portugal,' said the great Brazilian, 'apparently irritated by the comments they had received in the press for the way Morais played against me, were on their best behaviour, and on their best behaviour could not win. Still, only the excellent defence of Stiles in containing Eusebio kept England from losing.' It is difficult not to feel that Pele might have been more cautious with his compliments had he, and not Eusebio, been facing the little Mancunian.

The game may not quite have been a rose-tinted dream to Eusebio, but for Geoff Hurst it simply got better and better. 'I thought I played well,' he said, 'suddenly finding a confidence in myself in the second half that I had probably never felt before in my entire career. It was as though some small voice had whispered in my ear: 'Geoff Hurst, relax. These are great players on this pitch, but you have the right to be among them. Stop being overawed by what they can do, start showing what you can do.' Suddenly I felt a rush of belief in myself, I began holding on to the ball, taking on opponents, and not shoving passes hurriedly to some team-mate simply because he was far better known than I.'

With 12 minutes remaining George Cohen sent a through ball down the inside-right channel. Hurst chased it almost to the by-line with Jose Carlos, won the brief tussle for possession, and 'swung round him and waited for a full second before rolling the ball into Bobby Charlton's path. On that turf, with the ball running so straight and true, it was as easy as a shot in training for a marksman like Bobby. A match earlier I wouldn't have had the nerve to have waited for him to come up into position.'

Charlton connected with Hurst's lay-off without breaking stride two feet inside the Portuguese penalty area, and he thumped it first-time. The crowd, which had begun to roar as Charlton appeared in their vision, howled behind the ball like a following gale. The shot was just unstoppable. It passed Pereira's right hand a yard from the turf and rising, hit the back stanchion and thumped on to the ground at the back of the net. With his hands raised almost involuntarily, applauding his team-mates, the crowd, the occasion, the victory, and whatever incomprehensible genius had chosen to inhabit his own modest person, Charlton walked back to his own half through the embraces of his colleagues and the resigned, proffered hands of friendship of the Portuguese, and a bear-hug from his brother.

But it was still not over. Three minutes later Simoes slung a cross over from the right. Both Jack Charlton and Cohen lost the big figure of Torres, who rose at the back post and headed it back over the stranded Banks. 'I was determined to make sure that no matter what, this wasn't going to be a goal,' said Charlton. 'Anything rather than that. My hand shot out and stopped the ball squarely in its flight. I didn't try to argue, it would have been pointless. A penalty it was. I felt terrible.'

Thirty years later Charlton would have felt even more terrible. He would almost certainly have been sent off and would have missed the final. In 1966 he was not even booked. His worst punishment was to crouch miserably at the edge of his own penalty area (where he was charmingly if unintelligibly consoled by Alberto Festa), peeking through the hands which covered his face as Eusebio placed the ball on the spot, knowing in his heart of hearts that the Portuguese striker was too big a player to scorn this opportunity, idly watching a white-coated attendant on top of the huge scoreboard way above the goal, who was jumping about and waving his arms in an attempt to distract Eusebio ('What a good supporter!' thought Charlton) – and hoping that Gordon Banks would remember his pre-match briefing and dive the right way.

Eusebio struck his penalty exactly according to precedent: hard and waist-height to Banks's right. But the England goalkeeper had seen, just before the kick was taken, Coluna approach Eusebio and issue some instructions. Banks consequently chose to second-guess his opponent and – to the horror and astonishment of his team-mates – set off to his left just as Eusebio made contact. Eusebio picked the ball out of the back of the net, gave the 'keeper a pat on the cheek, and trotted off back to the centre circle.

They could have equalised. Coluna sent a screamer just wide and with just six minutes left Torres once more reached a high cross, which this time he knocked down to Simoes directly in front of goal. As Simoes had only Banks to beat the equaliser looked certain – until Stiles appeared to stick out a desperate right foot and deflect the Portuguese forward's shot wide of the post, and then turn and rant at his wayward defence. 'It didn't seem possible,' thought Alf Ramsey, 'that anyone could get to him [*Simoes*]. I thought the ball was sure to finish in the back of the net. It had to. Then Nobby Stiles came from nowhere . . .'

At the final whistle Eusebio, in tears, managed to smile his congratulations at the England players. (Later he would be found waiting outside a London cinema for Bobby Charlton to emerge so that he could present Charlton with a complimentary bottle of Portuguese wine.) In the England changing room Alf Ramsey – who was permitting himself an uncharacteristic display of boyish delight (he would later announce that this semi-final had been 'England's best game since I became manager') – gestured for silence from his babbling squad and announced: 'Gentlemen, I don't often talk about individuals. But I think you would all agree that Nobby has today turned in a very great professional performance.' Stiles's colleagues let loose a heartfelt extended cheer.

That night the players' wives were allowed up to Hendon Hall Hotel. Ramsey bought a round of drinks, but that was as far as it went. The women were allowed nowhere near the bedrooms. At midnight, on a signal from the manager, they were escorted away again like so many Cinderellas into the city night. The World Cup final against West Germany at the Empire Stadium, Wembley, was just four days away.

10 WEST GERMANY

'We are all cheats in some way.'

— ALF RAMSEY

Two renowned players were the subject of selection debate before the final. Would Jimmy Greaves, for almost ten years one of the greatest strikers in Europe and once more fit enough for consideration, be picked to play for England; and would the 20-year-old Franz Beckenbauer, a midfield player who had taken his first World Cup by the scruff of its neck, scoring four goals in his side's five games and leading such German stars of the past as Fritz Walter to suggest that 'he is going to be very, very great', be allowed to play for West Germany?

The Beckenbauer controversy provoked surprisingly little comment at the time. The Bayern player was actually ineligible to represent his country in the final, because he had picked up his second booking in the tournament in Germany's semi-final against the Soviet Union. That, then as later, meant a minimum of a one-match suspension, with immediate application.

But no exceptional player had ever before been prevented from playing in the final of the World Cup because of disciplinary action. That principle – unthinkable just a few years later – was as emblematic of the Age of Innocence as anything else. Four years earlier in Chile Garrincha had been sent off in the semi-final, but the Brazilian winger had been given a special dispensation to play in the big match. By 1966 FIFA had even developed a formula to allow themselves to bend the rules. Each caution by a referee had, after the game, to be 'confirmed' by a FIFA meeting. The absence of a 'confirmation' did

177

not necessarily suggest that the referee had made a mistake, or that the booking was wiped from the record books. It merely meant that in so far as the FIFA officials were concerned no further action was necessary. An 'unconfirmed' caution was a caution with a blind eye turned upon it.

At their meeting on Wednesday, 27 July, the day after England's semi-final, two days after Germany's semi-final, and three days before the final, FIFA met in London. They announced afterwards that the Russian Igor Chislenko, who had been sent off against West Germany, would be banned from the next three internationals. But they refused to confirm referee Lobello's caution of Franz Beckenbauer. Franz was therefore free to play. The news was greeted with enormous relief at the Germans' Welwyn Garden City training camp. 'It means a great deal to us,' said the tall, courteous German manager Helmut Schoen. 'Beckenbauer is one of the greatest talents of Europe. And he is better than he shows. There is more to come from him.'

'We were worried,' admitted Herman Joch, the secretary of the West German FA, 'because it was the second time that Beckenbauer had been cautioned and must have been an error.' The young midfielder had probably, added the secretary disingenuously, been confused by the referee with Wolfgang Overath, and Beckenbauer did not protest at the time 'because we do not encourage our players to do so'. This last comment would have been by way of salt in the wounds of the Soviets, who had become accustomed in the semi-final to watching the Germans stand and stare at the referee and point like an expectant chorus line at the changing rooms every time one of their number had been fouled.

Alf Ramsey's response to the news was to assure his players that Franz Beckenbauer was more worried about Bobby Charlton than any English footballer need be of Beckenbauer. England were not, in 1966, afraid of West Germany. The Germans counted as part – a strong part, but no more than that – of the European opposition which the players reckoned they knew well enough to overcome at Wembley at least nine times out of ten. As a united country previous to the Second World War Germany had hardly bothered England at all. They had been dismissed 3–0 at Wembley in 1935, and then 6–3 in Berlin in 1938 in that famous contest when the English players were instructed by the FA's officials (who in turn had been advised by the British Ambassador) to give the 'normal courtesy' of the Nazi salute to Hermann Goering.

Since the war, and the separation of Germany into east and west, West Germany had recorded one simply sensational achievement: spearheaded by the brilliant Helmut Rahn and Fritz Walter they had won the World Cup at their first attempt in 1954 in Switzerland, beating the supposedly invincible Hungarians in the final. They had been semi-finalists in Sweden in 1958, and quarter-finalists in 1962, but all four engagements with England since the constitution of the West German national side in 1950 had resulted in English wins. (The English bookmakers had Ramsey's team, in the hours before kick-off, at the ridiculous odds of 2–1 on.)

And there was an unavoidable resonance to the prospect of England playing West Germany in the final of the World Cup, an echo from just 20 years earlier. There was even something strangely fitting in the appointment of Gottfried Dienst, a German speaker from traditionally neutral Switzerland, as referee; and of Tofik Bahkramov, a Russian veteran of his country's Western Front, as one of the linesmen. Both the English and the West German camps knew that references to the Second World War might have been tasteless and misplaced, but they were inevitable and – not to put too fine a point on it – they benefited the winners of the 1939–45 clash. It was unthinkable to many Englishmen of a certain generation that, having won the war, they should lose a game of football. And the players were consequently aware of an extra dimension of responsibility, they were conscious that England Expected victory in a way that England would not have Expected had the final opponents been Portugal, say, or Brazil. Jack Charlton was not as unusual as he may have thought when he found himself, in the minutes before kick-off, reflecting that: 'For six years we had waged a war against Germany; now we were preparing to do battle on the football field. A strange thought, just before a vital match. But that's how it was with me.'

And that is how it was with a lot of English people. Some Germans professed to find this reawakened militant English nationalism disturbing. 'Everywhere you look in the [*English*] newspapers,' said the television commentator Werner Schneider rather priggishly, 'they are saying "England is going to win, England is going to rule the football world." This nationalism is surely more than football. Perhaps we have learned our lesson because of the Second World War. Perhaps we think more than other people of how mad this thinking is. You would expect this from countries who have nothing else. You could understand it in Ghana, or in the South American countries like the Argentine and Brazil where football is just about all they have. But in England it is strange and sad.

'They want to fly flags and beat drums because they are winning at football. Look at that band at Wembley. Tin soldiers, I call them. It is said that the Germans are the most militaristic people in the world but it is not so. The British are. Even winning at football is treated like a victory in battle.'

Schneider's comments were contradicted by one or two of his countrymen who suggested that German attitudes towards the trophy were little less chauvinistic ('I know that if we win,' said Ulrich Kaiser of the Dusseldorf Sports Information Agency, 'some of our people are going to say, "We have beaten the world." I hate that. Eleven German footballers will have won a cup and I will be glad to see it. But I am not saying I have beaten anybody. Of those eleven players how many at home would I have in my apartment for coffee or beer? Maybe two.'), but they hit a nerve. Across the rest of Europe, not to mention Latin America, England were deeply unpopular finalists.

They were unpopular in France, where the sports newspaper *L'Equipe* carried a cartoon showing Bobby Charlton and a ferocious Nobby Stiles driving a Rolls-Royce while referees in British bobbies' uniforms held back the Argentine, France and other teams. The cartoon was captioned: 'Let us pass, please.' They were unpopular even in Holland, a country with no apparent axe to grind in this tournament, and one with no historical reason to favour West Germany. They were, naturally, unpopular in the remainder of Great Britain. After the semi-final with Portugal one London-based Scottish journalist noticed that 'Scottish reporters sat in a smouldering sulk in corners in the Press Centre in Kensington and insisted that they did not know what all the carry on was about. People like myself who betrayed their birthright sufficiently to suggest that England played rather well to beat Portugal were accused of defecting to "the caramel chewers".'

Most, if not all, of the rest of the world wanted West Germany to win the 1966 World Cup. That was due in part to the widespread perception that the tournament had been loaded in England's favour; it was due in part to certain countries' – such as France – grievances at the manner of their own dismissal; it was due in smaller part to the neo-colonial arrogance which the city of London seemed to exude in the last week of July (an arrogance which struck ugly chords with those who recalled the British sides' complacent reluctance to enter international competitions at the level of both club and country until decades after their launch elsewhere); but it was mainly thanks to the tedious, plodding, cautious football which Ramsey's side had displayed for most of the championships. Football fans will forgive almost anything in an entertaining football team, and condemn everything in a boring one. Until the semi-final England's football had been indisputably boring. Deep fears which dated back to the 1950s were being aroused in the breasts of soccer supporters from Rio to Roumania, fears that their formerly free-running sport was being stultified and corrupted by a cult of coaching, discipline, physical strength and the horror of defeat. And more than any other side, the English team of 1966 appeared to embody all of those shameful characteristics. Their contrast with the reigning champions and pre-tournament favourites, Brazil, could not have been more stark. West Germany may not have been the most popular World Champions back in 1954, but that was conveniently forgotten as the world willed defeat on Ramsey's Robots.

All of which, of course, had an entirely positive effect on English morale. The players had felt strong enough before the Portugal match; afterwards they were simply sure that their names were on the Jules Rimet Trophy. Some of them, such as Bobby Charlton, felt this almost as a matter of divine providence. They played in what was still regarded as the strongest League in the world, they were in their own country, they had an unmatchable strength in depth and they believed in each other. It was just meant to be. Charlton in particular feared no individual opponent and would have been surprised, like anybody of natural brilliance, to learn that not all of his team-mates shared his assurance. But even the likes of George Cohen, an unpretentious full-back from Fulham FC, caught the infection. How do you feel? Cohen was asked at Hendon Hall in the days between the semi-final and the final. The full-back waved his arms about, searching fruitlessly for the appropriate phrase, and finally settled for: 'We feel . . . really good.'

For the first time in the tournament the whole country felt really good. If the Nobby Stiles affair and the Argentina game had induced a familiar sensation that when English backs were up against the wall, Englishmen gave of their best, the Portugal semi-final had apparently confirmed this posture. And now, just as we had always suspected, the rest of the world was opposed to an English victory. Well, bring on the rest of the world. Who invented this game anyway? . . . Previously in the tournament the players had noticed on their occasional brief excursions into the suburbia outside their hotel that not many people other than youthful autograph hunters paid them much attention. England, as the Wembley crowds had indicated, had been at a low level of expectation.

On the morning of Friday 29th, the day before the final, Bobby Charlton and Ray Wilson went shopping in Hendon. The difference was utterly startling. 'We found it almost impossible to move without being halted by well-wishers. We could see that England winning meant so much to people. Even the shop girls were full of England and the desire to win the World Cup. Suddenly it was more than a football competition. It was the greatest day that had ever dawned for the English game.'

Despite all of their optimism it was accepted in the England camp that West Germany were likely to present a sterner test than Portugal. Their football may have been short on Latin fantasy, but they were skilled and well-drilled professionals who, Ramsey emphasised to his team, were – like England – never beaten until the final whistle. And in case England were in danger of overlooking the difference between their final opposition and what had gone before, Helmet Schoen reminded them. 'Portugal,' he said, 'use the Mediterranean individualism. They ask Eusebio to do it alone. We will not do that. We will have at least two strikers running parallel, with powerful units backing up from behind.'

The most dangerous, if not the most powerful, of those 'units backing up from behind' was Franz Beckenbauer. The solution to his threat was tried and tested and surely obvious. On the deceptive face of the team-sheet Beckenbauer was directly up against Bobby Charlton. In fact, should the tall, young German start ambling forward, Ramsey had another player altogether marked down to take him out. 'In our book,' recalled Bobby Moore, 'the key to the whole situation seemed to rest with Beckenbauer. We had preparation ready for him. If he had started coming hard at us from his free-moving midfield role, then Nobby Stiles was picked out to nail him.' In a private room at Hendon Hall they watched film of the Germans, and paid attention to them individually. And that was it. 'The preparations virtually took care of themselves. There wasn't much for Alf to say by then.'

Other than to say who was in the team.

Jimmy Greaves had been pronouncing himself fit since before the Portugal game. He was due to take a full fitness test on the afternoon of Friday 29th, 24 hours before the final, but it was confidently expected that he would pass it (he did).

The country of England, which was united on just about every other issue concerning the game of association football in those last days of July 1966, was split down the middle on the matter of Jimmy Greaves – split down the middle, and fascinated by Ramsey's dilemma. More, far more than the vexed question of whether or not wingers should be deployed in an England team, the Greaves question became the issue of the day. Later, it would be portrayed unfairly as a defining point in Ramsey's direction of the national side: as a perfect exemplar of his preference for brawn over brain and workrate over inspiration. In 1966 it had not yet achieved such proportions. Jimmy Greaves had, after all, received half of his 54 caps from Alf Ramsey. In 1966 it was simply the biggest talking point in town.

The players were similarly divided, and similarly tense with anticipation. The captain, and Greaves's room-mate, Bobby Moore felt that Greaves should be and would be selected for the final even at the expense of Moore's West Ham team-mate Geoff Hurst. According to the Moore camp, 'one or two of us felt that Jimmy would be brought back as a psychological weapon – a dangerous finisher to frighten the Germans'.

With hindsight it is plain that Greaves was finished, and that in their secret hearts everybody – Moore and Greaves included – knew it. Alf Ramsey of all managers was not about to break up a physically effective winning side which had just taken itself with full battle honours through two contrasting but equally testing trials into the World Cup final. Ramsey was not alone in this inclination: virtually every disinterested international manager who was polled by the British press offered the same conclusion: 'Greaves is not on form. In modern football, even a great player has to work a lot.' At training on Wednesday and Thursday Ramsey kept the eleven who had won the last two matches separate from the remainder of the squad. Ostensibly, having just played a semi-final they needed different treatment from the rest. But in fact he was keeping them together as a unit: the select of the select. The World Cup finalists.

But whatever their private fears and hopes, whatever their inner-most convictions, not one of the players could possibly know for certain where Ramsey would come down. Who could gauge the thinking behind that Cheyenne mask; who could sense the inflection at the back of those clipped and proper commands? 'If you have ever been sentenced to death,' Geoff Hurst requires of a small percentage of the population, 'and then spent three days waiting for the Governor to walk in and announce a reprieve, you might know how I was feeling during the three days between England's victory over Portugal and the World Cup final. If not, you can't.

'Obviously I was the man who was likely to be dropped from the attack. As I saw it, Mr Ramsey would not change his defence for this final match, a defence that had conceded one goal from the penalty spot in five World Cup matches was hardly likely to be altered now.

'But the attack was something else again. Greaves had played in the first three games, then been injured. I had played in the last two, scored once and made a goal for Charlton. That was my claim. Then there was Roger Hunt, the bloke who had been doing a similar job to mine for England, but for a darn sight longer. Roger was reliable, experienced and the sort of man who would run until he dropped, and then make tackles with his teeth.

'So I sat and stewed. I had wanted nothing in my life more than I now wanted to play for England in this final. I wanted it so badly I literally ached at the thought of not being in. And every one of the 22 of us locked up in Hendon felt exactly the same as I did. Even those who had not played in the series, and must have known they had no chance of being picked . . .

'Again and again I went over the permutations in my mind, and always I came racing to the same conclusion: Greaves must play. He'd over 50 caps for England, no one had ever scored more goals. For four years I had read and been happy to accept that if anyone was going to win the World Cup for England it would be Jimmy.'

So Hurst sleepwalked through those 72 hours, unable even to bring himself to ask Greaves – whom he liked and respected – how his injury was healing, in case the answer was 'fine'. Greaves, he knew, must be suffering similar agonies. 'Remember since he was about ten years old Jimmy had never really had to look at a team-sheet – he knew his name would always be there . . . now suddenly, probably for the first time in his life, he was wondering, "Will I be chosen?"'

Hurst was rooming with Martin Peters, and at first they could not raise the courage to ask the other anything about Saturday's final. What if you asked, do you think I'll be picked, and your mate said no? Then the ice broke, one of them broached the subject, and after that they talked of little else, convincing each other that they were sure to be in, they were now indispensible, Alf would never change a winning team. And in the silences between their mutual self-assurance, they lay on their backs on their beds and stared at the ceiling and – like small boys – day-dreamed of scoring one spectacular World Cup-winning goal after another . . .

Players in such a condition would do anything to relieve the tension. They went shopping in Hendon for no real reason, picking up bits and pieces that they neither wanted nor needed until some hotel rooms seemed to be occupied by travelling cosmetics salesmen. They watched Ramsey 'with a sort of scared fascination', reading oceans of meaning into the manager's slightest action, such as passing them the sugar at tea-time ('Is he trying to build up my strength?'). If Alf left a newspaper on a seat it would be seized upon and scoured by the squad for the vaguest hint, through a sports report that he may have just been studying, of his intentions.

Ramsey, who had decided immediately after the semi-final that he would be sticking with exactly the same team for the final, knew that he had to break with precedent and tell his players the side on the Friday before the game, otherwise 'they wouldn't sleep'.

'Then, having decided to tell them, I had to think of the best way to do it. If I called in eleven players everyone would know the team had been selected, and I wanted this kept quiet for as long as possible.'

After training at Roehampton on the Friday morning the squad was due to go to the Odeon cinema in Hendon to watch a film called *Those Magnificent Men In Their Flying Machines* ('The greatest film I have ever seen,' thought Ramsey).

Between training and lunch and entering the cinema, the manager approached ten of the eleven players who had turned out against Portugal and Argentina and told them that they would be representing their country in the World Cup final. 'Nobby,' he said to Stiles, 'are you ready for tomorrow?'

'I hope so,' replied Eusebio's nemesis.

'You'd bloody well better be,' said his manager.

Others were more discreetly told: 'If it will help you to sleep tonight, you're playing tomorrow.' Geoff Hurst was informed as he was leaving the training field. 'Alf drifted casually over and said: "Geoff, you will be playing tomorrow. I thought you'd want to know, but please keep it to yourself. I am not telling the rest."

'Knowing,' thought Hurst, 'was almost worse than not knowing.' He resisted an impulse to kiss Ramsey and shout out his news to the world, muttered 'Thank you, I'll do my best,' went for a bath, and spent several hours trying to keep his delight hidden from the rest of the squad.

Ramsey told all of the selected players other than Bobby Moore, Jimmy Greaves's room-mate ('If Bobby didn't know he was playing without me telling him so, he's not the Bobby Moore I know.'). His expressed intention was to keep the bad news from all of the rejected 11 until the official announcement at noon on Saturday.

It was a naive hope, and he must have known it. There was a level of unintentional cruelty in such unspoken segregation. He was not especially dodging the unpleasant task of giving bad news to the disappointed. Ramsey's only purpose in telling the eleven that they would be playing was to allow them to relax and get a decent night's sleep. The well-being of the other eleven certainly entered his head, but as a remote, secondary consideration. How could it be otherwise? He was on the eve of the World Cup final, and he was keen to keep his secrets for as long as possible from the press and from Helmut Schoen. There was also the outside possibility that one of the chosen eleven might yet have to call off, in which case Ramsey would have to approach a substitute, and he did not want to tell a player one day that he was excluded and the next day tell him he was playing.

So he attempted clumsily to let exactly one-half of a tightly-knit group of anxious young men know the answer to the most widely discussed question in England, while keeping it from the other half. Inevitably, they found out. Bobby Moore woke up on Saturday to find a dejected Greaves packing his bags. 'Jimmy was hurt. I don't care what people say about Jimmy, about how he didn't work and didn't care, how his attitude was all wrong. I knew the man and I knew what he was going through. All he wanted was to play in the World Cup final. He believed he could get the goals to win it for England. He believed he was something special and it broke his heart not to have the chance to prove it.

'That moment began Jimmy's disenchantment with football. I knew that if he'd stayed fit or got his place back the Germans would have been frightened of him. I believed Jimmy Greaves could have won us the cup. But I also knew Alf Ramsey couldn't change the team. Geoff had come in and done too well. It was helpful to have someone else in the team who knew me and Martin Peters as players. From the start he had a good understanding with Roger Hunt and their running had opened the way for Bobby Charlton to start scoring vital goals. Alf had been given that bonus out of nothing. He couldn't turn it down now. Not for this match.'

On Friday night, while eleven English footballers tried to contain their excitement at the prospect of the next day's match and another eleven lay in differing degrees of despondency on their beds at Hendon Hall Hotel, their parents and wives – who had all been invited to the final by the Football Association – were taken to see the *Black and White Minstrel Show*. In deference to them the performers began and ended the evening with *When The Saints Go Marching In*.

Back at Hendon Alf Ramsey tucked himself into bed. 'My own job was done. The responsibility was now theirs, and I was able to sleep well that night – even though I don't normally sleep well in strange beds away from home.'

On Saturday morning most of the players woke up to an almost unbearable tension. 'I thought of games which had been won and lost before by cruel strokes of fate,' recalled Jack Charlton, whose wife Pat was expecting a baby back at home in Leeds, 'injuries on that Wembley turf; unhappy, accidental deflections which meant that despite all your striving you had given a goal away . . . I said to myself, "Get a grip on things." Nerves, excitement, tension – all these played havoc with my state of mind that Saturday morning. I almost wished I could have gone on sleeping all day.'

Charlton's bedside telephone rang, and the receptionist told him that his parents were downstairs. He did not want to see them: he did not want to see anybody from outside the squad; but he dutifully went downstairs and his doubts proved, of course, to be groundless. Cissie Charlton had a lifetime's experience of dealing with young men in the hours before important football games – 'We knew each other so well that we could read one another like books, instead of passing on the tension we relied upon each other for a bit of morale-boosting.' This immensely attractive cameo – Jackie Milburn's sister and the mother of two World Cup finalists sitting with her coalminer husband in the alien lounge of a posh London hotel talking in soft, calming, purposeful and vitally familiar Northumbrian tones to one of their sons, while outside the world waited upon them – was broken when the players went to a lunch which many of them could not swallow.

From the uneaten meal the eleven players filed into the private hotel room for a final briefing. Ramsey spoke for about 30 minutes – watch out for Emmerich's left foot, it's all he has . . . keep a respectful eye on Uwe Seeler. He may be getting on, but his influence on them is enormous . . . look out for Held's speed . . . watch Helmut Haller closely . . . Nobby, don't forget that if Beckenbauer starts coming forward, he's yours . . . and above all, don't forget their patience.

Remember how many times the Germans have been apparently out-played and beaten, but have fought their way back into a game just by sticking in there and keeping their pattern, keeping their resolve. 'You're better than them. You can beat them. But never forget they're not beaten until the final whistle goes and you're one goal in front.' And as the players began to rise from their chairs their manager said: 'Well, that's it then. The best of luck.'

Jack Charlton packed his boots and put his money in with them. Silver in the bag; silver for luck. Other players carefully put in the same order as before the same socks on the same feet that had worn them since the tournament began, or ritually carried each other's bags, or sat beside the same companion. The coach journey to Wembley was unusually subdued, missing the normal footballers' banter, but not uncomfortable – 'We all felt keyed up and confident going to the stadium. Alf seemed all right. Everyone seemed more or less in control of themselves.'

Wembley Way was packed. Nobody had seen it so busy before, not even on the afternoon of FA Cup finals. And as the team coach edged towards the twin towers great roars went up on all sides of 'Eng-land! Eng-land!' The few West German flags waving in the vast concourse seemed solitary and pointless. The England players thrilled despite themselves, and felt instantly both the joy of the people's affection and the responsibility which rested on their own fallible, mortal shoulders. The crowd – the paying English customers who had booed them off the field following a game against West Germany just five months earlier – was clearly out to influence the outcome of this game to the full extent that possibly only a passionate and partisan football crowd can affect a sporting event. It is an influence whose tribal power everybody – the home support, home players and the unfortunate opposition – acknowledges. That day it was worth more than just, as the cliché has it, a one-goal start. It delivered to the England players the extraordinary sensation that as many as 80,000 people out there would not let them lose.

Hardened observers had never before seen the cold grey terraces of Wembley in this condition. 'It was impossible,' wrote Hugh McIlvanney later, 'to define the atmosphere precisely but it was palpable, and it was unique. It was like walking into an ordinary, familiar room and knowing instinctively that something vital and unbearably dramatic was happening, perhaps a matter of life and death. The people hurrying and jostling and laughing nervously inside had a flushed, supercharged look, but if they were high it was with excitement. "It's bloody electric," said one of the doormen. He had found the word.'

'Football players like to tell you they don't hear the crowd,' reflected Geoff Hurst later, 'and in the sense you ignore the bloke who bellows "Hurst, you nit", this is true. But you can sense instantly whether the stadium is with you or not. At no time during that long, long afternoon did they falter . . . It was not so much they wanted you to win, it was the feeling that they were certain that you would succeed. With their belief pouring down to support our own conviction, we could hardly fail to have confidence in ourselves. The goals might have given us the game, but the crowd gave us the goals. There have been times I have loathed the fans, not when they jeered the misses, but when they failed to appreciate what we were trying to do. Not this time.'

The England changing-room was bedlam. It was crammed with photographers, officials, arc lights, journalists, hangers-on, and television cameras. The squad went out to wander around the pitch, walking from goal to goal (some of them in ritual order from one post to the other), and then went back in and attempted to read some of the pile of goodwill telegrams. It was still chaos in there. Some players could not understand why Ramsey did not kick the whole circus out and allow them half an hour of peace, but he did not, and at 2.30pm, 15 minutes before the players were due to leave for the pitch, there were still 100 people in the room. At 2.35 Bobby Moore turned to Jack Charlton and said: 'I've never seen anything like this before. I can't even start getting changed yet. And to think this is the number one cup final in all football.'

Charlton grinned. 'That's why it's like this, because it is the number one final.' Then the big Geordie followed his third-last superstition of the tournament: as before every other game, he changed his studs at the last minute. It kept his hands busy, and it had not yet let him down. The signal came for the players to leave, and Charlton's penultimate ritual was acted out. He waited for Nobby Stiles to get up off the bench, and then he took his place at the end of the queue. 'It was like repeating an act of faith . . . I didn't want to take any chances.'

Alf Ramsey went along the row from man to man, shaking hands with his players and repeating: 'Good luck.' He had never done that before, some players noted. They started moving. Somebody somewhere quipped: 'These boots were made for walking.' The noise from the crowd as they emerged from the tunnel momentarily took their breath away – 'I have never, ever heard a crowd roar as it did that day.' Bobby Moore was in a kind of trance, going through the motions. Jack Charlton went to perform his final act of faith: scoring during the kick-in. His first shot went high and he grabbed another ball, walloped it towards Banks's goal, and was absurdly relieved to see it float in.

The bands of the Portsmouth Command and the Portsmouth Group, Royal Marines, marched off, having delivered a musical number associated, however tenuously, with each of the 16 nations who had competed in the closing rounds of the 1966 World Cup (North Korea got *Oriental Patrol*). Moore hardly remembered the exchange of pennants with Uwe Seeler, nor the Swiss referee Gottfried Dienst showing both captains both sides of the coin, nor calling and winning the toss and opting not to change ends. Then the whistle shrilled and Siggy Held kicked off and Bobby Moore came to his full senses, and was happy to find himself still confident of winning.

After 12 minutes fate took its first swing at his confidence. Siggy Held took possession out wide on the left, stepped inside and delivered from deep in his own half an optimistic cross towards the far side of the England penalty area. The ball drifted slowly and harmlessly towards a deserted region. Helmut Haller gave up on it and Ray Wilson, ten yards clear of any other player, rose to head it clear.

'I got up too early,' he would say. He made a weak and mistimed contact and knocked the ball straight back into the inside-right channel a yard inside the box, where the astonished but duly grateful Haller brought it down with his right foot and – just as an alert, avenging Moore came hurtling at him – swept it with no especial power under the tumbling, unsighted Banks and into the England goal.

Jack Charlton suddenly felt both angry and scared, and stopped believing in omens. He had run in to cover in front of Banks, but at the last moment he had scorned a fleeting opportunity to stick out a telescopic leg and deflect Haller's shot. He had decided in that fatal split second not to do so because surely Banks would collect such a feeble strike. But the England 'keeper had seen it too late. 'Well, it's up to me,' thought Charlton, and shamefacedly avoided the eyes of his colleagues. He was surprised when nobody recriminated. Then he pulled himself together, clapped his hands and yelled, so that the others would see that he at least was unperturbed: 'Let's forget it. Get one back.'

Good footballers take a lot of responsibility upon themselves. Neither Charlton nor Banks nor Moore looked to blame Ray Wilson, from whose amazingly untypical error the goal had stemmed. Each felt either that the goal was quite unworthy, or that they themselves would normally have stopped it, or both. Wilson himself was momentarily overwhelmed by a surge of depression, but knew enough about himself and about the game to realise that, if he allowed it to do so, the incident would finish him and possibly his country's chances for the rest of the match. And so, like an army medic performing field surgery on himself, this unflappable man, whose function was more usually to relax his own team-mates, began to calm himself down, began to talk to himself softly and urgently out of the earshot of others: 'That's it. There's nothing that can be done about it. Just get on with it. Things'll come right.'

'All I thought,' remembered Bobby Moore, 'was that Haller shouldn't be the sort of player to score against us and certainly isn't the class of player to win a World Cup final. It wasn't right. So I still feel confident . . .'

Six minutes later he justified his own faith. He received a square ball from Bobby Charlton, strode forward and, knowing that he would never beat the challenging Overath for speed, turned quickly to shield the ball. Overath tripped the England captain, Moore grabbed the ball with his hands as he fell and as the referee's whistle blew, and as he rose to his feet he placed it on the ground 40 yards from the German goal and addressed it like a golfer. He took one deliberate step back, and covering Germans, sensing the sudden threat, raced past him towards their own penalty area. Waving his players forward, Moore went to take the kick quickly, and then he checked himself. Geoff Hurst was moving, mysteriously unmarked, across the edge of the German six-yard box. Immediately, Moore struck the ball with perfect accuracy over the scrambled German defence and Hurst met it cleanly with his temple and nodded it down past the stationary Hans Tilkowski. 'That's better,' thought Moore.

In the changing-room at half-time no mention was made of the German goal. There was no point. Ramsey talked quietly and soberly about the threat which was still posed by some of the German forwards – Held had looked particularly dangerous in the last quarter of the first half – and then he congratulated his own players. In many games it would have been a dangerous tactic. England were not playing so well, and West Germany so badly, that victory was assured. But it worked. 'You're doing very well,' he said. 'But you can improve. And if you do that you will win the cup.'

At least one player took the manager at his word. Alan Ball, who had been dogged by Karl-Heinz Schnellinger throughout the first 45 minutes, celebrated the start of the second half by quickly losing his marker and releasing first Charlton and then Cohen and Stiles into threatening positions down the right flank. He progressed to skipping past Schnellinger with an ease and a confidence which grew as the game grew old, and would prove decisive to its outcome.

With Beckenbauer too engrossed in the thankless task of covering Bobby Charlton in midfield to pose any threat of his own; with Jack Charlton fired up and intercepting everything that came his way; with Moore looking increasingly majestic; the game edged England's way. 'Going nicely,' thought Moore. The fitness of the English players may have been a controversial part of their preparation, it may have been criticised by some as being held in higher esteem than skill, but the players began, in the last quarter of normal time, to be thankful for it. 'Were we the fitter, stronger side?' wondered Ray Wilson. 'We certainly felt that way.'

Thirteen minutes from full-time they seemed to have won the World Cup. Ball won a corner on the right and took it himself. It fell to Hurst just outside the penalty area, and the West Ham striker controlled it, jockeyed for position and hit a harmless shot through a ruck of players directly at Tilkowski. Once again, a full-back intervened. Horst Hottges decided to play safe and clear the ball eight yards from his own goal line. He swiped at it with his weak left foot, slipped on the Wembley mud, fell backwards, and his clearance looped directly up into the air and began to fall to his left and behind him . . . into the path of Roger Hunt, Martin Peters and Jack Charlton, who had moved forward for the corner and were still standing there in a desperately ominous row as this gift from Heaven fell slowly towards them out of the sky. They were all played onside by the residual German full-back on the goal-line and the earth's rotation seemed to pause as the ball fell to earth in agonising slow-motion, and bounced once.

'Suddenly I was frightened,' recalled Charlton, 'in case I was the man on the spot.'

He need not have worried. The earth began to turn again. There was a rush of red shirt to his left. Martin Peters raced forward as Charlton was pondering his responsibilities and smacked the ball exuberantly, fearlessly into the back of the West German net from seven yards out.

'At that moment,' said Bobby Moore, 'I felt we'd won the World Cup, and I felt proud. Time was running out nicely. For the first time I noticed the crowd.'

Back on the halfway line Bobby Charlton was screaming for concentration, shouting above the torrential roar from the terracing around them that there were just minutes to go, that the cup was England's if they gave nothing away.

He could himself have put the matter beyond doubt. With four minutes to go Moore, under pressure on his own by-line, played an exquisite short ball out of defence to Peters, who found Roger Hunt free on the halfway line. Hunt turned and raced for goal, and laid it off at the last moment to Charlton at the edge of the penalty area. The crowd ceased its tuneful assurances that 'Britons never never never shall be slaves,' and held its breath, but Bobby stumbled, scuffed his shot wide and measured his length on the turf.

Never might a miss have been so costly. With 90 minutes gone Jack Charlton leaned robustly over Siggy Held to head clear. Charlton and his colleagues were convinced that Held had backed into Charlton, or had at best failed to jump for the ball, but referee Dienst blew – not for full time, as they thought at first, but for a German free-kick ten yards outside the English box. The English players looked across at their managerial dug-out and got the message: seconds to go. This is it. This is their last chance.

Emmerich hammered it low into the area, it sneaked through the wall to Held, who turned, jinked to his left and fired a shoulder-high cross-cum-shot into the six-yard box. The ball hit Schnellinger on the upper arm and bounced down and out across the front of goal two yards from the line, past Banks and the lunging Wilson, and Wolfgang Weber slid in to scoop the equaliser home at the post.

'How the hell did you let that happen?' Moore stood, arms akimbo, addressing his team. Nobody replied. Bobby Charlton kicked off, Hurst played it back to Jack Charlton, and Gottfried Dienst blew for full time. Jack Charlton waved his right arm angrily, bitterly, resentfully at the referee – 'Had away, man,' the expression said, 'had away t' hell' – and Nobby Stiles booted the ball violently upfield.

'Angry?' says Charlton. 'Here we were on the edge of time and the brink of victory. Angry? I couldn't trust myself to speak to anybody. Suddenly the realisation dawned . . . 30 more slogging minutes, 30 minutes when I felt so down that I couldn't run a yard.'

Charlton looked around him, at Martin Peters 'almost in a state of collapse', Gordon Banks pacing up and down, Nobby Stiles on the ground with cramp, Bobby Moore expressionlessly replacing divots in the grass, Bobby Charlton pale as a ghost, his face sunk and anguished. 'I thought: "This is it, we've had it now."'

Ray Wilson 'felt shattered . . . All I could feel was my tiredness. My legs were sore. My heart was heavy. All the nervous tension had drained me to a standstill.'

They were not stupid, the England players, nor were they incapable even at that stricken time of rationality: they knew that the Germans also were tired. But they knew as well that 'they must have been given a tremendous psychological boost by their goal. They must have been as happy and relieved as men who had come back from death.' The Englishmen, on the other hand, were 'pig sick'.

Bobby Moore watched Alf Ramsey and the trainer Harold

195

Shepherdson approach the players from the bench, and he feared for what was about to be said. 'Never forget,' Ramsey had punched into these England players, 'never forget they're not beaten until the final whistle goes.'

'If he'd gone on about that right then,' said Moore later, 'he would have killed half our team stone dead. They were gutted enough as it was. I didn't know what he would do. You never know absolutely and for certain how people are going to react until the really big moment comes. He could have come on screaming and shouting, hollering and hooting, saying: "I thought you'd know better. I thought you'd have learned . . ."'

Moore was right to be concerned. 'I was absolutely furious,' Ramsey would say later of his feelings at that moment. 'I knew exactly how many chances of scoring we had missed. But I knew that I must not show my anger. I also realised that I must not indicate, either by word or expression, the least degree of sympathy for the team because they had to go on playing. I knew they could do it; they knew they could do it. But even a casual "hard luck" might have put a doubt in their minds.'

Alf Ramsey approached his group of players, some sprawled on the grass, some being massaged, the others standing and looking disconsolately at him, and with beads of sweat standing out on his brow he began to talk softly. It was almost mesmerical. Gradually his voice became the only sound in that seething stadium.

'Forget it,' he was saying. 'Forget what's just happened. Forget the last 90 minutes. You've been the better team. Look at the Germans.' They did look at the Germans. 'They're flat out. Down on the grass. Flat on their backs.' They were. 'Just have a look at them. They can't live with you. Not for another half an hour. Not through extra time. 'You've won the World Cup once. Now go out and win it again.'

It may have been the most effective team talk in the long history of English football. 'Although no-one said a word as we lined up for the kick-off,' remembered Jack Charlton, 'somehow every man-jack of the England team seemed suddenly to have a streak of tempered steel in his make-up. Our motto had become: "They shall not pass."'

'The West Germans were as tired as us,' noted Ray Wilson. 'Both sides had their socks rolled down. Cramp was taking its grip. Our shorts and shirts were soaked and stained with perspiration. Yet with an incredible surge of spirit I sensed that we in the England team were rising to the occasion more completely than the opposition. All those hard days of training under the whip of Ramsey, Shepherdson and Cocker were paying off.'

Up at the FA's training ground at Lilleshall the warden, unable to bear any more, got up and left his television set and took his dog for a walk. Somewhere in the Indian Ocean Jack and Bobby's brother Gordon Charlton walked out of the radio room and took refuge down below among the thundering engines of his merchantman.

They need not have worried. The contrast between the two sides at the start of extra time was quickly evident. West Germany had shot their bolt. The crowd, which had fallen into a muttering, disillusioned silence, quickly sensed blood and began to bay again. For England it became, once more, 'just a matter of getting on with it'.

Moore and Ball pointed the way. Even in the furnace of extra time the England captain refused to be wrenched away from his normal pattern of play, refused to relinquish thoughtful, stylish football. Moore was something more than arrogant: he was an expression of scornful superiority. He played as if the game was five rather than 95 minutes old. His every touch was a mocking challenge to the opposition to find a similar level of self-belief. And the opposition, at this late stage in the day, could not. Within minutes he was robbing Seeler on the edge of the England box and finding Ball with a beautifully measured pass to the halfway line – from where the little midfield player, his socks rolled down to his ankles, galloped through the German defence and released a shot which Tilkowski did well to tip over the bar. Two minutes later Bobby Charlton hit a 20-yard drive against the inside of Tilkowski's left-hand post, from where it bounced back, hit the keeper's chest and rolled to safety. England were back in business and the crowd was back in voice.

After ten minutes of extra time, it came. Stiles took possession in the centre circle and slung a long ball out for Ball to chase down the right wing. 'As I saw it run free,' Ball recalled later, 'I thought: "Oh no! I can't get that one. I'm finished." I'd already died twice and been looking for a chance to have a breather for ten minutes. That Schnellinger was already shooting after it. Well, I'd been beating him all afternoon and there was no reason why I couldn't do it again. "Here we go again," I thought. "This time I really am finished . . ."'

Ball reached it first and curled a low cross towards Hurst. The big forward had to stretch out a long right leg to bring it down, then he turned and while falling sent a shot from ten yards high over Tilkowski. 'I watched it hit up in the roof of the net, touching where the crossbar and net were joined,' he would say. 'I felt sure in my own mind it was over when it touched down.'

In fact the ball hit the underside of Hans Tilkowski's crossbar, which in turn shivered the net slightly. It then cannoned down to the ground and landed with between a half and two-thirds of its circumference over the thick white goal-line. The rules of association football dictate that the whole of the ball must be over the line before a goal is allowed. The backspin put on the ball by its contact with the crossbar caused it to bounce back out into play, where Wolfgang Weber headed it over to what the Germans considered to be safety.

Gottfried Dienst had blown, because one way or the other the ball was out of play. His Russian linesman Tofik Bahkramov raised his flag. With German and English eyes anxiously upon them, the two men conferred.

'I asked him,' recalled Dienst, 'is the ball behind the line? Bahkramov said: "Yes."' Then Dienst wheeled away sharply, blowing his whistle once more and pointing to the centre spot. He was briefly surrounded by despairing German players, but it was a goal. England were in the lead again.

It was a goal. If the referee gives it, it is a goal. But it should not have been. The whole of the ball did not cross the line, either when it struck the crossbar or when it bounced on the line. Most England players have ever since cited Roger Hunt's reaction as their authority for the ball having crossed the line. Hunt, who was following up on Hurst's shot, and was apparently in a position to knock it into the empty net behind Tilkowski, did not do so. Instead he turned away, both arms held aloft, and claimed the goal. No professional foot-baller, the familiar argument goes, would have left that ball alone if there had been the slightest doubt in his mind as to whether or not it had crossed the line. 'He was only a yard away,' said Hurst, 'and knowing Roger he could have "died" on the ball if necessary, hurling

198

himself at it to get it back if there had been any doubt. But he stood there, and his hands made a little gesture as though to say "That's good enough . . . that's in." '

Back on the halfway line Jack Charlton called out to Hunt: 'Was it a good 'un?' Hunt held up his hands a couple of feet apart, like an angler indicating the size of the one that got away. It was that far over.

But Roger Hunt could not have scored once the ball had hit the goal-line. He was running in towards goal a foot in front of Wolfgang Weber when Geoff Hurst struck his shot. But when the ball hit the underside of the bar Hunt checked slightly in premature anticipation. It was only an instant's pause, but Weber did not pause at all, and when the ball bounced up off the line the German was himself a foot in front and had displaced Hunt as firm favourite to reach it first. Roger Hunt, at that stage, was behind Weber's shoulder. So Hunt did not bother to compete for it. It would have been a waste of time. His instincts took him onward for a yard or so and then he turned away, claiming the goal, as Weber headed it over the bar.

'We won the World Cup,' Bobby Moore admitted much later to the *Daily Mail*'s Jeff Powell, 'on the best appeal of all time. I believe Roger Hunt got us the verdict. I was 50 yards away on the halfway line and in no position to offer an honest opinion at the time. From my viewpoint it had to be a goal because of Roger's reaction . . . he made no attempt to knock it back in. Just turned round with his arms in the air . . . I believe old Bahkramov was convinced by that reaction.

'I don't know how the linesman could decide. At the time I was in no doubt, but on reflection I've got to say I wouldn't have liked a goal like that to be given against England.'

Moore's interpretation of the event, that Bahkramov had been seduced by Hunt's appeal, was certainly more charitable than that of the West Germans, who would claim for decades afterwards that the Russian linesman's Second World War experiences had affected his judgement. Which begged the question: from which European country could soccer officials be trusted to handle a game involving Germany? Moore's reading of the situation was also almost certainly correct. Bahkramov may not have been able to see the ball well, but any cursory glance showed it to be more over the line than not, and why did Hunt not finish the job? Tofik Bahkramov was not aided by slow-motion replays. He saw no check in the striker's stride, he saw no overtaking German full-back . . .

'In situations like this,' Ray Wilson confessed, 'I accept that what you want to believe is part of the belief itself. I wanted that to be a goal, so I honestly believed that it was; the Germans wanted it to be disallowed and so were quite sincere in believing that the ball had been only half across the line. Neither side would be lying, just describing what they were sure they had seen . . .'

The stiff-limbed players hirpled through a further 20 minutes of agonising football, and as the final seconds of extra time brought wishful whistles from the Wembley crowd West Germany threw all players forward, and English defenders dizzy with exhaustion noticed with astonishment that the forwards they were tackling were German full-backs, and Ball and Peters and Hunt jogged painfully between defence and midfield in gasping efforts to relieve the pressure, and Jack Charlton was just thinking, 'This time we'll make it', when Bobby Moore took a cross from Willi Schulz on his chest near his own penalty spot and played a wall pass with Roger Hunt to take himself and the ball out of the left-hand side of the English box, and with Charlton screaming at him to kick the fucking thing out of the stadium the England captain spotted Geoff Hurst alone on the halfway line, making a slight gesture with his arm.

Referee Dienst put his whistle into his mouth, and the crowd roared, and the players faltered, and three English fans burst on to the pitch, but Dienst waved play on.

Moore already had played on. His pass was looping over 40 yards of turf towards Hurst. 'It came straight as an arrow to the position just over halfway where I was beginning to turn. As I went round I sensed rather than saw the white shirt of a German coming in from my right and I knew I could scoot past him. He was gone . . .'

('Any second now, it will all be over,' Kenneth Wolstenholme told the television audience.)

'Even as I straightened out towards the German goal I wasn't thinking of scoring. I thought I was all alone. The thought flew through my mind: "They won't get it back again . . . they won't . . . they won't . . ." I wondered if it would look a bit off if I just slammed the ball at the crowd at the far end of the stadium . . .'

('Here comes Hurst . . .')

'I risked another glance, even though I could feel a tackle looming up on my right. The goal had miraculously shifted to within 25 yards in front of me. It was on for me to have a bang. I didn't give a damn whether it went in or not. If I hit the ball hard enough it would hit the net – or the crowd I could see heaving in the background . . .'

('Some people are on the pitch. They think it's all over . . .')

'So I whacked it. I knew I would never hit a better shot so long as I lived. The feel, the sound of leather on leather were exactly right. Over the tip of my left boot, raised chest high on the follow-through, I could see the ball speeding for the top corner. Tilkowski had no chance.'

('. . . it is now!')

West Germany never touched the ball again in the final, there was no time for them to kick off. Bobby and Jack Charlton, the former's face streaming with tears, embraced. 'I wish I could cry,' thought Jack. Nobby Stiles and George Cohen fell into each other's arms and on to the ground. Ray Wilson was slapping his hands on the grass. Alan Ball turned cartwheels. Bobby Moore wanted vaguely to wander around his team and say: 'All right. It's okay. We've done it.' Geoff Hurst tried to repress giggles, his legs shook, and as faces loomed up in front of him he kept asking, 'Did that third one count?', but nobody seemed to understand him, or if they did, he could not understand their replies. One of the England players kept saying, 'Fuck, shit, fuck, shit', over and over again, laughing as he did so.

Alf Ramsey sat on the bench at the touchline, watching. 'It was because I did not want to forget that I stayed as I did,' he would explain, 'not jumping up with the rest shouting, "Wahoo, we've won, we've won!" My pleasure was to see what was happening. I was looking at the players. Amazed at their reaction, getting so much enjoyment just out of watching them.'

As Bobby Moore walked towards the steps to the Royal Box to collect the cup Ramsey got to his feet and approached his captain, and with a huge smile on his face he embraced him. Moore climbed the steps feeling 'misty and unreal', and noticed the Queen's lily white gloves, and quickly wiped his hands on the velvet-lined front of the Royal Box.

'The colours of those flowers were right, after all,' said Elizabeth II.

'Yes. Thank heaven,' said Moore. (What flowers?) 'Your Majesty.'

Back down on the pitch some players tried to persuade Ramsey to allow them to chair him around Wembley on a lap of honour. He refused, smiling quietly and saying: 'This is your day. You won the World Cup.' Photographers posed the team for a group shot which Ramsey also refused to join. Finally, Stiles and Moore forced him to look at the trophy so that the press had something for their front pages. In the resultant photographs the manager looked reluctant and slightly unhappy, like a middle-aged vicar judging a wet T-shirt competition for charity.

Nobby Stiles also stared at the Jules Rimet trophy, and then he looked around at his team-mates, and he made the only truly illustrative, and the most paranoid, and the most poignant, and the most significant, and the saddest statement of England's World Cup win.

'Nobody can take this away from us,' he said.

11 THE PARTY

'When I first came back to Brazil after the World Cup games of 1966, my heart wasn't in playing football. The games had been a revelation to me in their unsportsman-like conduct and weak refereeing. England won the games that year, but in my opinion she did not have the best team in the field.'

— PELE

On a golf course at Chorlton-cum-Hardy in the north of England, the Manchester United and Scotland footballer Denis Law had elected the afternoon of 30 July 1966 to play a round for a £25.00 stake with a Manchester businessman named John Hogan.

All afternoon long, Law and Hogan had the course to themselves. The clubhouse was packed with Englishmen watching television. Law knew that it would be a bad day: normally he would have beaten Hogan comfortably, but that afternoon he could not play a decent stroke. He lost the bet, and as the two of them came round the corner from the 18th green at about 5.30pm a crowd of members were at the clubhouse window cheering frantically. 'England,' Denis Law knew then, 'had won the World Cup. It was the blackest day of my life.'

At exactly the same time, down in the changing-room beneath the Empire Stadium George Cohen was sitting on a bench muttering: 'It's bloody ridiculous. I don't feel anything. I don't. I really don't.' Bobby Moore was thinking: 'Is this true?' Bobby Charlton turned once more to his brother Jack and said: 'That's it. What can you win after that?' In the dazzling beam of the arc lights and the hum of the cameras and the gabble of reporters and the pop of champagne corks,

203

Geoff Hurst heard through his dizziness an FA official come up and shout into his ear: 'It counted, Geoff . . . that third goal . . . it counted.'

All the same, before the coach left to take them back to Hendon Hall to get changed for the post-match celebrations, Hurst walked up the tunnel at Wembley and out on to the pitch to look at the scoreboard. It read: ENGLAND 4 WEST GERMANY 2. He knew then that he had become the first player ever to score a hat-trick in a World Cup final. A few fans were still scattered around the terraces, singing and chanting, and a white-coated attendant called over to him: 'Great, Geoff, great! How does it feel?' Hurst waved to him and said nothing.

Jack Charlton was meantime feeling aggrieved. For the fourth time in six matches his name had been drawn out of a hat to take a random dope test. Having given, he was returning to the changing room when one of the testers approached him with a grave expression and asked to see him later on. He was still fretting about this (what had they found? a mystery illness?) when all four testers walked into the changing-room and up to Charlton, and one of them pulled from behind his back a baby's potty inscribed with the words: 'Presented to J Charlton, who gave his best for his country.'

They tumbled aboard the coach, all order gone, all superstitions ditched, to Hendon Hall Hotel, from where they travelled through streets lined with Union flags and bunting and cheering crowds, down the Edgware Road through Paddington and Shepherd's Bush to Kensington High Street – which was closed by the police to traffic at both ends – and the official reception at the Royal Garden Hotel. The three other semi-finalists, the Soviets, the Portuguese and the West Germans, were there, as was prime minister Harold Wilson, cabinet ministers Jim Callaghan and George Brown, and every FA official who was fit to walk. The players' wives and girlfriends, needless to say, were not invited to the official banquet. They dined separately, like country house servants, in an ante-room.

Before the occasion began Jack Charlton wrote on a card, 'This body is to be returned to Room 508, Royal Garden Hotel', and put it in his top pocket. (The body was not returned: Charlton found himself next morning sitting in the sunshine on the lawn of a friendly family in Walthamstow. A next-door neighbour leaned over the fence and said: 'You're Jack Charlton! I know you. I knew your mother!')

204

In between courses – in between bites – at the banquet, the players walked out on to the balcony to receive the ovation of the crowd below. The redoubtable Mrs Cissie Charlton, who had somehow been exempted from the ban on players' womenfolk, was commiserating with Harold Wilson on the latter's youthful failure to get a job at Ashington Colliery; telling the Portuguese that, after England, they had been the best side in the tournament; and being charmed by Uwe Seeler's admission that he felt no disgrace in losing such a final.

Then they left to go their separate ways into London, to meet up with their wives and girlfriends and enjoy the longest night. All but one of the squad fought for taxis in Kensington, or sneaked out behind Harold Wilson's limousine . . . all but one. Jimmy Greaves was not there. Immediately after the game Greaves picked up his bags and carried his immense burden of sorrow and disappointment far away, to some quiet, private place. Alf Ramsey felt personally slighted, and asked Moore why Greaves had chosen to boycott the ceremonies. 'Jimmy's hurt,' said Moore. 'Accept it, Alf. He's better off away from all the fuss.'

The party was not over yet. It would not properly end until some seven years later, when a dreadful mistake by Bobby Moore's replacement Norman Hunter let the Polish player Domarski through to score past Peter Shilton and put England out of the qualifying rounds of the 1974 World Cup. It had not even ended in 1970, when a better England side to that of 1966 was stripped of its trophy in the heat and hostility of Mexico. Nor had it really finished in the late 1960s, when the upward surge of domestic soccer attendances which had followed the victory began, once more, their inexorable decline; when the goals dried up and players of quality were lucky to get a sniff of an international place; when all of the stark fears which had been stoked up by Ramsey's tactics and attitude began to seem to be real, and people began to ask themselves, would it have been better in the long term if Hungary, or Portugal, or even West Germany had won in 1966? What roads have we driven down since then? Where were we going? But by the end of 1973 it was over, and Alf Ramsey's days were numbered, and the most successful manager that English football had ever known was about to be dumped brutally out of the game, because the system whose only virtue was that it got results no longer got results.

'It was a bad thing for British football,' said Denis Law when he had collected up his golf clubs and left Chorlton-cum-Hardy far behind. 'It was the beginning of the end of football as we knew it. We had seen the beautiful, attacking, flowing football of Spurs; now we had 4–3–3, a system without wingers.

'That was the worst thing that ever happened to the game, because it killed the art of scoring goals. You can't blame Ramsey for the decline of British football as a spectacle, you must blame the people who followed his example. He set the pattern and he was successful with it because he had the players to make it work. If every team had three front men like Hurst, Hunt and Ball, then they might have been successful too; but no team had. It worked for a time for England, but it was always going to be disastrous for the bread-and-butter stuff.

'I've always said that England only won the World Cup because they had six matches at home. Getting to the final was all about getting results; about not getting beaten in the early rounds. All right, the system worked in that limited context for England, in favourable circumstances, but to play football like that on a permanent basis would be fatal. With no wingers, attacks were coming just from midfield, negative to watch and negative to play. You didn't need to be a Jimmy Greaves to play football like that.

'After 4–3–3, the next logical step was 4–4–2, where we now had four men in midfield. Then of course the system went back to the schools and everybody wanted to become a midfield player. I had hoped that when Brazil won the World Cup in 1970 things might change, but for the first time that I could remember that didn't happen: teams didn't start to adopt the style of the World Champions. The reason was that they couldn't, because they hadn't got the players to make the change.

'The year 1966 saw the start of eight or ten years of bad football. It took a couple of seasons to work its way thoroughly into the League system, but within a few years British football had become, for the most part, boring and predictable. Skill was being stifled at birth.'

There are flaws in such a blanket condemnation. If England did not deserve to win the 1966 World Cup, who did? Not Brazil, who were twice well beaten in their first round group. Not Hungary, who were also defeated twice. Surely not Portugal, who were deservedly eliminated by England in the semi-finals. West Germany? West Germany, who may have lost the final as the result of a goal which was not a goal, but who were in fact the lesser team over 120 minutes that afternoon at Wembley? West Germany, who also played just three forwards, often retracted to two, and who fielded a five-man defence? Were West Germany more suitable apostles than England of attacking football?

Probably not. The odium which was heaped upon Alf Ramsey's team more than any other was compounded by the resentments which festered around the tournament's appallingly ill-chosen number of British referees, by the apparent bias displayed in the switching of England's semi-final from Liverpool to Wembley, by the arrogance displayed in England (which seemed at times to be personified as much in Bobby Moore's annoyingly hitched-up shorts as in the chauvinism of the English media), and by the fact that Alf Ramsey chose to select and then support with all of his might a footballer who was widely perceived to be a destroyer.

Those were its compounds, but it had its base material in the unfortunate fact that football's Age of Innocence was over, and the team which briefly profited from that death, the team which adapted most quickly and most effectively to Alfredo Di Stefano's new age of 'bowing to the knee of coaches', was the host nation and the inventor of the game. To English men and women Alf Ramsey's side were sturdy, yeoman champions. To the emergent nations England was a sick, cynical old man prepared to resort to almost any iniquity – including the desecration of the game he had fathered – to reclaim his former eminence.

It was only a game, wasn't it? Only a job. On the day after the World Cup final the England squad and its manager assembled for a final party at the ITV studios at Borehamwood. They were breaking up. 'Suddenly it was over. We tried to drag it out. A few strained jokes and silly laughs and handshakes. But that was that.'

It was a Sunday. Alf Ramsey was greeted at the studios by two reporters, who asked him how he felt.

'This,' he told them in reply, 'is my day off.'

A few hours later, following an uncomfortable lunch, the happy band of brothers left Hendon Hall Hotel for the last time. A prominent, well-respected journalist was waiting at reception for Ramsey. When the manager appeared the sportswriter stepped forward and said politely: 'I just want to congratulate you, Alf, and thank you on behalf of all the press for your co-operation.'

Alf Ramsey's brow clouded over. He looked the man suspiciously in the eye. 'Are you taking the piss?' he asked.

12 WHERE ARE THEY NOW?

'While it would be wrong to accuse Ramsey of inaugurating what was to become the stifling style of much of English football in the late sixties . . . there is some truth in the argument that he retained the system too long and was slow to appreciate the development, at home and abroad, of more positive ideas.'

— DAVID LACEY, *THE GUARDIAN*, MAY 1974

They played together as a team once more at Wembley: in a dull 0–0 friendly draw with Czechoslovakia on 2 November 1966. And then the time for sentiment was gone; the exigencies of competition took over; Scotland arrived in the capital to inflict a hubristic but humiliating (and entirely predictable) 3–2 defeat upon the new World Champions; and the 1970 World Cup in Mexico – for which England, as holders, would not have to qualify – beckoned to Alf Ramsey.

Gordon Banks played in those finals. He had transferred from Leicester to Stoke and was by then 32 years old, but still rated as the best goalkeeper in the world: a ranking which he promptly confirmed by pulling off the save of the century from Pele in a Group Three game at Guadalajara. He was absent with food-poisoning a week later when England squandered a two-goal lead over West Germany in the quarter-finals. Banks's replacement Peter Bonetti gifting at least two and arguably all three of the goals which knocked England out and gave West Germany sweet revenge. Gordon Banks continued to play for Stoke until he damaged an eye in a car crash in 1972. He played, half-sighted, in the emergent North American soccer league, and he managed non-League Telford United, and then he was lost to the game He presently runs hls own PR company, GB Sales and Promotions.

George Cohen concluded both his life as an international and his unassuming career with Fulham just two years later, due to knee trouble at the age of 28 in 1968. After this early retirement from a game which he served widely and well, he worked, and still works, as an estate agent in Tunbridge Wells in Kent. He does not go to football matches any more.

Ray Wilson was signed from Everton by Oldham Athletic in 1969. After a season there he went to Bradford City, and then – at the age of 35 – he retired from Valley Parade after only two fourth division matches. He went straight out of football and into the family undertaking business which he still runs.

Bobby Moore played in Mexico in 1970. Three years later, on 14 November 1973, he played his last game for his country. It was a month after England had failed to qualify for the 1974 World Cup following the home draw with Poland for which Moore had been dropped. His 108th and last cap came during a dismal, unsuitable 1–0 friendly defeat by Italy at Wembley. In 1974 he transferred – after 16 seasons and 642 matches – from West Ham to Fulham. In the summer of '76 he played in the North American Soccer League, in '77 he retired from Fulham, but in '78 – at the age of 37 – he played for Seattle Sounders in the USA. Between 1979 and '81 he managed non-league Oxford City, and he did the same job between 1984 and '86 for Southend United. He died on 24 February 1993 of cancer of the colon. 'He made himself a great player,' said Geoff Hurst, 'and the bigger the stage, the better he performed. If the world had played Mars, he would have been man of the match.'

Jack Charlton, at the age of 34 and still stopping for Leeds, also travelled to Mexico in 1970, where he played one match – England's 1–0 win over Czechoslovakia. After retiring as a player he embarked on a solid career in club management, most notably at Middlesbrough and Sheffield Wednesday. During one of England's post-Ramsey turmoils Charlton applied in writing for the job of manager of England, and did not receive so much as a reply from the Football Association. But in 1986 he was given control of the international squad of the Republic of

Ireland. Under Charlton, Eire qualified for the finals of the 1988 European Championship (where they beat England 1–0) and for the finals of the World Cup in 1990 and 1994. In both of the latter competitions their first at this altitude – they won through their first round group to reach the last eight.

Nobby Stiles was also taken to Mexico by Ramsey in 1970 ('a beautiful gesture,' said one acquaintance of the England manager. When I saw that selection I almost cheered. It was saying: thanks for all you've done for me.') But he was not used in the tournament, and he never played for England again. Shortly afterwards he was transferred by Matt Busby from Manchester United to Middlesbrough oddly, without the benefit of an Old Trafford testimonial – and he finished his playing days with Preston North End in 1974, at the age of 32. Apart from a brief spell back under the rainbow as Manchester United's youth team coach, he then left professional football.

Martin Peters, the footballer whom Alf Ramsey burdened with the tag of being 'ten years ahead of his time', transferred from West Ham to Tottenham in 1970. He played in all four of England's World Cup games in Mexico. In 1975 he moved on to Norwich City, and then to Sheffield United in 1980. He retired after some 20 games for United and, at the age of 37, became briefly the manager at Bramall Lane, before being succeeded there by Ian Porterfield. He presently works in automobile insurance in Dagenham, Essex, alongside Geoff Hurst. Alan Ball, with notable skills enhancing by then his work-rate, also turned out in all four of England's 1970 World Cup matches. His club playing career took him from Blackpool to Everton after the 1966 victory, and then throughout the 1970s to Arsenal, Southampton and the Vancouver Whitecaps. He became the player/manager at Blackpool in 1980 and he played his last 17 matches of professional football at the age of 38 for Bristol Rovers in 1983. His real successes as a manager – successes which, out of this group of distinguished players, he shares only with Jack Charlton began at Exeter City, where he was manager between 1991 and 1994. From Exeter he moved to Southampton, and in the summer of 1995 he was attracted back to Lancashire to manage Manchester City.

Bobby Charlton added to his World Cup winner's medal two years later, when he won the European Cup with Manchester United in 1968. (Charlton scored twice in the Wembley final against a Benfica side which included, still, Coluna, Eusebio, Torres, Simoes . . .) That result made Bobby Charlton and – less predictably – his United team-mate Nobby Stiles the only British footballers ever to have won soccer's two greatest trophies, and consequently the most successful British footballers of all time. He was also present in Mexico, and his substitution against West Germany was blamed by many for giving Beckenbauer the extra freedom required to bring the Germans back into the game. He concluded his career for England after that tournament, with 106 caps under his belt and a standing record of 49 goals. In 1973, after 20 years, 17 of them in the first team, and 751 games, he took off his Manchester United shirt for the last time. He was 35 years old. At the end of that season he embarked on a short and unsuccessful spell as manager of Preston North End. In 1980 he returned, Sir Bobby Charlton, to become a director of Manchester United. 'Bobby Charlton,' says Nobby Stiles, 'is every-thing that's good in this game. He's an ordinary working lad is Bobby.'

Jimmy Greaves, as we have seen, finally brought down the curtain on his England career during the European Nation's Cup in Italy in 1968, when after one frustration too many he presented Alf Ramsey with the ultimatum which demanded that he be selected for the team or left out of the squad altogether. He was 28 years old, he had won 57 caps (only three of them in the two years since 1966), and he had scored 44 international goals. In 1970 he transferred from Tottenham to West Ham, for whom he played 36 games before finish-ing his career at non-league Barnet in the season of 1972–73. After a successful struggle against alcoholism he carved out in the 1980s a new and entirely winning role for himself as a witty and forthright television pundit. The disenchantment of the most venomous striker that England has ever produced with his own international career is perhaps best illustrated by the fact that, when asked many years later, he would nominate as his favourite match Tottenham Hotspur's 1963 Cup-Winners' Cup final against Atletico Madrid, and as his favourite goal one scored for Barnet.

Roger Hunt scored the eighteenth and last goal of his brief international career against Sweden at Wembley in May 1968. Thereafter the 29-year-old bowed out of Alf Ramsey's squad. After ten years with Liverpool as a darling of the Anfield crowd, he finished his club career at Bolton in 1971. He has his own haulage contracting company in that Lancashire town.

Geoff Hurst played three games and scored one goal for England in Mexico in 1970. He went on to contribute substantially, at the age of 29, to his country's European Nation's Cup campaign in 1971–72, after which he bowed out of the international game with 24 goals. In 1972 he signed for Stoke City from West Ham, and after three years in the Potteries he moved on to West Bromwich Albion, for whom he appeared ten times. His top-flight career spanned 16 years. He made no attempt to move into club management, and he now works with Martin Peters in the insurance business. In the summer of 1992 Hurst took a flight out of Glasgow to the European Nation's Cup competition in Sweden, where both Scotland and England were taking part. His plane was consequently filled with celebratory members of the Tartan Army. Nervously, Hurst made his way to his seat through a gauntlet of ribald comments and proffered drinks. He sat down and instantly noticed an elderly Scottish supporter gazing at him sternly and silently from across the aisle. After a long, pregnant pause the Scot finally leaned over and stated confidentially: 'It wisnae in, y'know.'

Alf Ramsey was made a knight in the 1967 New Year's Honours List. 'The players always called me Alf, and I hope they will continue to do so,' he said. Sir Alf Ramsey suffered no real disgrace in the 1970 World Cup, but his qualifying campaign – the first that he had been obliged to endure – for the 1974 World Cup finals was a disaster. England, still featuring Moore, Peters and Ball, took just one win (in Wales) from their four group games. They were eliminated when Poland arrived at Wembley needing a draw to qualify and withstood a lengthy seige of their goal to achieve it. This humiliation, coupled with the festering national resentment at Ramsey's stodgy approach to football, did for Sir Alf. He was sacked by the Football Association on 1 May 1974, at the age of . . . 54. During 113 matches in charge of his country's national team, he had lost just 17 times. He worked briefly and unsuccessfully as a television sports pundit, he represented a sportswear company, and he took an ill-defined advisory post with Birmingham City. But effectively, the man who won England the World Cup was subsequently lost to soccer. He retired early to the small suburban Ipswich house in which he still lives, he played golf occasionally and he gave interviews even more occasionally. He never chose to publish his memoirs. On 28 April 1999 this most enigmatic and successful of England managers died at the age of 79 at an Ipswich nursing home. 'He was a winner,' said Bobby Charlton. 'Without Alf Ramsey England would not have won the World Cup in 1966. He gave us our proudest moment.'

By 1999 Charlton and Ramsey were no longer the only two Knights from 1966. In the Queen's Birthday Honours List of 1998 Geoff Hurst became Sir Geoff in honour of what was then the only English hat-trick to have been scored against Germany. For a few years it would remain the most important hat-trick to be scored against them.

And in the New Year's Honours List of 2000 the rest of the squad got their gongs. Moore, Banks, Jack Charlton and Peters had earlier accepted the Order of the British Empire. Stiles, Ball, Hunt, Wilson and Cohen – dubbed the 'forgotten five' – were rounded up with an MBE as the third millennium dawned. Some people wondered aloud why it had taken so very long for this elementary courtesy to be extended to all the footballers who had given their country its greatest sporting triumph. In reply it was suggested that for several years after 1966 the government had been reluctant to reward World Cup winners because it was considered a serious possibility that England might go on to win one World Cup after another, every 48 months, and an overly liberal dishing out of knighthoods and OBEs would consequently result in a devaluation of the honours system and with the House of Lords being stuffed with retired professional footballers.

APPENDIX

ENGLAND'S GAMES UNDER ALF RAMSEY

From February 1963 to July 1966

27/2/63 European Nation's Cup, round one
(with the FA's International Selection Committee)

France 5	*England 2*
Wisnieski (2)	Bobby Smith
Douis	Tambling
Cossou (2)	

6/4/63 Home Championships
(with the FAISC)

England 1	*Scotland 2*
Douglas	Baxter (2)

8/5/63

England 1	*Brazil 1*
Douglas	Pepe

29/5/63

Czechoslovakia 2	*England 4*
Scherer	Greaves (2)
Kadraba	Bobby Smith
	Bobby Charlton

2/6/63

East Germany 1   *England 2*
Ducke   Hunt
                          Bobby Charlton

5/6/63

Switzerland 1   *England 8*
Bertschi   Bobby Charlton (3)
                          Byrne (2)
                          Douglas
                          Kay
                          Melia

12/10/63 Home Championships

Wales 0   *England 4*
                          Bobby Smith (2)
                          Greaves
                          Bobby Charlton

23/10/63 FA Centenary Match

England 2   *Rest Of The World 1*
Paine   Law
Greaves

20/11/63 Home Championships

England 8   *Northern Ireland 3*
Greaves (4)   Crossan
Paine (3)   Wilson (2)
Bobby Smith

11/4/64 Home Championships

Scotland 1   *England 0*
Gilzean

6/5/64

England 2
Byrne (2)

Uruguay 1
Spencer

17/5/64

Portugal 3
Torres (2)
Eusebio

England 4
Byrne (3)
Bobby Charlton

24/5/64

Eire 1
Strahan

England 3
Eastham
Byrne
Greaves

27/5/64

USA 0

England 10
Hunt (4)
Pickering (3)
Paine (2)
Bobby Charlton

30/5/64 Little World Cup

Brazil 5
Rinaldo (2)
Pele
Julinho
Roberto Dias

England 1
Greaves

4/6/64 Little World Cup

Portugal 1
Peres

England 1
Hunt

6/6/64 Little World Cup

Argentina 1   *England 0*
Rojas

3/10/64 Home Championships

Northern Ireland 3   *England 4*
Wilson   Pickering
McLaughlin (2)   Greaves (3)

21/10/64

England 2   *Belgium 2*
Pickering   Cornelis
Hinton   Van Himst

18/11/64 Home Championships

England 2   *Wales 1*
Wignall (2)   Jones

9/12/64

Holland 1   *England 1*
Moulijn   Greaves

10/4/65 Home Championships

England 2   *Scotland 2*
Bobby Charlton   Law
Greaves   St John

5/5/65

England 1   *Hungary 0*
Greaves

9/5/65

Yugoslavia 1   *England 1*
Kovacevic   Bridges

12/5/65

West Germany 0

England 1
Paine

16/5/65

Sweden 1
Erikson

England 2
Ball
Connelly

2/10/65 Home Championships

Wales 0

England 0

20/10/65

England 2
Bobby Charlton
Connelly

Austria 3
Fritsch (2)
Flogel

10/11/65 Home Championships

England 2
Baker
Peacock

Northern Ireland 1
Irvine

8/12/65

Spain 0

England 2
Baker
Hunt

5/1/66

England 1
Moore

Poland 1
Sadek

23/2/66

England 1   *West Germany 0*
Stiles

2/4/66 Home Championships

Scotland 3   *England 4*
Law   Hurst
Johnstone (2)   Hunt (2)
                                     Bobby Charlton

4/5/66

England 2   *Yugoslavia 0*
Greaves
Bobby Charlton

26/6/66

Finland 0   *England 3*
                                     Peters
                                     Hunt
                                     Jack Charlton

29/6/66

Norway 1   *England 6*
Sunde   Greaves (4)
                                     Connelly
                                     Moore

3/7/66

Denmark 0   *England 2*
                                     Jack Charlton
                                     Eastham

5/7/66

Poland 0   *England 1*
                                     Hunt

THE 1966 WORLD CUP FINALS

11/7/66 Round One, Group One. Wembley, 75,000

England (0) 0   *Uruguay (0) 0*

Banks
Cohen   J Charlton   Moore   Wilson
Ball   Stiles   R Charlton
Greaves   Hunt   Connelly

16/7/66 Round One, Group One. Wembley, 85,000

England (1) 2   *Mexico (0) 0*
Bobby Charlton
Hunt

Banks
Cohen   J Charlton   Moore   Wilson
Peters   Stiles   R Charlton
Greaves   Hunt   Paine

20/6/66 Round One, Group One. Wembley, 92,500

England (1) 2   *France (0) 0*
Hunt (2)

Banks
Cohen   J Charlton   Moore   Wilson
Peters   Stiles   R Charlton
Greaves   Hunt   Callaghan

23/7/66 Quarter-final. Wembley, 88,000

England (0) 1   *Argentina (0) 0*
Hurst

Banks
Cohen   J Charlton   Moore   Wilson
Peters   Stiles   R Charlton   Ball
Hurst   Hunt

26/6/77 Semi-Final. Wembley, 90,000

England (1) 2   *Portugal (0) 1*
Bobby Charlton (2)   Eusebio (pen.)

Banks
Cohen   J Charlton   Moore   Wilson
Peters   Stiles   R Charlton   Ball
Hurst   Hunt

30/6/66 Final. Wembley, 93,000

England (1) 4   *West Germany (1) 2*
(After extra time, Full time 2-2)
Hurst (3)   Haller
Peters   Weber

Banks
Cohen   J Charlton   Moore   Wilson
Peters   Stiles   R Charlton   Ball
Hurst   Hunt